Software Project Management

Mike Cotterell
Bob Hughes

Tutorial Guides in Computing and Information Systems

Series Editors

Professor David Howe, De Montfort University
Dr Martin Campbell-Kelly, University of Warwick

About the series

The Tutorial Guides in Computing and Information Systems series covers the first and second year undergraduate programme and the Higher National Diploma courses in these subjects. The essentially practical nature of the books is particularly appropriate to today's courses where examinations reflect an increasing emphasis on problem-solving skills. The books are characterised by a high proportion of worked examples, practical exercises and frequent friendly tutorial-style notes in the margins of the text. The problem-solving approach also addresses the requirements of practitioners in business and industry.

Each book stands alone in its subject area; the series as a whole provides comprehensive coverage of the first two years of the undergraduate or Higher National programme.

About the Series Editors

David Howe is Head of Department of Information Systems at De Montfort University. He specializes in the analysis and design of information systems and is the author of *Data Analysis for Database Design*.

Martin Campbell-Kelly is Senior Lecturer in Computer Science at Warwick University. He teaches a number of subjects of the undergraduate programme and is a recognized authority on the history and development of computing.

Other titles in the series

Beginning Unix™
Mike Joy

Z: A Beginner's Guide
David Rann, John Turner and Jenny Whitworth

Introduction to C++
David Dench and Brian Prior

Human Computer Interaction for Software Designers
Linda Macauly

The Relational Database
John Carter

Programming in C
John Gray and Brian Wendl

Information Systems: Strategy to Design
Chris Claire and Gordon Stuteley

Systems Analysis Techniques
Barbara Robinson and Mary Prior

Foundation Discrete Mathematics for Computing
Dexter J. Booth

Software
Project Management

Mike Cotterell
Bob Hughes

INTERNATIONAL THOMSON COMPUTER PRESS

I(T)P An International Thomson Publishing Company

London • Bonn • Boston • Madrid • Melbourne • Mexico City • New York • Paris • Singapore
Tokyo • Toronto • Albany, NY • Belmont, CA • Cincinnati, OH • Detroit, MI

Software Project Management
Copyright ©1995 Mike Cotterell & Bob Hughes

I(T)P   A division of International Thomson Publishing Inc.
          The ITP logo is a trademark under licence

British Library Cataloguing-in-Publication Data
A catalogue record for this book is available from the British Library

First printed 1995

Typeset by Mouse Nous, Cross-in-Hand
Printed at Alden Press Limited, Oxford and Northampton, Great Britain

ISBN 1-850-32190-6

International Thomson Publishing
Berkshire House
168–173 High Holborn
London WC1V 7AA
UK

Contents

Appendices

Preface

The effective management of projects in IT environments has increasingly been seen to be important in recent years. In the UK, some aspects of this have been:

- the development of the government-sponsored PRINCE standard
- the setting up of the PROMS-G project management special interest group of the British Computer Society
- the provision of a Certificate of Proficiency in project management by the Information Systems Examinations Board.

Our contacts with industry and commerce have underlined for us the significance of what might be regarded as very basic project management measures. It is our belief that these fundamental practices need to be stressed so that they become first nature for IT practitioners, as a very important part of the foundations of their professional education. While it is hoped that there may be something of interest in this book for the experienced project manager, it is targeted more directly at students about to enter the world of IT development, either through an industrial placement or a first job, and those already in software development who are just starting to take on project management responsibilities and who seek guidance.

Bearing in mind this audience, we have made extensive reference to two imaginary scenarios which explore the concerns of two new project leaders, Amanda and Brigette, who are undertaking their first project management roles.

We touch upon many techniques that may be of assistance when planning and controlling projects. Some of these may be more appropriate than others in particular circumstances. To give coherence we have provided Step Wise, a general framework compatible with PRINCE, for project planning into which the various techniques can be fitted.

We would especially like to thank Ken I'Anson of the CCTA for his helpful suggestions about the Appendix on PRINCE, and also Dave Hatter and Chris Clare for their guidance. The early advice of David Howe and Martin Campbell Kelly on the basic content and format of this book is also gratefully acknowledged. Thanks, too, to Barbara Kitchenham of the NCC, Manchester for her permission to us to use a project data set shown in the Chapter 5. We know that we have picked up many ideas from our colleagues and we acknowledge this particularly in the case of John Williams, Garth Glynn and Heinz Seefried. The work of putting together a textbook inevitably encroaches on family life and we would like to thank Audrey and Cleo Cotterell and Heather, Katherine and Tom Hughes for their forbearance.

Most of the material presented here has been developed in teaching, and learning from, students over a number of years. To those former students who are now grappling with the problems of IT development in the 'real world', this book is dedicated.

Chapter 1

Introduction to software project management

OBJECTIVES

When you have completed this chapter you will be able to:

- [ ] define the scope of 'software project management'

- [ ] distinguish between software and other types of development project

- [ ] understand some problems and concerns of software project managers

- [ ] define the usual stages of a software project

- [ ] explain the main elements of the role of management

- [ ] appreciate the need for careful planning, monitoring and control

- [ ] identify the stakeholders of a project and their objectives and ways of measuring the success in meeting those objectives

- [ ] measure the success of a project in meeting its objectives.

Introduction

What exactly do we mean by 'software project management'? To answer this we need to look at some key ideas about the planning, monitoring and control of software projects.

We are then going to look at how we can identify the stakeholders in a project and their objectives. Identifying those objectives and checking that they are met lays a foundation for a successful project. This, however, cannot be done unless there is accurate information; the importance of this is discussed.

What is a project?

Dictionary definitions of 'project' include:
'A specific plan or design'
'A planned undertaking'
'A large undertaking: e.g. a public works scheme'
Longman Concise English Dictionary, 1982.

The dictionary definitions clearly put the emphasis on the project being a planned activity.

Another key aspect of a project is that the undertaking is non-routine: a job which is repeated a number of times is not a project. There is a hazy boundary in between. The first time you do a routine task it will be very like a project. On the other hand, a project to develop a system which is very similar to previous ones that you have developed will have a large element of the routine.

We can summarize the key characteristics which distinguish projects as follows:

- non-routine nature of the tasks involved
- planning is required
- specific objectives are to be met or specified product is to be created
- the project has a predetermined time span (which may be absolute or relative)
- work is carried out for someone other than yourself
- work involves several specialisms
- work is carried out in several phases
- the resources that are available for use on the project are constrained
- the project is large or complex.

In general, the more each of these factors apply to a task, the more difficult it is going to be to complete it successfully. Project size is particularly important. It should not be a surprise that a project that employs 200 project personnel is going to be rather trickier to manage than one which involves just two people. The examples and exercises used in this book usually relate to smaller projects. This is just to make them more manageable from a learning point of view: the techniques and issues discussed are of equal relevance to larger projects.

Exercise 1.1

Consider the following:

- producing an edition of a newspaper
- building the Channel Tunnel
- getting married
- amending a financial computer system to start the financial year on January 1st rather than April 1st
- a research project into what makes a good human–computer interface
- an investigation into the reason why a user has a problem with a computer system
- a second year programming assignment for a computing student
- writing an operating system for a new computer
- installing a new version of a word processing package in an organization.

Some would appear to merit the description 'project' more than others. Put them into an order that most closely matches your ideas of what constitutes a project. For each entry in the ordered list, describe the difference between it and the one above which makes it less worthy of the term 'project'.

There is no one correct answer to this exercise, but a possible solution to this and the other exercises you will come across may be found at the end of the book.

Software projects versus other types of project

Many of the techniques of general project management are applicable to software project management, but Frederick Brooks pointed out that the products of software projects have certain characteristics which make them different.

Invisibility – when a physical artefact such as a bridge or road is being constructed the progress being made can actually be seen. With software, progress is not immediately visible.

Complexity – per pound spent, software products contain more complexity than other engineered artefacts.

Flexibility – the ease with which software can be changed is usually seen as one of its strengths. However this means that where the software system interfaces with a physical or organizational system, it is expected that, where necessary, the software will normally change to accommodate the other components rather than vice versa. This means the software systems are likely to be subject to a high degree of change.

> Brooks, F. P. (1987). 'No silver bullet: essence and accidents of software engineering', *IEEE Computer* 20(4) pages 10–20 is recommended background reading. One way of perceiving software project management is as the process of making visible that which is invisible.

Activities covered by software project management

A software project is not only concerned with the actual writing of software. In fact, where a software application is bought in 'off-the-shelf', there may be no software writing as such. This is still fundamentally a software project because so many of the other elements associated with this type of project are present. Individual projects are likely to differ considerably but will typically have the following phases.

> Chapter 4 on project analysis and technical planning looks at some alternative life cycles.

- **Project evaluation** – before a project is embarked upon, there must be a careful investigation of its feasibility. This evaluation may be done as part of a strategic planning exercise where a whole range of potential software developments are evaluated and put into an order of priority, or alternatively a study may be carried out to check the feasibility of the one project under consideration. This phase may be regarded as a project in its own right.

The PRINCE method which is described elsewhere takes this planning by stages approach.

- **Planning** – by definition we would expect the project to be planned! In fact, for a large project, we would not do all our detailed planning right at the beginning. We would formulate an outline plan for the whole project and a detailed one for the first stage. More detailed planning of the later stages would be done as they approach. This is because we will have more detailed and accurate information upon which to base our plans nearer to the start of the later stages.

- **Requirements analysis** – this is finding out in detail what the users require of the system that the project is to implement. Some work along these lines will almost certainly have been carried out when the project was evaluated but now the original information obtained needs to be updated and supplemented. Several different approaches to the users' requirements may be explored. For example, a small system which satisfies some, but not all, of the users' needs at a low price may be compared to a system with more functions but at a higher price.

- **Specification** – detailed documentation of what the proposed system is to do.

- **Design** – a design has to be drawn up which meets the specification. This design will be in two stages. One will be the external or user design. This lays down what the system is to look like to the users in terms of menus, screen and report layouts and so on. The next stage produces the physical design which tackles the way that the data and software procedures are be structured internally.

- **Coding** – this may refer to writing code in a procedural language such as C or Ada, or may refer to the use of a '4th Generation Environment' which may require techniques such as screen painting. Even where software is not being built from scratch, some modification to the base package may be required to meet the needs of the new application.

- **Verification and validation** – whether software is developed specially for the current application or not, careful testing will be needed to check that the proposed system meets its requirements.

- **Implementation** – some system development practitioners refer to the whole of the project after design as 'implementation' (i.e. the implementation of the design) while others insist that the term refers to the installation of the system after the software has been developed. In this case it encompasses such things as setting up data files and system parameters, writing user manuals and training users of the new system.

- **Maintenance and support** – once the system has been implemented there will be a continuing need for the correction of any errors that may have crept into the system and for extensions and improvements to the system. Maintenance and support activities may be seen as a series of minor software projects. In many environments, most software development is in fact maintenance.

Brightmouth Higher Education (HE) College which used to be managed by a local authority has been made autonomous. Its payroll is still administered by the local authority and pay slips and other output are produced in the local authority's computer centre. The authority now charges the college for this service. The college management are of the opinion that it would be cheaper to obtain an 'off-the-shelf' payroll package and do the payroll processing themselves.

    What would be the main stages of the project to convert to independent payroll processing by the college? Bearing in mind that an off-the-shelf package is to be used, how would this project differ from one where the software was to be written from scratch?

Exercise 1.2

Some ways of categorizing software projects

It is important to distinguish between the main types of software project because what is appropriate in one context may not be so in another. For example, SSADM, the Structured Systems Analysis and Design Method, is suitable for developing information systems but not necessarily other types of system.

Information systems versus industrial systems

A distinction may be made between **information systems** and **industrial systems.** Very crudely, the difference is that in the former case the system interfaces with the organization, whereas in the latter case the system interfaces with a machine! A stock control system would be an information system which controls when the organization reorders stock. An industrial, or process control, system might control the air conditioning equipment in a building. Some systems may have elements of both so that the stock control system might also control an automated warehouse.

Would an operating system on a computer be an information system or an industrial system?

Exercise 1.3

Objectives versus products

Projects may be distinguished by whether their aim is to produce a **product** or to meet certain **objectives.**

    A project may be to create a product the details of which have been specified by the client. The client has the responsibility for justifying the product.

Service level agreements are becoming increasingly important as organizations contract out functions to external service suppliers.

On the other hand, the project may be required to meet certain objectives. There may be several ways of achieving these objectives in contrast to the constraints of the product-driven project. One example of this is where a new information system is implemented to improve some service to users inside or outside an organization. The level of service that is the target would be the subject of an agreement rather than the characteristics of a particular information system.

Many software projects have two stages. The first stage is an objectives-driven project which results in a recommended course of action and may even specify a new software system to meet identified requirements. The next stage is a project to actually to create the software product.

Exercise 1.4

Would the project to implement an independent payroll system at the Brightmouth HE College described in Exercise 1.2 above be an objectives-driven project or a product-driven project?

The project as a system

A project is concerned with creating a new system and/or transforming an old one and is itself a system.

Systems, subsystems and environments

A simple definition of the term 'system' is 'a set of interrelated parts'. A system will normally be part of a larger system and will itself comprise subsystems.

Outside the system there will be the system's environment. This will be made up of things that can affect the system but over which the system has no direct control. In the case of Brightmouth HE College, the bankruptcy of the main supplier of IT equipment would be an event happening in the system's environment.

Exercise 1.5

Identify the possible subsystems of the installed Brightmouth HE College payroll system.

What important entities exist in the payroll system's environment?

Open versus closed systems

Open systems are those that interact with the environment. Nearly all systems are open. One reason that engineered systems and the projects to construct them often fail is that the technical staff involved do not appreciate the extent to which systems are open and are liable to affected by outside changes.

Suboptimization

This is where a subsystem is working at its optimum but having a detrimental affect on the overall system. An example of this might be where software developers deliver a system to the users which is very efficient in its use of machine resources, but is also very difficult to modify.

Sociotechnical systems

Software projects belong to this category of systems. Any software project requires both technological organization and also the organization of people. Software project managers therefore need to have both technical competence and also be able to interact persuasively with other people.

What is management?

The Open University Software Project Management module (1987) suggests that management involves the following activities.

- Planning – deciding what is to be done
- Organizing – making arrangements
- Staffing – selecting the right people for the job etc.
- Directing – giving instructions
- Monitoring – checking on progress
- Controlling – taking action to remedy hold-ups
- Innovating – coming up with new solutions
- Representing – liaising with users etc.

A convenient way of accessing this OU material is in D. Ince, H. Sharp, and M. Woodman, *Introduction to Software Project Management and Quality Assurance*, McGraw-Hill, 1993.

Paul Duggan is the manager of a software development section. On Tuesday at 10.00 am he and his fellow section heads have a meeting with their group manger about the staffing requirements for the coming year. Paul has already drafted a document 'bidding' for staff. This is based on the work planned for his section for the next year. The document is discussed at the meeting. At 2.00 pm Paul has a meeting with his senior staff about an important project his section is undertaking. One of the programming staff has just had a road accident and will be in hospital for some time. It is decided that the project can be kept on schedule by transferring another team member from less urgent work to this project. A temporary replacement is to be brought in to do the less urgent work but this may take a week or so to arrange. Paul has to phone the personnel manager about getting a replacement and the user for whom the less urgent work is being done to explain that it is likely to be delayed.

Exercise 1.6

Identify which of the eight management responsibilities listed above Paul was responding to at different points during his day.

Another way of looking at the management task is to ask managers what their most frequent challenges are. A survey of software project managers produced the following list:

The results of this survey were published by H. J. Thamhain and D. L. Wilemon in June 1986 in *Project Management Journal* under the title 'Criteria for controlling software according to plan' (pp 75–81).

- coping with deadlines (85%)
- coping with resource constraints (83%)
- communicating effectively among task groups (80%)
- gaining commitment from team members (74%)
- establishing measurable milestones (70%)
- coping with changes (60%)
- working out project plan agreement with their team (57%)
- gaining commitment from management (45%)
- dealing with conflict (42%)
- managing vendors and subcontractors (38%).

The percentages relate to the numbers of managers identifying each challenge. A manager could identify more than one.

Problems with software projects

One way of deciding what ought to covered in 'software project management' is to consider what the problems are that need to be addressed.

Traditionally, management has been seen as the preserve of a distinct class within the organization. As technology has made the tasks undertaken by an organization more sophisticated, many management tasks seem to have become dispersed throughout the organization: there are management systems rather than managers. Nevertheless the successful project will normally have one person who is charged with its success. Their concern is likely to be with the key areas which are most likely to prevent success – they are primarily trouble-shooters and their job is likely to be moulded by the problems that confront the project. A 1981 survey of managers published by Thayer, Pyster and Wood identified the following commonly experienced problems:

Further details of the survey can be found in 'Major issues in software engineering project management' in *IEEE Transactions on Software Engineering*, Volume 7, pp 333–342.

- poor estimates and plans
- lack of quality standards and measures
- lack of guidance about making organizational decisions
- lack of techniques to make progress visible
- poor role definition – who does what?
- incorrect success criteria.

The above list looks at the project from the manager's point of view. What about the staff who make up the members of the project team? Below is a list of the problems identified by a number of Computing and Information Systems degree students who had just completed a year's industrial placement:

- inadequate specification of work
- management ignorance of IT
- lack of knowledge of application area
- lack of standards
- lack of up-to-date documentation
- preceding activities not completed on time – including late delivery of equipment
- lack of communication between users and technicians
- lack of communication leading to duplication of work
- lack of commitment – especially when a project is tied to one person who then moves
- narrow scope of technical expertise
- changing statutory requirements
- changing software environment
- deadline pressure
- lack of quality control
- remote management
- lack of training.

Note how many of the problems identified by the students stemmed from poor communications. Another common problem identified by this and other groups of students is that of the many different IT specialisms – an organization may be made up of lots of individuals who will be expert in one set of software techniques and tools but ignorant of those used by their colleagues. Communication problems are therefore bound to arise.

What about the problems faced by the customers of the products of computer projects? A review of leading stories over a twelve month period in a leading UK trade paper included the following:

- a local authority had to send out incorrect council tax bills because the software supplier had not delivered a complete benefits package on time
- a leading insurance company abandoned a £40 million client-server project as it turned out to be over-ambitious
- a major heritage charity abandoned a three-year project to develop a membership system
- a computer project at one of the world's largest insurance-broking organizations was reported as being £7 millions over budget
- a police crime recording system was reported as being delayed for another year
- a report on a fire brigade said of its computer applications branch '...users have little confidence in its ability to deliver'

These stories appeared in *Computing* over a 12 month period spanning 1993 to 1994.

- the Public Accounts Committee of the House of Commons blamed poor management and spurious procurement procedures for the waste of at least £20 millions on the information systems development programme of a regional health authority
- several references were made to the failed Taurus stock exchange project (estimated at £75 millions)
- the Performing Rights Society had to abandon a £8 million membership services computer project
- a £12 million student loans IT project was abandoned (note that the £12 million was spent on IT, not student loans!)

On balance it may be a good idea not to survey users about their problems with IT projects!

Management control

Management, in general, can be seen as the process of setting objectives for a system and then monitoring the system to see what its true performance is. Having obtained this feedback, the actual performance can be compared with the objectives and remedial action can be taken when a discrepancy is found between the two (Figure 1.1).

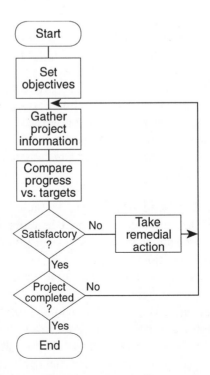

Figure 1.1 *The project control cycle.*

Objectives

To have a successful software project the manager and the project team members must know what will constitute success. This will make them concentrate on what is essential to project success.

Project objectives should be clearly defined.

There may be more than one set of users of a system and there may be different groups of staff who are involved its development. There is a need for well defined objectives that are accepted by all these people. Where there is more than one user group then a **project authority** needs to be identified which has overall authority over what the project is to achieve.

This authority is often held by a **project steering committee** which has overall responsibility for setting, monitoring and modifying objectives. The project manager still has responsibility for running the project on a day to day basis, but has to report to the steering committee at regular intervals. Only the steering committee can authorize changes to the project objectives and resources.

This committee is likely to contain user, development and management representatives.

Measures of effectiveness

Effective objectives are concrete and well defined. Vague aspirations such as 'to improve customer relations' are unsatisfactory. Objectives should be such that it is obvious to all whether the project has been successful or not. Ideally there should be **measures of effectiveness** which tell us how successful the project has been. For example, 'to reduce customer complaints by 50%' would be more satisfactory as an objective than 'to improve customer relations'.

The measure can, in some cases, be an answer to simple yes/no question, e.g. 'Did we install the new software by 1st June?'

Subobjectives and goals

In order to keep things manageable, objectives may need be broken down into subobjectives. Here we say that in order to achieve A we must achieve B, C and D first. These subobjectives are also known as **goals**, steps on the way to achieving an objective, just as goals scored in a football match are steps towards the objective of winning the match.

Identify the objectives and subobjectives of the Brightmouth HE College payroll project. What measures of effectiveness could be used to check the success in achieving the objectives of the project?

Exercise 1.7

Stakeholders

These are people who have a stake or interest in the project. It is important that they be identified as early as possible, because you need to set up adequate communication channels with them right from the start. The project leader also has to be aware that not everybody who is involved with a project has the same motivation and objectives. The end-users may, for instance, be concerned about the ease of use of the system while their managers may be interested in the staff savings the new system may allow.

Stakeholders may be internal to the project team, external to the project team but in the same organization, or totally external to the organization.

- **Internal to the project team** – this means that they will be under the direct managerial control of the project leader.
- **External to the project team but within the same organization** – for example, the project leader may need the assistance of the data base administration group in order to add some additional data types to a data base or the assistance of the users to carry out systems testing. Here the commitment of the people involved has to be negotiated .
- **External to both the project team and the organization** – external stakeholders may be customers (or users) who will benefit from the system that the project implements or contractors who will carry out work for the project. One feature of the relationship with these people is that it is likely to be based on a legally binding contract.

Within each of the general categories there will be various groups. For example, there will be different types of user with different types of interests e.g. users and user management

B. W. Boehm and R. Ross 'Theory W Software Project Management: Principles and Examples', in B. W. Boehm (ed.) *Software Risk Management*.

Different types of stakeholder may have different objectives and one of the jobs of the successful project leader is to recognize these different interests and to be able to reconcile them. It should therefore come as no surprise that the project leader needs to be a good communicator and negotiator. Boehm and Ross proposed a 'Theory W' of software project management where the manager concentrates on creating situations where all parties involved in a project benefit from it and therefore have an interest in its success. (The 'W' stands for Everyone a Winner.)

Exercise 1.8

Identify the stakeholders in the Brightmouth HE College payroll project.

Requirement specification

Very often, especially in the case of product-driven projects, the objectives of the project are carefully defined in terms of functional requirements, quality requirements, and resource requirements.

- **Functional requirements** – these define what the system that will be the end-product of the project is to do. SSADM, the government approved analysis and design method, is designed primarily to provide functional requirements.

- **Quality requirements** – there will be other attributes of the system to be implemented that do not relate so much to what the system is to do but how it is to do it. These are still things that the user will be able to experience. They include, for example, response time, the ease of using the system and its reliability.

  These are sometimes called non-functional requirements.

- **Resource requirements** – a record of how much the organization is willing to spend on the system. There may be a trade-off between this and the time it takes to implement the system. In general it costs disproportionately more to implement a system by an earlier date than a later one. There may also be a trade-off between the functional and quality requirements and cost. We would all like exceptionally reliable and user-friendly systems which do exactly what we want but we may not be able to afford them.

Information and control in organizations

With a small project, the project leader is likely to be working very closely with the other team members and may even be carrying out many non-managerial tasks themselves. Therefore they should have a pretty good idea what is going on. When projects are larger, many separate teams will be working on different aspects of the project and the overall managers of the project are not going to have day-to-day direct contact with all aspects of the work.

The larger the project, the bigger the communication problems.

Larger projects are likely to have a **hierarchical** management structure (Figure 1.2). Each project team member will have a group leader who allocates them work and to whom they report progress. In turn the group leader, along with several other group leaders, will report to a manager at the next higher level. That manager may have to report to another manager at a higher level, and so on.

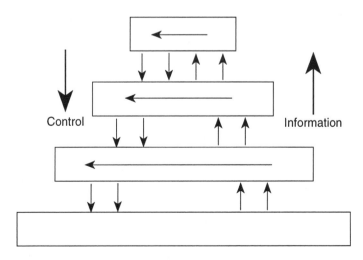

Figure 1.2 *Management information flows up the organizational structure and control flows down.*

The referral of disagreements to a higher level is sometimes known as escalation.

There may be problems that cannot be resolved at a particular level. For example, additional resources may be needed for some task, or there may be a disagreement with another group. These will be referred to the next higher level of management.

At each higher level more information will be received by fewer people. There is thus a very real danger that managers at the higher levels may be overloaded with too much information. To avoid this, at each level the information will have to be summarized.

As a result of examining the progress information and comparing it against what was planned, some remedial action may need to be taken. Instructions may be formulated and passed down to a lower level of management. The lower level managers will have to interpret what needs to be done and formulate more detailed plans to fulfil the directive. As the directives filter down the hierarchy, they will be expanded into more detail at each level.

For example, a programmer will receive a specification from an analyst and may then seek clarification.

Not all information flows concerning a project will be going up and down the hierarchy. There will also be lateral flows between groups and individuals on the same level.

Levels of decision making and information

Each decision made in a project environment should be based on adequate information of the correct sort. The type of information needed depends on the level of decision making. Decisions can be grouped at three levels: strategic, tactical, and operational.

Strategic decision making is essentially about deciding objectives. In the case of the Brightmouth HE College payroll, the decision to become administratively independent could be regarded as a strategic decision. In our example we were only interested in the payroll, but this may have been part of a wider programme which may have affected many other administrative functions.

Tactical decision making is needed to ensure that the objectives will be fulfilled. The project leader who has the responsibility for achieving objectives will have to formulate a plan of action to meet those objectives. The project leader will need to monitor progress to see whether these objectives are likely to be met and to take action where needed to ensure that the things remain on course.

Operational decisions relate to the day-to-day work of implementing the project. Deciding the content of the acceptance tests might come under this heading.

Differences in types of information

Table 1.1 gives some idea of the differences in the kind of information needed. There is a kind of continuum for most of the qualities suggested and what is needed for tactical decision making comes somewhere in the middle.

Table 1.1 *The types of information required for decision making*

Characteristic	Operational	Strategic
Viewpoint	efficiency	effectiveness
Orientation	internal	internal & external
Coverage	specific to a function	specific to organization
Detail	detailed	summarized
Response	fast	not so fast
Access paths	standard	flexible
Up-to-dateness	essential	desirable
Accuracy	essential	approximate
Certainty	essential	often predictive
Objectivity	high	more subjective
Information type	mainly quantitative	often qualitative

Effectiveness is concerned with doing the right thing. Efficiency is carrying out a task making the best possible use of the resources.

Measurement

The leader of a small project will have direct contact with many aspects of the project. With a larger project, the project leader would have to depend on information being supplied to them. This information should not be vague and ideally should be quantitative. This ties in with our need for unambiguous measures of effectiveness.

The quantification of measures of effectiveness reduces ambiguity.

Software development deals largely with intangibles and does not easily lend itself to quantitative measures, but attempts are increasingly being made to introduce measurement into the software process.

Many software engineers use the term software metrics interchangeably with software measurement. Some specialists distinguish between a **metric** that characterizes in numerical terms some simple attribute of an object such as the number of lines of code in a program, and a **measure** which is dependent on the values of more than one attribute (e.g. the productivity of a programmer measured in lines of code produced per day).

We will try to avoid the use of the term metric because of the arguments over what it really means!

Software measurements can be divided into **performance measures** and **predictive measures.**

Performance measures

These measure the characteristics of a system that has been delivered. They are important when we are trying to specify unambiguously the **quality requirements** of a proposed system.

Performance measures include mean time between failures (reliability) and time to learn a package (usability).

Predictive measures

The trouble with performance measures is that you need to have a system actually up and running before you can take measurements. As a project leader what you want to be able to do is to get some idea of the characteristics during its development of the final system. **Predictive measures** are taken during development and indicate what the performance of the final system is likely to be.

For example, the errors found per KLOC (i.e. thousand lines of code) at different stages of the project may help to predict the correctness and reliability of the final system. Keystrokes required to carry out a particular transaction may help predict what the operator time to carry out the transaction is likely to be. Modularity, the degree to which the software is composed of self-contained manageable components, may help predict how easy changes to the final system will be.

Conclusion

This chapter has laid a foundation for the remainder of the book by defining what is meant by various terms such as 'software project ' and 'management'. Among some of the more important points that have been made are the following.

- Projects are by definition non-routine and therefore more uncertain than normal undertakings.
- Software projects are similar to other projects but have some attributes that present particular difficulties, e.g. the relative invisibility of many of their products.
- A key factor in project success is having clear objectives. Different stakeholders in a project, however, are likely to have different objectives. This points to the need for a recognized overall project authority.
- For objectives to be effective there must be practical ways of testing that the objectives have been met. Hence there is a need for measurement.
- Where projects involve many different people, effective channels of information have to be established. Having objectives measures of success helps unambiguous communication between the various parties to a project.

Further exercises

1. List the problems you experienced when you carried out a recent programming assignment. Try and put these problems into some order of magnitude. For each problem consider whether there was some way in which the problem could have been reduced by better organization and planning by yourself.

2. Identify the main types of personnel employed in an information systems department. For each stage of a typical IS development project, list the types of personnel who are likely to be involved.

3. A local authority is considering the implementation of a computer-based system to help administer book loans at libraries. Identify the stakeholders in

such a project. What might be the objectives of such a project and how might the success of the project be measured in practical terms?

4. Suggest objectives for the following types of staff. In each case suggest two measures of efficiency or effectiveness:
    (a) a data preparation clerk
    (b) a programmer/analyst
    (c) a computer software sales person
    (d) a systems analyst
    (e) a software project leader.

Chapter 2

'Step Wise' An overview of project planning

OBJECTIVES

When you have completed this chapter you will be able to:

☐ approach project planning in an organized step-by-step manner

☐ see where the techniques described in other chapters fit into an overall planning approach

☐ repeat the planning process in more detail for sets of activities within a project as the time comes to execute them.

Introduction to 'Step Wise' project planning

This chapter describes a framework of basic steps in project planning and control upon which the following chapters build. There are many different techniques which can be used in project planning and this chapter gives an overview of the points at which these techniques can be used during project planning. Chapter 4 will illustrate how different projects may need different approaches, but this framework should always apply to the planning process used.

Appendix A adds some further details about the PRINCE approach.
The framework described is called the Step Wise method to help to distinguish it from other methods such as PRINCE. PRINCE is the set of IT project management standards that have been developed and promulgated by the Central Computing and Telecommunications Agency (CCTA) for use on British government IT projects. The standards are also being more widely being used on non-government projects in the United Kingdom. Step Wise should be compatible with PRINCE. It should be noted, however, that Step Wise only covers the planning stages of a project and not monitoring and control.

In order to illustrate the Step Wise approach and to show how it may have to be adapted to deal with different circumstances, two parallel examples are used. Let us assume that there are two former Computing and Information Systems students who now have several years of software development experience under their belts.

Brigette has been working for the Management Services department of a local authority when she sees an advertisement for the position of Information Systems Development Officer at Brightmouth HE College. She is attracted to the idea of being her own boss, working in a relatively small organization and helping them to set up appropriate information systems from scratch. She applies for the job and gets it. One of the first tasks that confronts her is the implementation of independent payroll processing! (This scenario has already been used as the basis of some examples in Chapter 1.)

Amanda works for International Office Equipment (IOE), which manufactures and supplies various items of high-technology office equipment. An expanding area of their work is the maintenance of IT equipment. They have now started to undertake maintenance of equipment for which they were not originally the suppliers. A computer-based batch processing system deals with invoicing on a job-by-job basis. An organization may have to call IOE out several times to deal with different bits of equipment and there is a need to be able to group the invoice details for work done into 'group accounts' for which monthly statements will be produced. Amanda has been given her first project management role, the task of implementing this extension to the invoicing system.

Case study examples: Brightmouth HE College Payroll and International Office Equipment Group Maintenance Accounts

---

In Table 2.1 we outline the general approach that might be taken to planning these projects. Figure 2.1 provides an outline of the main planning activities. Steps 1 and 2 'Identify project scope and objectives' and 'Identify project infrastructure' may be tackled in parallel in some cases. Steps 5 and 6 will need to be repeated for each activity needed to complete the project.

A major principle of project planning is to plan in outline first and then in more detail as the time to carry out an activity approaches. Hence the lists of products and activities that are the result of Step 4 will be reviewed when the tasks connected with a particular phase of a project are considered in more detail. This will be followed by a more detailed iteration of Steps 5 to 8 for the phase under consideration.

Table 2.1 *An outline of Step Wise planning activities*

Step	Activities within step
0	Select project
1	Identify project scope and objectives
	1.1 Identify objectives and measures of effectiveness in meeting them
	1.2 Establish a project authority
	1.3 Stakeholder analysis
	1.4 Modify objectives in the light of stakeholder analysis
	1.5 Establish methods of communications with all parties
2	Identify project infrastructure
	2.1 Establish relationship between project and strategic planning
	2.2 Identify installation standards and procedures
	2.3 Identify project team organization
3	Analyse project characteristics
	3.1 Distinguish the project as either objective- or product-driven
	3.2 Analyse other project characteristics
	3.3 Identify high level project risks
	3.4 Take into account user requirements concerning implementation
	3.5 Select general life-cycle approach
	3.6 Review overall resource estimates
4	Identify project products and activities
	4.1 Identify and describe project products (including quality criteria)
	4.2 Document generic product flows
	4.3 Recognize product instances
	4.4 Produce ideal activity network
	4.5 Modify ideal to take into account need for stages and checkpoints
5	Estimate effort for each activity
	5.1 Carry out bottom-up estimates
	5.2 Revise plan to create controllable activities
6	Identify activity risks
	6.1 Identify and quantify activity-based risks
	6.2 Plan risk reduction and contingency measures where appropriate
	6.3 Adjust plans and estimates to take account of risks
7	Allocate resources
	7.1 Identify and allocate resources
	7.2 Revise plans and estimates to account for resource constraints
8	Review/publicize plan
	8.1 Review quality aspects of project plan
	8.2 Document plans and obtain agreement
9/10	Execute plan/lower levels of planning
	This may require the reiteration of the planning process at a lower level

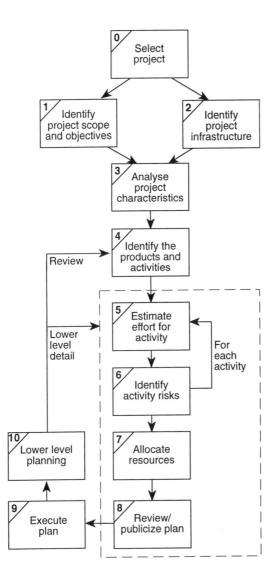

Figure 2.1 *An overview of Step Wise.*

Step 0: Select project

This is called Step 0 because in a way it is outside the main project planning process. Projects are not initiated out of thin air – some activity may have to take place which decides that this project is worth undertaking as opposed to others. This project evaluation may be done on an individual basis or as part of strategic planning.

Step 1: Identify project scope and objectives

The activities in this step ensure that all the parties to the project agree on the objectives and are committed to the success of the project. A danger to be avoided is overlooking people who are affected by the project.

Step 1.1: Identify objectives and practical measures of the effectiveness in meeting those objectives

We discussed earlier the need for agreed objectives for a project and ways of measuring the success in achieving those objectives.

Case Study Example: Project objectives

The project objectives for the Brightmouth HE College payroll project have already been discussed in Exercise 1.7.

Amanda at IOE has the objectives clearly laid down for her in the recommendations of a feasibility study report which have been accepted by IOE management. The main objectives are to allow a detailed monthly statement to be sent to group account clients and to be able to reallocate the cash received to individual jobs when the client has paid on the monthly statement. Other objectives are laid down that refer to expected timescales and the resources that may be used.

Step 1.2: Establish a project authority

A single overall project authority needs to be established so that there is unity of purpose between all those concerned.

Case Study Examples: Project authorities

Throughout the text we use capitalized initial letters to indicate a term that has a precise meaning in the PRINCE standards, e.g. Project Board.

Amanda finds that her manager and the main user management have already set up a Project Board which will have overall direction of the project. She is a little concerned as the equipment maintenance staff are organized with different sections dealing with different types of equipment. This means that a customer may have work done by several different sections. Not all the sections are represented on the Project Board and Amanda is aware that there are some differences of opinion between the different sections. It is left to the user representatives on the board to resolve those differences and to present an agreed policy to the systems developers.

Brigette finds that effectively she has two different clients for the payroll system: the finance and personnel departments. To help resolve conflicts, it is agreed that the managers of both departments should attend a monthly meeting with the Vice-Principal which Brigette has arranged in order to steer the project.

Step 1.3: Stakeholder analysis – identify all stakeholders in the project and their interests

Recall that this was the basis of a discussion in Chapter 1. Essentially all the parties who have an interest in the project need to be identified. In that chapter we listed as an example the stakeholders in the Brightmouth HE College Payroll project.

What important stakeholders outside the IOE organization might be considered in the case of the IOE Maintenance Group Accounts System?

Exercise 2.1

Step 1.4: Modify objectives in the light of stakeholder analysis

In order to gain the full cooperation of all concerned, it may be necessary to modify the project objectives. This may mean adding new features to the system which give a benefit to some stakeholder as a means of assuring their commitment to the project. This is potentially dangerous as the system size may be increased and the original objectives obscured. Because of these dangers, it is suggested that this process be done consciously and in a controlled manner.

The IOE maintenance staff are to be given the extra task of entering data about completed jobs. They do not benefit from this additional work. To give some benefit, the system is to be extended to automatically reorder spare parts when required.

Case Study Examples: Modified project objectives

At Brightmouth HE College, the personnel department may have a lot of work preparing payroll details for finance. It may be tactful to agree to produce some management information reports for personnel from the payroll details held on the computer.

Step 1.5: Establish methods of communication with all parties

For internal staff this should be fairly straightforward, but a project leader implementing a payroll system would need to find a contact point with BACS (Bankers Automated Clearing Scheme) for instance.

Step 2: Identify project infrastructure

Projects are rarely initiated in a vacuum. There is usually some kind of existing infrastructure into which the project can fit. If they do not know already, the project leader must find out the precise nature of this infrastructure.

Step 2.1: Identify relationship between the project and strategic planning

Some of the issues of
strategic planning are
addressed in Chapter 3.
As well as identifying projects to be carried out, an organization needs to decide in what order these projects are to be carried out. It also needs to establish the framework within which the proposed new systems are to fit. Hardware and software standards, for example, may be needed so that various systems can communicate with each other. These strategic decisions may be documented in a strategic business plan or in an information technology plan that is developed from the business plan.

**Case Study Examples:
Role of existing
strategic plans**

Amanda finds at IOE that there is a well-defined rolling strategic plan which has identified her group accounts subsystem as an important required development. Because it is an extension of an existing system, the hardware and software platforms upon which the application are to run are dictated.

Brigette at Brightmouth HE College finds that there is an overall College strategic plan which describes new courses to be developed, and so on, and mentions in passing the need for 'appropriate administrative procedures' to be in place. There is a recommendation that independent payroll processing be undertaken in a short section in a consultant's report from an accountancy firm concerning the implications of financial autonomy. Although the college has quite a lot of IT equipment for teaching purposes, there is no machine set aside for payroll processing and the intention is that the hardware to run the payroll will be acquired at the same time as the software.

Step 2.2: Identify installation standards and procedures

Each installation that develops software should promulgate development procedures. As a minimum, the normal stages in the software life cycle to be carried out should be documented along with the products created at each stage.

See Chapter 9 on
Monitoring and Control.
Change control and **configuration management** standards should be in place to ensure that changes to requirements are implemented in a safe and orderly way.

The procedural standards may lay down the quality checks that need to be done at each point of the project life cycle or these may be documented in a separate **quality standards and procedures** manual.

The organization as part of its monitoring and control policy may have a **measurement programme** in place which dictates that certain statistics have to be collected at various stages of a project.

Finally the project manager should make sure they are aware of any **project planning and control standards**. These will relate to the way that the project is controlled: for example, the way that the hours spent by team members on individual tasks are recorded on time-sheets

Amanda at IOE finds that there is a very weighty volume of development standards which, among other things, specifies that SSADM will be the analysis and design method used. She finds that a separate document has been prepared which lays down quality procedures. This specifies when the reviews of work will be carried out and describes detailed procedures about how the reviews are to be done. Amanda also finds a set of project management guidelines modelled closely on PRINCE.

Brigette finds no documents of the nature that Amanda found at IOE except for some handouts for students that have been produced by different lecturers at different times and which seem to contradict each other.

As a stop-gap measure, Brigette writes a brief document which states what the main stages of a 'project' (perhaps 'job for the user' would be a better term in this context) should be. This happens to be very similar to the list given in Chapter 1. She stresses that:

- no job of work to change a system or implement a new one is to be done without there being a detailed specification first
- the users must 'sign off' (i.e. agree to) each specification in writing before the work is carried out.

She draws up a simple procedure for recording all changes to user requirements.

Brigette, of course, has no organizational quality procedures, but she dictates that each person in the group (including herself) has to get someone else to check through their work when they finish a major task and that, before any new or amended software is handed over to the users, someone other than the original producer should test it. She sets up a simple system to record errors found in system testing and their resolution. She also creates a log file of reported user problems with operational systems.

Brigette does not worry about time sheets but arranges an informal meeting with her colleagues each Monday morning to discuss how things are going and also arranges to see the Vice-Principal, who is her official boss, and the heads of the finance and personnel sections each month to review progress in general terms.

**Case Study Examples:
Identifying standards**

Step 2.3: Identify project team organization
The project leader, especially in the case of large projects, may have some control over the organizational structure of the project team. More often, though, the organizational structure will be dictated to them. For example, a high level managerial decision may have been taken that programmers and systems analysts will be in different groups, or that the development of PC applications will not be done within the same group as that responsible for 'traditional' main-frame applications.

Some of these issues will be discussed in Chapter 10 – Team organization and managing people.

If the project leader does have some control over the project team organization then this would best be considered at a later stage (see Step 7: Allocate resources).

Case Study Examples:
Project organization

At IOE, there are groups of systems analysts set up as teams which deal with individual user departments. Hence the users always know whom they should contact within the information systems department if they have a problem. Programmers, however, work in a 'pool' and are allocated to specific projects on an 'ad hoc' basis.

At Brightmouth HE College, Brigette has seconded to her a programmer who has been acting as a technician supporting the computing courses in the college. She is also allowed to recruit a trainee analyst/programmer. She is not unduly worried about the organizational structure that is needed.

Step 3: Analyse project characteristics

Chapter 4 elaborates on the process of analysing project characteristics.

The general purpose of this part of the planning operation is to ensure that the appropriate methods are used for the project.

Step 3.1: Distinguish the project as either objective- or product-driven

This has already been discussed in the first chapter. A general point to note is that as system development advances it tends to become more product-driven, although the underlying objectives always remain and must be respected.

Step 3.2: Analyse other project characteristics (including quality-based ones)

For example, is this an information system that is being developed or a process control system, or does it have elements of both? Is it a safety-critical system, i.e. could human life be threatened by a malfunction?

Step 3.3: Identify high level project risks

Consideration must be given to the risks that threaten the successful outcome of the project. Generally speaking most risks can be attributed to the operational or development environment, the technical nature of the project or the type of product being created.

Case Study Example:
High level risks

At IOE Amanda identifies the danger of there being resistance to the new system by maintenance engineers, especially as a new centralized group accounts office is to be set up. Amanda decides therefore that additional efforts are needed to consult all sections involved and that the new procedures should be introduced in small increments to accustom staff to them gradually.

Brigette at Brightmouth HE College considers the application area to be very well-defined. There is a risk, however, that there may be no package on the market which caters for the way that things are done at the moment. Brigette, therefore, decides that an early task in the project is to obtain information about the features of the main payroll packages that are available.

Step 3.4: Take into account user requirements concerning implementation

The clients may have their own procedural requirements. For example, work for government departments may require the use of SSADM.

Step 3.5: Select general life-cycle approach in the light of the above

The project life cycle to be used for the project will be influenced by the issues raised above. For example, a prototyping approach may be used where the user requirements are not clear.

Chapter 4 discusses life cycles in more detail.

Step 3.6: Review overall resource estimates

Once the major risks have been identified and the broad project approach has been decided upon, this would be a good point at which to reestimate the effort and other resources required to implement the project. Where enough information is available a function point-based estimate might be appropriate.

Chapter 5 goes into more detail on this topic. Function points are an attempt to measure system size without using lines of code.

Step 4: Identify project products and activities

The more detailed planning of the individual activities that will be needed now takes place. The longer term planning is broad and in outline, while the more immediate tasks are planned in some detail.

Step 4.1: Identify and describe project products (or deliverables)

In general there can be no project products which do not have activities which create them. Wherever possible, we ought also to ensure the reverse: that there are no activities which do not produce a tangible product. Making sure we have identified all the things the project is to create helps us to ensure that all the activities we need to carry out are accounted for.

Chapter 7 goes into this in more detail.

These products will include a large number of **technical** products including training material and operating instructions, but also products to do with the **management** and the **quality** of the project. Planning documents would, for example, be management products.

PRINCE suggests that the PBS be presented as a hierarchy diagram. In practice it may be more convenient to produce a structured list.

The products will form a hierarchy. The main products will have sets of component products which in turn may have subcomponent products and so on. These relationships can be documented in a Product Breakdown Structure (PBS).

This part of the planning process draws heavily on the standards laid down in PRINCE. These specify that products at the bottom of the PBS should be documented by **Product Descriptions** which contain:

- the **name/identity** of the product
- the **purpose** of the product
- the **derivation** of the product (i.e. the other products from which it is derived)
- the **composition** of the product
- the **form** of the product
- the relevant **standards**
- the **quality** criteria that should apply to it.

Case Study Example: Product breakdown structures

At IOE, Amanda finds that there is a standard PBS that she can use as a check-list for her own project.

Brigette at Brightmouth HE College has no installation standard PBS, although she can, of course, refer to various books for standard check-lists. She decides that one part of the PBS should contain the products needed to help select the appropriate hardware and software for the payroll application (Figure 2.2).

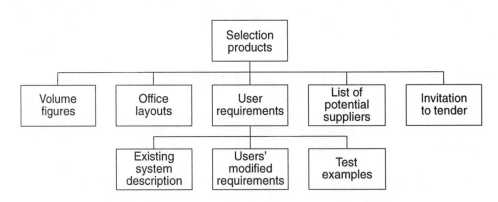

Figure 2.2 *A fragment of the PBS for the Brightmouth HE College Payroll Project.*

Step 4.2: Document generic product flows

Some of the products will need some other product to exist first before they can be created. For example, a program design must be created before the program can be written and the program specification must exist before the design can be commenced. These relationships can be portrayed in a **Product Flow Diagram** (PFD). Figure 2.3 gives an example.

At IOE, Amanda has a standard installation PFD. Many of the products that will make up Amanda's application will be of the same type: hence the same generic PFD will apply to each instance. It is pointless in these circumstances to draw up a separate PFD for each instance of the product.

Case Study Example: IOE has standard PFD

Draw up a possible Product Flow Diagram (PFD) based on the Product Breakdown Structure (PBS) shown in Figure 2.2. This represents the products that will be produced when gathering information to be presented to potential suppliers of the hardware. The volume figures are for such things as the number of employees for whom records will have to be maintained.

Exercise 2.2

Step 4.3: Recognize product instances

Where the same generic PFD fragment relates to more than one instance of a particular type of product, an attempt should be made to identify each of those instances.

This may be delayed to later in the project when more information is known.

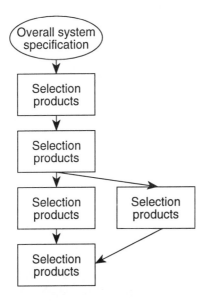

Figure 2.3 *A fragment of a PFD.*

Case Study Example: identifying product instances

Amanda decides that there are likely to be four major software modules needed in her application for which the PFD fragment in Figure 2.3 would be appropriate The products that Brigette can identify at the present are all unique.

Step 4.4: Produce ideal activity network

In order to generate one product from another there must be one or more activities which carry out the transformation. By identifying these activities we can create an activity network which shows the tasks that have to be carried out and the order in which they have to be executed.

Case Study Example: Activity network for IOE Maintenance Accounts

Part of the initial activity network for the IOE Maintenance Group Accounts project might look like Figure 2.4.

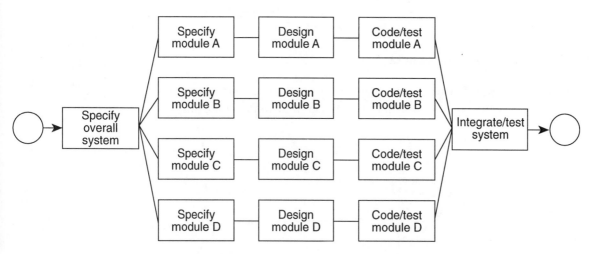

Figure 2.4 *An activity network fragment for the IOE Maintenance Group Accounts project.*

Exercise 2.3

Draw up an Activity Network for the Product Flow Diagram that you created in Exercise 2.2 (or the PFD given in the solution if you prefer!).

The activity networks are 'ideal' in the sense that no account has been taken of resource constraints. For example in Figure 2.4, it is assumed that resources are available for all four software modules to be developed in parallel.

Step 4.5: Modify the ideal to take into account need for stages and checkpoints

The approach to sequencing activities described above encourages the formulation of a plan which will minimize the elapsed time for the project (i.e. the overall duration). It assumes that an activity will start as soon as the preceding ones upon which it depends have been completed.

There may, however, be a need to modify this by dividing the project into stages and introducing checkpoint activities. These are activities which draw together the products of preceding activities to check that they are compatible. These are sometimes referred to as **milestone** events. This could potentially delay work on some elements of the project – there has to be a trade-off between efficiency and quality.

Amanda decides that after the four modules have been specified, the four specifications need to be carefully checked to see that they are consistent and compatible. Redraw the activity network in Figure 2.4 to reflect this.

Exercise 2.4

Step 5: Estimate effort for each activity

Step 5.1: Carry out bottom-up estimates

Some top-down estimates of effort, cost and duration will already have been done (see Step 3.6).

At this point, estimates of the staff effort required, the probable elapsed time and the other resources needed for each activity will need to be produced. The method of arriving at each of these estimates will vary depending on the type of activity.

Chapter 5 on Software Estimation deals with this topic in more detail.

The individual activity estimates of effort should be summed to get an overall bottom-up estimate which can be reconciled with the previous top-down estimate.

The activities on the activity network can be annotated with their elapsed times so that the overall duration of the project can be calculated.

Step 5.2: Revise plan to create controllable activities

The estimates for individual activities may reveal that some are going to take quite a long time. Long activities may make a project difficult to control. If an activity involving system testing is to take 12 weeks, it may be difficult after six weeks to judge accurately whether 50% of the work is completed. It would be better to break this down into a series of smaller subtasks.

Case Study Example:
IOE Maintenance Group
Accounts – breaking
activities down into
manageable tasks

At IOE, Amanda has to estimate the lines of code for each of the software modules. She looks at programs that have been coded for similar types of application at IOE in the past to get some idea of the size of the new modules. She then refers to some conversion tables that the information systems development department at IOE have produced which convert the lines of code into estimates of effort. Other tables allow her to allocate the estimated effort to the various stages of the project.

Although Brigette is aware that some additional programs may have to be written to deal with local requirements, the main software is to be obtained 'off-the-shelf' and so estimating based on lines of code would clearly be inappropriate. Instead, she looks at each individual task and allocates a time. She realizes that in many cases these represent 'targets' as she is uncertain at the moment how long these tasks will really take (see Step 6 below).

Step 6: Identify activity risks

Step 6.1: Identify and quantify activity-based risks

Chapter 7 on Risk
touches on this topic in
more detail.

Risks inherent in the overall nature of the project have already been considered in Step 3. We now want to look at each activity in turn and assess the risks to its successful outcome. The seriousness of each risk and likelihood of it occurring have to be gauged. At individual task level some risks are unavoidable, and the general effect if a problem materializes is to make the task longer or more costly. A range of estimates may be produced which take into account the possible occurrence of the risks.

Step 6.2: Plan risk reduction and contingency measures where appropriate

It may be possible to avoid or at least reduce some of the identified risks. Contingency plans specify action that is to be taken if a risk materializes. For example, a contingency plan could be to use contract staff if a member of the project team is unavailable at a key time because of serious illness.

Step 6.3: Adjust overall plans and estimates to take account of risks

We may change our plans, perhaps by adding new activities which reduce risks. For example, a new programming language may mean we schedule training courses and time for the programmers to practise their new programming skills on some non-essential work.

As well as the four new software modules that will have to be written, Amanda has identified several existing modules that will need to be amended. The ease with which the modules can be amended will depend upon the way that they were originally written. There is therefore a risk that they may take longer than expected to modify. Amanda takes no risk reduction measures as such but notes a pessimistic elapsed time for the amendment activity.

Brigette identifies as a risk the possible absence of key staff when investigating the user requirements as this activity will take place over the holiday period. To reduce this risk, she adds a new activity, 'arrange user interviews', at the beginning of the project. This will give her advance notice of any likely problems of this nature.

Case Study Example: Identifying risks

Step 7: Allocate resources

Step 7.1: Identify and allocate resources

The type of staff needed for each activity is recorded. The staff available for the project are identified and are provisionally allocated to tasks.

Chapter 8 on Resource allocation covers this topic in more detail.

Step 7.2: Revise plans and estimates to take into account resource constraints

Some staff may be needed for more than one task at the same time and, in this case, an order of priority is established. The decisions made here may have an effect on the overall duration of the project when some tasks are delayed while waiting for staff to become free.

Ensuring someone is available to start work on an activity as soon as the preceding activities have been completed may mean that they are idle while waiting for the job to start and are therefore used inefficiently.

Amanda has now identified four major software modules plus two existing software modules that will need extensive amendment. At IOE the specification of modules is carried out by the lead systems analyst for the project (who in this case is Amanda) assisted by junior analyst/designers. Four analyst/programmers are available to carry out the design, coding and unit testing of the individual modules. After careful consideration and discussion with her manager, Amanda decides to use only three analyst/programmers so as to minimize the risk of staff waiting between tasks. It is accepted that this decision, while reducing the cost of the project, will delay its end.

Brigette finds that she herself will have to carry out many important activities. She can reduce the workload on herself by delegating some work to her two colleagues, but she realizes that she will have to devote more time to specifying

Case Study Example: Taking resource constraints into account

exactly what they will have to do and to checking their work. She adjusts her plan accordingly.

Step 8: Review/publicize plan

Step 8.1: Review quality aspects of the project plan

A danger when controlling any project is that an activity can reveal that an earlier activity was not properly completed and needs to be reworked. This, at a stroke, can transform a project that appears to be progressing satisfactorily into one that is badly out of control. It is important to know that when a task is reported as completed, it really is – hence the importance of quality reviews. Each task should have 'exit requirements'. These are quality checks that have to be passed before the activity can be 'signed off' as completed.

Case Study Example: IOE existing quality standards

Amanda finds that at IOE, the Quality Standards and Procedures Manual lays down quality criteria for each type of task. For example, all module design documentation has to be reviewed by a group of colleagues before the coding of that module can commence.

Exercise 2.5

Brigette has no installation standards to help her apart from the minimal ones she has written herself. What quality checks might Brigette introduce to ensure that she has understood the users requirements properly?

Step 8.2: Document plans and obtain agreement

It is important that the plans be carefully documented and that all the parties to the project understand and agree to the commitments required of them in the plan.

Steps 9 and 10 Execute plan/lower levels of planning

Once the project is under way, plans will need to be drawn up in greater detail for each activity as it becomes due. Detailed planning of the later stages will need to be delayed because more information will be available nearer the start of the stage. Of course, it is necessary to make provisional plans for the more distant tasks, because thinking about what needs to be done can help unearth potential problems, but sight should not be lost of the fact that these plans are provisional.

While work is going on with the specification of the individual modules, Amanda has some time to start planning the integration tests in some detail. She finds that, in fact, integration testing of two of the six new or amended modules will be independent of the others. Testing of these two can start when they are ready without waiting for the remainder.

When Brigette comes to consider the activity 'draft invitation to tender', she has to familiarize herself with the detailed institutional rules and procedures that govern this process. She finds that in order to draft this document she will need to obtain some additional pieces of information from the users.

Case Study Examples:
Lower level planning

Conclusion

This chapter has presented a framework into which the techniques described in the other parts of the book should slot. It is suggested that any planning approach should have the following elements:

- the establishment of project objectives
- the analysis of the characteristics of the project
- the establishment of an infrastructure consisting of an appropriate organization and set of standards, methods and tools
- the identification of the products of the project and the activities needed to generate those products
- the allocation of resources to activities
- the establishment of quality controls.

Project management is an iterative process. As the time approaches for particular activities to be carried out they should be replanned in more detail.

Further Exercises

1. List the products created by the Step Wise planning process.

2. What products must exist before the activity 'test program' can take place? What products does this activity create?

3. An employee of a training organization has the task of creating case study exercises and solutions for a training course which teaches a new systems analysis and design method. The person's work plan has a three-week task 'learn new method'. A colleague suggests that this is unsatisfactory as a task as there are no concrete deliverables or products from the activity. What can be done about this?

4. In order to carry out usability tests for a new word processing package, the software has to be written and debugged. User instructions have to be available describing how the package is to be used. These have to be scrutinized in order to plan and design the tests. Subjects who will use the package in the tests will need to be selected. As part of this selection process, they will have to complete a questionnaire giving details of their past experience of, and training in, typing and using word processing packages. The subjects will carry out the required tasks using the word processing package. The tasks will be timed and any problems the subjects encounter with the package will be noted. After the test, the subjects will complete another questionnaire about what they felt about the package. All the data from the tests will be analysed and a report containing recommendations for changes to the package will be drawn up. Draw up a Product Breakdown Structure, a Product Flow Diagram and a preliminary activity network for the above.

5. Identify the actions that could prevent each of the following risks from materializing or could reduce the impact if it did occur:
    (a) a key member of the programming team leaving
    (b) a new version of the operating system being introduced which has error in it
    (c) a disk containing copies of the most up-to-date version of the software under development being corrupted
    (d) system testing unearths more errors than were expected and takes longer than planned
    (e) the government changes the taxation rules which alter the way that VAT is to be calculated in an order processing system under development.

6. Read Appendix A on PRINCE. To what extent could the PRINCE project management standards be usefully applied to the Brightmouth HE College payroll?

Chapter 3

Project evaluation

OBJECTIVES

When you have completed this chapter you will be able to:

☐ carry out an evaluation and selection of projects against strategic, technical and economic criteria

☐ use a variety of cost-benefit evaluation techniques for choosing between competing project proposals

☐ evaluate the risk involved in a project and select appropriate strategies for minimizing potential costs.

Introduction

Deciding whether or not to go ahead with a project is really a case of comparing a proposed project with the alternatives and deciding whether to proceed with it. That evaluation will be based on strategic, technical and economic criteria and will normally be undertaken as part of a strategic planning or feasibility study for any information system development. We shall also need to evaluate the risks involved.

'Do nothing' is an alternative which should always be considered.

In this chapter we shall be using the term project in a broader sense than elsewhere in the book. Our decision as to whether or not to proceed with a project is a decision based upon whether or not it is desirable to carry out the development and operation of a software system. The term project will therefore be used to describe the whole life cycle of a system from conception through to final decommissioning.

Project evaluation is normally carried out in Step 0 of Step Wise (Figure 3.1). The subsequent steps of Step Wise are then concerned with managing the development project that stems from this project selection.

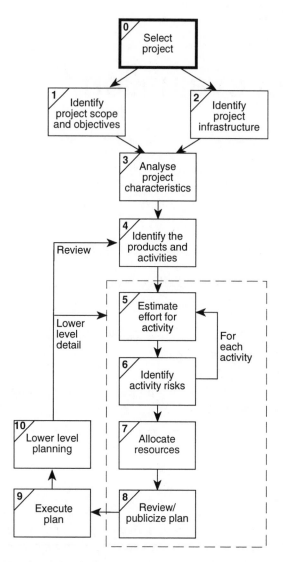

Figure 3.1 *Project evaluation is carried out in Step 0.*

Strategic assessment

For a more detailed
exploration of the
strategic implications see
Chris Clare & Gordon
Stutely, *Information
Systems: A Strategy to
Design*, in this series.

In an information system's environment, any potential software system will form part of the user organization's overall information system and should be evaluated within that context rather than as an isolated system. In order to carry out this strategic assessment of a potential project there must be a strategic plan clearly defining the organization's objectives and, ideally, the role and plans for information systems development (Table 3.1).

Table 3.1 *Typical issues and questions to be considered during strategic assessment*

Issue	Typical questions
Objectives	How will the proposed system contribute to the organization's stated objectives? How, for example, might it contribute to an increase in market share?
IS plan	How does the proposed system fit into the IS plan? Which existing system(s) will it replace/interface with? How will it interact with systems proposed for later development?
Organization structure	What effect will the new system have on existing departmental and organization structure? Will, for example, a new sales order processing system overlap existing sales and stock control functions?
MIS	What information will the system provide and at what levels in the organization? In what ways will it complement or enhance existing management information systems?
Personnel	In what way will the proposed system affect manning levels and the existing employee skill base? What are the implications for the organization's overall policy on staff development?
Image	What, if any, will be the effect on customers' attitudes towards the organization? Will the adoption of, say, automated systems conflict with the objectives of providing a friendly service?

Where an organization such as a software house is developing a software system they may be asked to carry out a strategic and operational assessment on behalf of the customer. Whether or not this is the case, they will require an assessment of any proposed project themselves. They will need to ensure that carrying out the development of a system is consistent with their own strategic plan – it is unlikely, for example, that a software house specializing in financial and accounting systems would wish to undertake development of a factory control system unless their strategic plan placed an emphasis on diversification.

Where a well-defined information systems strategy does not exist, system development and the assessment of project proposal will be based on a more piecemeal approach – each project being individually assessed early in its life cycle. In such cases it is likely that cost–benefit analysis will have more importance and some of the questions of Table 3.1 will be more difficult to answer.

Third party developers must also carry out strategic and operational assessment of project proposals.

Technical assessment

Technical assessment of a proposed system consists of evaluating the required functionality against the hardware and software available. Where an organization has a strategic information systems plan this is likely to place limitations on the nature of solutions that might be considered. The constraints will, of course, influence the cost of the solution and this must be taken into account in the cost–benefit analysis.

Cost–benefit analysis

The most common way of carrying out an economic assessment of a proposed information system, or other development, is by comparing the expected costs of development and operation of the system with the benefits of having it in place.

Any project requiring an investment must, as a minimum, provide a greater benefit than putting that investment in a building society or bank.

Assessment is based upon the question of whether the estimated costs are exceeded by the estimated income and other benefits. Additionally it is usually necessary to ask whether or not the project under consideration is the best of a number of alternatives. There may be more candidate projects than can be undertaken at any one time and, in any case, projects will need to be prioritized so that any scarce resources may be allocated effectively.

The standard way of evaluating the economic benefits of any project is to carry out a cost–benefit analysis which consists of two steps.

- **Identifying and estimating all of the costs and benefits of carrying out the project**. This includes development costs of the system, the operating costs and the benefits that are expected to accrue from the operation of the system. Where the proposed system is replacing an existing one these estimates should reflect the costs and benefits due to the new system. A sales order processing system, for example, could not claim to benefit an organization by the total value of sales – only the increase due to the use of the new system.
- **Expressing these costs and benefits in common units.** We must evaluate the net benefit which is the difference between the total benefit and the total cost. To do this we must express each cost and each benefit in monetary terms.

Many costs are easy to identify and measure in monetary terms.

Most costs are relatively easy to identify and quantify in approximate monetary terms. It is helpful to categorize costs according to where they originate in the life of the project.

- **Development costs** – include the salaries and other employment costs of the staff involved in the development project and all associated costs.
- **Setup costs** – include the costs of putting the system into place. These consist mainly of the costs of any new hardware and ancillary equipment but will also include costs of file conversion, recruitment and staff training.
- **Operational costs** – consist of the costs of operating the system once it has been installed.

Benefits, on the other hand, are often quite difficult to quantify in monetary terms even once they have been identified. Benefits may be categorized as follows.

- **Direct benefits** – these accrue directly from the operation of the proposed system. These could, for example, include the reduction in salary bills through the introduction of a new, computerized system.
- **Assessable indirect benefits** – these are generally secondary benefits, such as increased accuracy through the introduction of a more user-friendly screen design where we may be able to estimate the reduction in errors, and hence costs, of the proposed system.
- **Intangible benefits** – these are generally longer term or benefits that are considered very difficult to quantify. Enhanced job interest may lead to reduced staff turnover and, hence, lower recruitment costs.

> Indirect costs which are difficult to estimate are sometimes known as intangible costs.

Brightmouth HE College are considering the replacement of the local authority supplied payroll service with a tailored, off-the-shelf computer-based system. List some of the costs and benefits they might consider under each of the six headings given above. For each cost or benefit, explain how, in principle, it might be measured in monetary terms.

> **Exercise 3.1**

Any project that shows an excess of benefits over costs is clearly worth considering for implementation. However, as we shall see later, it is not a sufficient justification for going ahead: we may not be able to afford the costs; there may be even better projects we could allocate our resources to instead; the project may be too risky.

> If a proposal shows an excess of benefits over costs then it is a candidate for further consideration.

Cash flow forecasting

As important as estimating the overall costs and benefits of a project is the forecasting of the cash flows that will take place and their timing. A cash flow forecast will indicate when expenditure and income will take place (Figure 3.2).

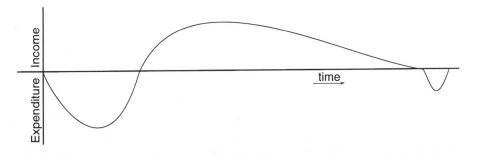

> Typically products generate a negative cash flow during their development followed by a positive cash flow over their operating life. There may be decommissioning costs at the end of a product's life.

Figure 3.2 *Typical product life cycle cash flow.*

The difficulty and importance of cash flow forecasting is evidenced by the number of companies that suffer bankruptcy because, although they are developing profitable products or services, they cannot sustain an unplanned negative cash flow.

We need to spend money, such as staff wages, during the development stages of a project. Such expenditure cannot be deferred until income is received (either from using the software if it is being developed for in-house use or from selling it). It is important that we know that we can fund the development expenditure either from the company's own resources or by borrowing from the bank. In any event, it is vital to have some forecast of when expenditure will take place (e.g. end of month salaries and bank interest payments) and when any income is to be expected (e.g. payment on completion and, possibly, stage payments).

Accurate cash flow forecasting is not easy as it generally needs to be done early in the project's life cycle (at least before any significant expenditure is committed) and many items to be estimated (particularly the benefits of using software or decommissioning costs) may be some years in the future.

When estimating future cash flows it is usual to ignore the effects of inflation. Trying to forecast the effects of inflation increases the uncertainty of the forecasts. Moreover, if expenditure is increased due to inflation it is likely that income will increase proportionately.

Table 3.2 illustrates cash flow forecasts for four projects. In each case it is assumed that the cash flows take place at the end of each year. For short-term projects or where candidate projects demonstrate significant seasonal cash flow patterns it may be advisable to produce quarterly, or even monthly, cash flow forecasts.

Cost–benefit evaluation techniques

We would only consider proceeding with a project where the benefits outweigh the costs. However, in order to choose between projects we need to take the timing of the costs and benefits into account as well as the benefits relative to the size of the investment.

Exercise 3.2

Consider the project cash flow estimates for four projects at IOE shown in Table 3.2. Negative values represent expenditure and positive values income.

Rank the four projects in order of financial desirability and make a note of your reasons for ranking them in that way before reading further.

In the following sections we will take a brief look at some common methods for comparing projects on the basis of their cash flow forecasts.

Net profit

The net profit of a project is the difference between the total costs and the total income over the life of the project. Project 2 in Table 3.2 shows the greatest net profit but this is at the expense of a large investment. Indeed, if we had £1m to invest, we might undertake all of the other three projects and obtain an even greater net profit. Note also, that all projects contain an element of risk and we might not be prepared to risk £1m. We shall look at the effects of risk and investment later in this chapter.

Table 3.2 *Four project cash flow projections – figures are end of year totals (£)*

Year	Project 1	Project 2	Project 3	Project 4
0	−100,000	−1,000,000	−100,000	−120,000
1	10,000	200,000	30,000	30,000
2	10,000	200,000	30,000	30,000
3	10,000	200,000	30,000	30,000
4	20,000	200,000	30,000	30,000
5	100,000	300,000	30,000	75,000
Net profit	50,000	100,000	50,000	75,000

Cash flows take place at the end of each year. The year 0 figure represents the initial investment made at the start of the project.

Moreover, the simple net profit takes no account of the timing of the cash flows. Projects 1 and 3 each have a net profit of £50,000 and therefore, according to this selection criteria, would be equally preferable. The bulk of the income occurs late in the life of project 1, whereas project 3 returns a steady income throughout its life. Having to wait for a return has the disadvantage that the investment must be funded for longer. Add to that the fact that, other things being equal, estimates in the more distant future are less certain that short-term estimates and we can see that the two projects are not equally preferable.

Payback period

The payback period is the time taken to break even or pay back the initial investment. Normally the project with the shorter payback period will be chosen on the basis that an organization will wish to minimize the time that a project is 'in debt'.

Consider the four project cash flows given in Table 3.2 and calculate the payback period for each of them.

Exercise 3.3

The advantage of the payback period is that it is simple to calculate and is not particularly sensitive to small forecasting errors. Its disadvantage as a selection technique is that it ignores the overall profitability of the project – in fact, it totally ignores any income (or expenditure) once the project has broken even. Thus the fact that projects 2 and 4 are, overall, more profitable than project 3 is ignored.

Return on investment

The return on investment (ROI), also known as the accounting rate of return (ARR), provides a way of comparing the net profitability to the investment required. There are some variations on the formula used to calculate the return on investment but a straightforward common version is

$$\text{ROI} = \frac{\text{average annual profit}}{\text{total investment}} \times 100$$

Exercise 3.4

Calculating the ROI for project 1, the net profit is £50,000 and the total investment is £100,000. The return on investment is therefore calculated as

$$\text{ROI} = \frac{\text{average annual profit}}{\text{total investment}} \times 100$$

$$= \frac{10,000}{100,000} \times 100 = 10\%$$

Calculate the ROI for each of the other projects shown in Table 3.2 and decide which, on the basis of this criteria, is the most worthwhile.

The return on investment provides a simple, easy to calculate measure of return on capital and is therefore quite popular. Unfortunately it suffers from two severe disadvantages. Like the net profitability, it takes no account of the timing of the cash flows. More importantly, it may be tempting to compare the rate of return with current interest rates. However, this rate of return bears no relationship to the interest rates offered or charged by banks or building societies (or any other normal interest rate).

Net present value

Net present value (NPV) and internal rate of return (IRR) are collectively known as discounted cash flow (DCF) techniques.

Net present value is a project evaluation technique that takes into account the profitability of a project and the timing of the cash flows that are produced. It does so by discounting future cash flows by a percentage known as the discount rate. This is based on the view that receiving £100 today is better than having to wait until next year to receive it because the £100 next year is worth less than £100 now. We could, for example, invest the £100 in a building society today and have £100 plus the interest in a year's time. If we say that the present value of £100 in a year's time is £91 we mean that £100 in a year's time is the equivalent of £91 now.

The equivalence of £91 now and £100 in a year's time means we are discounting the future income by approximately 10% – that is, we would need an extra 10% to make it worthwhile waiting for a year. An alternative way of considering the equivalence of the two is to consider that, if we received £91 now and invested for a year at an annual interest rate of 10%, it would be worth £100 in a year's time.

Similarly, £100 received in 2 years' time would have a present value of approximately £83 – £83 invested for 3 years at an interest rate of 10% would yield £100 in 2 years' time.

The present value of any future cash flow may be obtained by applying the following formula

$$\text{present value} = \frac{\text{value in year } t}{(1 + r)^t}$$

where r is the discount rate, expressed as a decimal value and t is the number of years into the future that the cash flow occurs.

Alternatively, and rather more easily, the present value of a cash flow may be calculated by multiplying the cash flow by the appropriate discount factor. A small table of discount factors is given in Table 3.3.

The NPV for a project is obtained by discounting each cash flow (both negative and positive) and summing the discounted values. It is normally assumed that any initial investment takes place immediately (indicated as year 0) and is not discounted. Later cash flows are normally assumed to take place at the end of each year and are discounted by the appropriate amount.

Table 3.3 *Table of NPV discount factors*

Year	Discount rate (%)					
	5	*6*	*8*	*10*	*12*	*15*
1	0·9524	0·9434	0·9259	0·9091	0·8929	0·8696
2	0·9070	0·8900	0·8573	0·8264	0·7972	0·7561
3	0·8638	0·8396	0·7938	0·7513	0·7118	0·6575
4	0·8227	0·7921	0·7350	0·6830	0·6355	0·5718
5	0·7835	0·7473	0·6806	0·6209	0·5674	0·4972
6	0·7462	0·7050	0·6302	0·5645	0·5066	0·4323
7	0·7107	0·6651	0·5835	0·5132	0·4523	0·3759
8	0·6768	0·6274	0·5403	0·4665	0·4039	0·3269
9	0·6446	0·5919	0·5002	0·4241	0·3606	0·2843
10	0·6139	0·5584	0·4632	0·3855	0·3220	0·2472
15	0·4810	0·4173	0·3152	0·2394	0·1827	0·1229
20	0·3769	0·3118	0·2145	0·1486	0·1037	0·0611
25	0·2953	0·2330	0·1460	0·0923	0·0588	0·0304

Note that this example uses approximate figures – when you have finished reading this section you should be able to calculate the exact figures yourself.

More extensive or detailed tables may be constructed using the formula

$$\text{Discount factor} = \frac{1}{(1 + r)^t}$$

for various values of r (the discount rate) and t (the number of years from now).

Assuming a 10% discount rate, the NPV for project 1 (Table 3.2) would be calculated as in Table 3.4. The net present value for Project 1, using a 10% discount rate is therefore £618. Using a 10% discount rate, calculate the net present values for projects 2, 3 and 4 and decide which, on the basis of this, is the most beneficial to pursue.

Table 3.4 *Applying the discount factors to project 1*

Year	Project 1 cash flow (£)	Discount factor @ 10%	Discounted cash flow (£)
0	−100,000	1·0000	−100,000
1	10,000	0·9091	9,091
2	10,000	0·8264	8,264
3	10,000	0·7513	7,513
4	20,000	0·6830	13,660
5	100,000	0·6209	62,090
Net Profit: £50,000			NPV: £618

It is interesting to note that the net present values for projects 1 and 3 are significantly different – even though they both yield the same net profit and both have the same return on investment. The difference in NPV reflects the fact that, with project 1, we must wait longer for the bulk of the income.

The main difficulty with NPV for deciding between projects is selecting an appropriate discount rate. Some organizations have a standard rate but where this is not the case, then the discount rate should be chosen to reflect available interest rates (borrowing costs where the project must be funded from loans) plus some premium to reflect the fact that software projects are inherently more risky than lending money to a bank or building society. The exact discount rate is normally less important than ensuring that the same discount rate is used for all projects being compared. However, it is important to check that the ranking of projects is not sensitive to small changes in the discount rate – have a look at the following exercise.

Calculate the net present value for each of the projects A, B and C shown in Table 3.5 using each of the discount rates 8%, 10% and 12%.

For each of the discount rates, decide which is the best project. What can you conclude from these results?

Alternatively, the discount rate may be thought of as a target rate of return. If, for example, we set a target rate of return of 15% we would reject any project that did not display a positive net present value using a 15% discount rate. Any project that displayed a positive NPV would be considered for selection – perhaps by using alternative criteria where candidate projects were competing for resources.

Table 3.5 *Three estimated project cash flows*

Year	Project A (£)	Project B (£)	Project C (£)
0	– 8,000	– 8,000	– 10,000
1	4,000	1,000	2,000
2	4,000	2,000	2,000
3	2,000	4,000	6,000
4	1,000	3,000	2,000
5	500	9,000	2,000
6	500	–6,000	2,000
Net Profit	4,000	5,000	6,000

Internal rate of return

One disadvantage of NPV as a measure of profitability is that, although it may be used to compare projects, it may not be directly comparable with earnings from other investments or the costs of borrowing capital. Such costs are usually quoted as a percentage interest rate. The internal rate of return (IRR) attempts to provide a profitability measure as a percentage return that is directly comparable with interest rates. Thus, a project that showed an estimate IRR of 10% would be worthwhile if the capital could be borrowed for less than 10% or if the capital could not be invested elsewhere for a return greater than 10%.

Table 3.6 *A project cash flow treated as an investment at 10%*

Year	Project cash flow forecast (£)	Capital at start of year (£)	Interest during year (£)	Capital at end of year (£)	End of year withdrawal (£)
		Equivalent investment at 10%			
0	–100,000	—	—	—	—
1	10,000	100,000	10,000	110,000	10,000
2	10,000	100,000	10,000	110,000	10,000
3	10,000	100,000	10,000	110,000	10,000
4	20,000	100,000	10,000	110,000	20,000
5	99,000	90,000	9,000	99,000	99,000
6		0	0	0	0

£100,000 invested at 10% may be used to generate the cash flows shown. At the end of the 5-year period the capital and the interest payments will be entirely consumed leaving a net balance of zero.

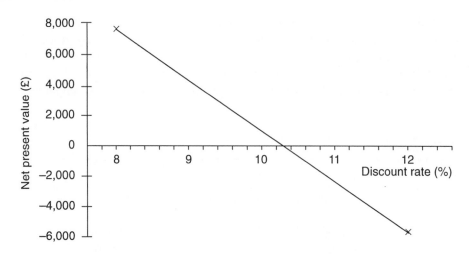

Figure 3.3 *Estimating the internal rate of return for project 1.*

The IRR is calculated as that percentage discount rate that would produce a NPV of zero. Consider the project shown in the left hand column of Table 3.6 – it has an IRR of 10% (we shall see how that is calculated in a moment). Saying that the IRR = 10% is equivalent to saying that if we were to invest £100,000 now at an annual interest rate of 10% it could generate the payments indicated in the cash flow forecast at the end of each year leaving a net balance of zero.

The IRR is most easily calculated using a spreadsheet or other computer program that provides functions for calculating the IRR. Microsoft Excel and Lotus, for example, both provide IRR functions which, provided with an initial guess (which may be zero), will search for and return an IRR. Manually it must be calculated by trial-and-error or estimated using the technique illustrated in Figure 3.3.

The internal rate of return is a convenient and useful measure of the value of a project in that it is a single percentage figure that may be directly compared with rates of return on other projects or interest rates quoted elsewhere. A project with an IRR greater than current interest rates will provide a better rate of return than lending the investment to a bank – or will be worth borrowing to finance.

One deficiency of the IRR is that it does not indicate the size of the return. A project with a NPV of £100,000 and an IRR of 15% may be more attractive than one with a NPV of £10,000 and an IRR of 18% – the return on capital is lower but the net benefits greater.

An often quoted objection to the internal rate of return is that, under certain conditions, it is possible to find more than one rate that will produce a zero NPV. This is not a valid objection since, if there are multiple solutions, it is always appropriate to take the lowest value and ignore the others. Spreadsheets will normally always return the lowest value if provided with zero as a starting value.

NPV and IRR are not, however, a complete answer to economic project evaluation. A total evaluation must also take into account the problems of funding the cash flows – will we, for example, be able to repay the interest on any borrowed money and pay development staff salaries? We must also consider any one project within the financial and economic framework of the organization as a whole – if we fund this one, will we also be able to fund other worthy projects?

Risk evaluation

Every project involves risk of some form. When assessing and planning a project we are concerned with the risk of the project not meetings its objectives. In Chapter 8 we shall discuss ways of analysing and minimizing risk during the development of a software system. In this chapter we are concerned with taking risk into account when deciding whether to proceed with a proposed project.

There is a risk that software may exceed the original specification and that a project will be completed early and under budget. That is not a risk that need concern us.

Risk identification and ranking

In any project evaluation we should attempt to identify the risks and quantify their potential effects. One common approach to risk analysis is to construct a project risk matrix utilizing a checklist of possible risks and to classify each risk according to its relative importance and likelihood. Note that the importance and likelihood need to be separately assessed – we may be less concerned with something that, although serious, is very unlikely to occur than with something less serious that is almost certain. Table 3.7 illustrates a basic project risk matrix listing some of the risks that might be considered for a project with their importance and likelihood classified as high (H), medium (M), low (L) or exceedingly unlikely (—). So that projects may be compared the list of risks must be the same for each project being assessed. It is likely, in reality, that it would be somewhat longer than shown and more precisely defined.

The project risk matrix may be used may be used as a way of evaluating projects (those with high risk high likelihood risks being less favoured) or as a means of identifying and ranking the risks for a specific project. In Chapter 7 we shall consider a method for scoring the importance and likelihood of risks that may be used in conjunction with the project risk matrix to score and rank projects.

Risk and net present value

Where a project is relatively risky it is common practice to use a higher discount rate to calculate net present value. This addition or risk premium, might, for example, be an additional 2% for a reasonably safe project or 5% for a fairly risky one. Projects may be categorized (e.g. high, medium or low risk) using a scoring method and risk premiums designated for each category. The premiums, even if arbitrary, provide a consistent method of taking risk into account.

Table 3.7 *A fragment of a basic project risk matrix*

Risk	Importance	Likelihood
Software never completed or delivered	H	—
Project cancelled after design stage	H	—
Software delivered late	L	M
Development budget exceeded $\leq 20\%$	L	M
Development budget exceeded $> 20\%$	M	L
Maintenance costs higher than estimated	L	L
Response time targets not met	L	H

Cost–benefit analysis

A rather more sophisticated approach to the evaluation of risk is to consider each possible outcome and estimate the probability of it occurring and the corresponding value of the outcome. Rather than a single cash flow forecast for a project, we will then have a set of cash flow forecasts, each with an associated probability of occurring. The value of the project is then obtained by summing the cost or benefit for each possible outcome weighted by its corresponding probability. Exercise 3.7 illustrates how this may be done.

Exercise 3.7

BuyRight, a software house is considering developing a payroll package for use in academic institutions and is currently engaged in a cost-benefit analysis. Study of the market has shown that, if they can target it efficiently and no competing products become available, they will obtain a high level of sales generating an annual income of £800,000. They estimate that there is a 1 in 10 chance of this happening. However, a competitor may launch a competing package before their own launch date and then sales may generate only £100,000 per year. They estimate that there is a 30% chance of this happening. The most likely outcome, they believe, is somewhere in between these two extremes – they will gain a market lead by launching before any competing product becomes available and achieve an annual income of £650,000. BuyRight have therefore calculated their expected net sales income as in Table 3.8.

   Total development costs are estimated at £750,000 and sales are expected to be maintained at a reasonably constant level for at least 4 years. Annual costs of marketing and product maintenance are estimated at £200,000 irrespective of the market share gained. Would you advise them to go ahead with the project?

This approach is frequently used in the evaluation of large public sector projects such as the building of new motorways where variables such as future traffic volumes, and hence the total benefit of shorter journey times, are subject to uncertainty. The technique does, of course, rely on being able to assign probabilities of occurrence to each scenario and, without extensive study, this may be difficult.

When used to evaluate a single project the cost–benefit approach, by 'averaging out' the effects of the different scenarios, does not take account an organization's reluctance to risk damaging outcomes. Because of this it is often considered more appropriate for the valuation of a portfolio of projects where overall profitability is the primary concern.

Table 3.8 *BuyRight's income forecasts*

Sales	Net Annual Income (£) *I*	Probability *p*	Expected Value (£) *I* ×*p*
High	800,000	0·1	80,000
Medium	650,000	0·6	390,000
Low	100,000	0·3	30,000
Expected Income			500,000

Risk profile analysis

An approach which attempts to overcome some of the objections to cost–benefit averaging is the construction of risk profiles using sensitivity analysis.

This involves varying each of the parameters that affect the project's cost or benefits to ascertain how sensitive the project's profitability is to each factor. We might, for example, vary one of our original estimates by plus or minus 5% and recalculate the expected costs and benefits for the project. By repeating this exercise for each of our estimates in turn we can evaluate the sensitivity of the project to each factor.

By studying the results of a sensitivity analysis we can identify those factors that are most important to the success of the project. We then need to decide whether we can exercise greater control over them or otherwise mitigate their effects. If neither is the case, then we must live with the risk or abandon the project.

Sensitivity analysis demands that we vary each factor one at a time. It does not easily allow us to consider the effects of combinations, of circumstances neither does it evaluate the changes of a particular outcome occurring. In order to do this we need to use a more sophisticated tool such as Monte Carlo simulation. There are a number of risk analysis packages available (such as Predict from Risk Decisions) that use Monte Carlo simulation and produce risk profiles of the type shown in Figure 3.4.

For an explanation of the Monte Carlo technique see any text book on operational research.

Projects may be compared as in Figure 3.4 which compares three projects with the same expected profitability. Project A is unlikely to depart far from this expected value compared to project B which exhibits a larger variance. Both of these have symmetric profiles which contrasts with project C. Project C has a skewed distribution which indicates that although it is unlikely to ever be much more profitable than expected, it is quite likely to be far worse.

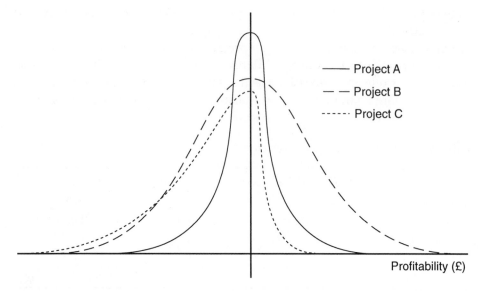

The profitability of project A is unlikely to depart greatly from its expected value (indicated by the vertical axis) compared to the likely variations for project B. Project A is therefore less risky than project B.

Figure 3.4 *A risk analysis profile.*

Using decision trees

The approaches to risk analysis discussed previously rather assume that we are passive by-standers allowing nature to take its own course – the best we can do is to reject over-risky projects or choose those with the best risk profile. There are many situations, however, were we can evaluate whether a risk is important and, if it is, indicate a suitable course of action.

Many such decisions will limit or affect future options and, at any point, it is important to be able to see into the future to assess how a decision will affect the future profitability of the project.

Prior to giving Amanda the job of extending their invoicing system, IOE must consider the alternative of completely replacing the existing system – which they will have to do at some point in the future. The decision largely rests upon the rate at which their equipment maintenance business expands – if their market share significantly increases (which they believe will happen if a rumours of a competitor's imminent bankruptcy are fulfilled) the existing system may need to be replaced within 2 years. Not replacing the system in time could be an expensive option as it may lead to lost revenue if they cannot cope with the increase in invoicing demand. Replacing it immediately will, however, be expensive as it will mean deferring other projects which have already been scheduled.

They have calculated that extending the existing system will have a NPV of £57,000, although if the market expands significantly, this will be turned into a loss with a NPV of –£100,000 due to lost revenue. If the market does expand, replacing the system now has a NPV of £250,000 due to the benefits of being able to handle increased sales and other benefits such as improved management information. If sales do not increase, however, the benefits will be severely reduced and the project will suffer a loss with NPV of –£50,000.

The company estimate the likelihood of the market increasing significantly at 20% – and, hence, the probability that it will not increase as 80%.

This scenario can be represented as a tree structure as shown in Figure 3.5.

The analysis of a decision tree consists of evaluating the expected benefit of taking each path from a decision point (denoted by D in Figure 3.5). The expected value of each path is the sum of the value of each possible outcome multiplied by its probability of occurrence. The expected value of extending the system is therefore £25,600 (75,000 × 0·8 – 100,000 × 0·2) and the expected value of replacing the system £10,000 (250,000 × 0·2 – 50,000 × 0·8). IOE should therefore choose the option of extending the existing system.

This example illustrates the use of a decision tree to evaluate a simple decision at the start of a project. One of the great advantages of using decision trees to model and analyse problems is the ease with which they may be extended. Figure 3.6 illustrates an extended version of Amanda's decision tree which includes the possibility of a later decision should they decide to extend the system and then find there is an early market expansion.

Conclusion

Some of the key points in this chapter are:

- projects must be evaluated on strategic, technical and economic grounds
- economic assessment involves the identification of all costs and income over the lifetime of the system, including its development and operation and checking that the total value of benefits exceeds total expenditure

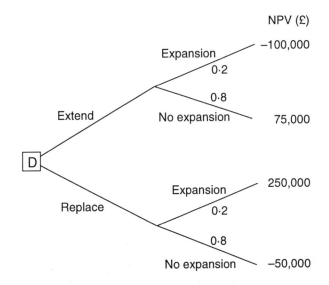

Figure 3.5 *A decision tree.*

The net present values
shown in italic are those
identified in Amanda's
original decision tree
shown in Figure 3.5.

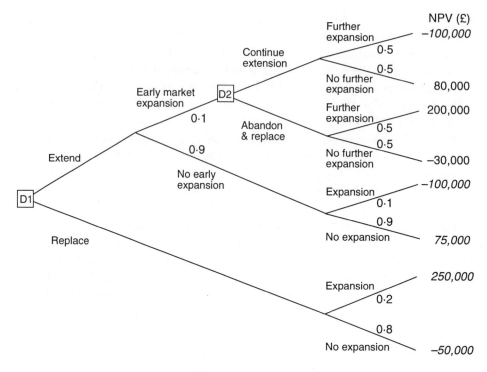

Figure 3.6 *An extension to Amanda's decision tree.*

- money received in the future is worth less than the same amount of money in hand now which may be invested to earn interest
- the uncertainty surrounding estimates of future returns lowers their real value measured now
- discounted cash flow techniques may be used to evaluate the present value of future cash flows taking account of interest rates and uncertainty
- cost–benefit analysis techniques and decision trees provide a tool for evaluating expected outcomes and choosing between alternative strategies.

Further exercises

1. Identify the major risks that could affect the success of the Brightmouth College Payroll project and try to rank them in order of importance.

2. Working in a group of three or four, imagine that you are about to embark upon a programming assignment as part of the assessed work for your course. Draw up a list of the risks that might affect the assignment outcome. Individually classify the importance and likelihood of each of those risk as high, medium or low. When you have done this compare your results and try to come up with an agreed project risk matrix.

3. Explain why discounted cash flow techniques provide better criteria for project selection than net profit or return on investment.

4. Consider the decision tree shown in Figure 3.6 and decide whether, given the additional possibilities, which option(s) IOE should choose.

Chapter 4

Project analysis and technical planning

OBJECTIVES

When you have completed this chapter you will be able to:

- ☐ take account of the characteristics of the system to be developed when planning a project

- ☐ select an appropriate process model

- ☐ make best use of the 'waterfall' process model where appropriate

- ☐ reduce risks by the creation of appropriate prototypes

- ☐ reduce other risks by implementing of the project in increments.

Introduction

The development of software in-house usually implies certain assumptions:

- the project team and the users belong to the same organization
- the projects being considered slot into a portfolio of existing computer-based systems
- the methodologies and technologies to be used are not selected by the project manager, but are dictated by an information technology plan.

Martyn Ould in *Strategies for Software Engineering: the Management of Risk & Quality*, John Wiley & Sons, Chichester, 1990, describes how technical planning was done at the software house, Praxis.

Where work is being carried out by a software house for an external customer, there is unlikely to be an information technology plan to guide the project leader. The methodologies and technologies to be used may have to be decided for each individual project. This decision-making process is called technical planning by some, although here we use the term project analysis. Even where development is in-house, it is important to spend some time looking for any characteristics of the new project which might make us take a different approach from that used on previous projects. It is this analysis that is the subject of this chapter.

The relevant part of the Step Wise approach is Step 3: Analyse project characteristics. The selection of a particular process model will add new products to the Project Breakdown Structure or new activities to the activity network. This will create outputs for Step 4: Identify the products and activities of the project (see Figure 4.1).

In the remainder of this chapter we will firstly look at how the characteristics of a project will influence the approach to the planning of a project. We will then look at some of the most common process models, namely the waterfall approach, prototyping and incremental delivery.

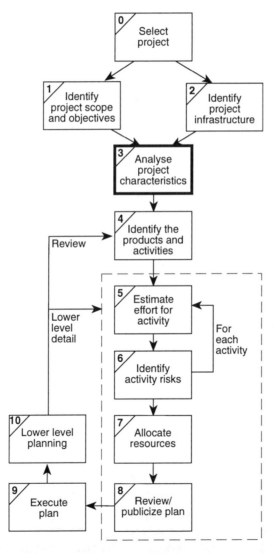

Figure 4.1 *Project analysis is the subject of Step 3.*

Choosing technologies

An outcome of project analysis will be the selection of the most appropriate methodologies and technologies. Methodologies include techniques like SSADM and JSP (Jackson Structured Programming) while technologies might include an appropriate fourth generation environment, or the use of a particular expert system shell and so on.

As well as the products and activities, the chosen technology will influence the following aspects of a project:

• training requirements for development staff
• type of staff recruited
• development environment – both hardware and software
• system maintenance arrangements.

We are now going to describe some of the steps of project analysis.

Identify project as either objectives-driven or product-driven

You may recall in Chapter 1 that we distinguished between objective-driven and product-driven projects. Very often a product-driven project will have been preceded by an objective-driven project which chose the general software solution that is to be implemented.

The soft systems approach is described in Peter Checkland's *Systems Thinking, Systems Practice*, Wiley and Sons, 1981.

There may be cases where things are so vague that even the objectives of the project are uncertain or are the subject of disagreement. People may be experiencing a lot of problems but no-one knows exactly what the solution to the problems might be. It may be that the IT specialists can provide help in some places but assistance from other specialisms is needed in others. In these kinds of situation a **soft systems** approach may need to be considered.

Analyse other project characteristics

The sorts of question that would need to be asked include the following.

We first introduced the difference between information systems and industrial systems in Chapter 1.

• **Is an information or industrial system to be implemented?** Information systems are sometimes referred to as data-oriented as they will have a considerable data base. Industrial systems refer to process control systems. These days it is not uncommon to have systems with components of both types.
• **Will the software that is to be produced be a general package or application specific?** An example of a general package would be a spreadsheet or a word processing package. An application specific package could be, for example, an airline seat reservation system.
• **Is the system to be implemented of a particular type for which specific tools have been developed?** For example:

does it involve concurrent processing? – if so the use of techniques appropriate to the analysis and design of such systems would be considered;

will the system to be created be knowledge based? – expert systems have a set of rules which result in some 'expert advice' when applied to a problem domain (sets of methods and tools have been developed to assist in the creation of such systems); or

will the system to be produced make heavy use of computer graphics?

- **Is the system to be created safety critical?** For instance, could a malfunction in the system endanger human life?
- **What is the nature of the hardware/software environment in which the system will operate?** It may be that the environment in which the final software will operate is different to that in which it will be developed. Process control software may be developed on a large development machine which has lots of supporting software tools in the way of compilers, debuggers, static analysers and so on, but may then be down-loaded to a small processor in the larger engineered product. A system destined for a personal computer may need a different approach to one destined for a main-frame or a distributed environment.

How would you categorize each of the following systems according to the classification above?

(a) a payroll system

(b) a system to control a bottling plant

(c) a system which holds details of the plans of plant used by a water authority to supply water to consumers

(d) a software package to support project managers

(e) a system used by lawyers to get hold of case law relating to company taxation.

Exercise 4.1

Identify high level project risks

When we first embark on a project we may be expected to work out elaborate plans even though we are at least partially ignorant of many important factors that will affect the project. For example, until we do a detailed investigation of the users' requirements we will not be able estimate how much effort will be needed to build a system to meet those requirements. The greater the uncertainties at the beginning of the project, the greater the risk that the project will be unsuccessful. Once we recognize a particular area of uncertainty we can, however, take steps to reduce its uncertainty.

One suggestion is that uncertainty can be associated with either the **products**, **processes**, or **resources** associated with the project.

Chapter 3 has already touched on some aspects of risk which are developed further in Chapter 8.

HOOD is an object-
oriented design approach.

- **Product uncertainty** – here we ask how well the requirements are understood. It may well be that the users themselves are uncertain about what a proposed information system is to do. The government, say, may introduce a new form of taxation but the way this is going to operate in detail may not be known until a certain amount of case law has been built up. Some environments may change so quickly that what was a precise and valid statement of requirements rapidly becomes out of date.
- **Process uncertainty** – it may be that the project under consideration is the first where an organization has tried to use a method such as SSADM or HOOD that is new to them. It may be that a new fourth generation language is being used. Any change in the way that the systems are developed is going to introduce uncertainty.
- **Resource uncertainty** – the main area of uncertainty here will almost surely be the availability of staff of the right ability and experience. A major influence on the degree of uncertainty in a project will be the sheer size of a project. The larger the number of resources needed or the longer the duration of the project, the more inherently risky it is likely to be.

Exercise 4.2

At IOE, Amanda has identified possible staff resistance as a risk to the maintenance group accounts project. Would you classify this as a product, process or resource risk? It may be that it does not fit into any of these categories and some other is needed.

Brigette at Brightmouth HE College identified the possibility that no suitable payroll package would be available on the market as a risk. What other risks might be inherent in the Brightmouth HE College payroll project?

Take into account user requirements concerning implementation

A user organization may lay down standards that have to be adopted by any contractor providing software for them. For example the UK Civil Service has the SSADM standard where information systems are being developed and the Ministry of Defence has Mascot as the real-time development standard for its real-time projects.

Chapter 11 on Software
Quality discusses BS EN
ISO 9001 and TickIT.

It is common for organizations to specify that suppliers of software have BS EN ISO 9001:1994 or TickIT accreditation. This will affect the way projects are conducted.

Select general life cycle approach

- **Control systems** – a real-time system will need to be implemented using an appropriate methodology, e.g. Mascot. Real-time systems that employ concurrent processing may have to use techniques such as Petri nets.

- **Information systems** – similarly, an information system will need a methodology, such as SSADM or Information Engineering, that matches that type of environment. SSADM will be especially appropriate where the project will employ a large number of development staff whose work will need to be coordinated: the method lays down in detail what needs to be done and what products need to be created at each step. Team members would therefore know exactly what is expected of them.
- **General packages** – where the software to be produced is of a general nature rather than being application specific, then a methodology such as SSADM would have to be thought about very carefully. This is because the framers of the method make the assumption that a specific user exists. Some parts in the method also assume that there is an existing system which can be analysed to yield what the logical features of the new, computer-based, system should be.
- **Specialized techniques** – these have been invented to expedite the development of, for example, **knowledge-based systems** and there are a number of expert systems shells and logic based programming languages that can be used to implement this type of system. Similarly a number of specialized techniques and tools have been developed to assist in the development of **graphics-based systems**.
- **Hardware environment** – the environment in which the system is to operate may put constraints on the way it is to be implemented. For instance, the need for a fast response time or for the software to take up only a small part of computer memory may mean that only low-level programming languages can be used.
- **Safety-critical systems** – where safety and reliability are of the essence, it may be possible to justify the additional expense of a formal specification using a notation such as Z or VDM. Really critical systems may call for expensive measures such as having independent teams develop parallel systems with the same functionality. The parallel systems can then run concurrently when the application is in operation so that the results of each of the parallel systems can be cross-checked.
- **Imprecise requirements** – uncertainties or a **novel hardware/software platform** may mean that a **prototyping** approach should be considered. If the environment in which the system is to be implemented is a rapidly changing one, then serious consideration would need to be given to **incremental delivery.** If the users have **uncertain objectives** in connection with the project, them a **soft systems** approach may be desirable.

The implications of prototyping and the incremental approach are explored later in the chapter.

Bearing in mind the discussion above, what, in broad outline, is the most suitable approach for each of the following?

Exercise 4.3

(a) a system which calculates the amount of a drug that should be administered to a patient who has a particular complaint

(b) a system to administer a student loans scheme
(c) a system to control trains in the Channel Tunnel

Technical plan contents list

The analysis described above will produce a number of practical requirements which will be fed into the next stage of the planning process. These requirements may add activities to the project and may involve the acquisition of items of software or hardware or the adoption of particular methodologies which may require staff training. As these recommendations imply certain costs, they should be recorded formally.

A preliminary version of this technical plan might be produced by a software house to help in the preparation of the bid for a contract. In some cases, it may actually be shown to the potential customer in order to show the basis for the bid price and to generally impress the customer with the soundness of the approach the software house intends to adopt.

The technical plan is likely to have the following contents.

1. **Introduction and summary constraints:**
    (a) character of the system to be developed
    (b) risks and uncertainties of the project
    (c) user requirements concerning implementation.
2. **Recommended approach:**
    (a) selected methodology or process model
    (b) development methods
    (c) required software tools
    (d) target hardware/software environment.
3. **Implementation:**
    (a) required development environment
    (b) required maintenance environment
    (c) required training.
4. **Implications:**
    (a) project products and activities – this will have an effect on the schedule and staff-time
    (b) financial – this report will be used to produce costings.

Choice of process models

The word 'process' is sometimes used to emphasize the idea of a system **in action**. In order to achieve an outcome, the system will have to execute one or more activities: this is a process. This idea can be applied to the development of computer-based systems where a number of interrelated activities have to be undertaken to create a final product. These activities can be organized in different ways and we can call these **process models**.

A major part of the planning will be the choosing of the development methods to be used and the slotting of these into an overall process model.

The planner needs not only to select methods but also to specify how the method is to be applied. With methods such as SSADM, there is a considerable degree of choice about how it is to be applied: not all parts of SSADM are compulsory. Many student projects have the rather basic failing that at the planning stage they claim that, say, SSADM is to be used: in the event all that is produced are a few SSADM fragments such as a top level data flow diagram and a preliminary logical data structure diagram. If this is all the particular project requires, it should be stated at the outset.

Structured methods

Although some 'object oriented' specialists may object(!), we include the OO approach as a structured method – after all, we hope it is not unstructured. Structured methods are made up of sets of steps and rules which when applied produce system products such as data flow diagrams. Each of these products is carefully documented. Such methods are often time consuming compared to more intuitive approaches and this implies some additional cost. The pay-off is such things as a less error prone and more maintainable final system. This balance of costs and benefits is more likely to be justified on a large project involving many developers and users. This is not to say that smaller projects cannot justify the use of such methods.

The waterfall model

This is the 'classical' model of system development. As can be seen in Figure 4.2, there is a sequence of activities working from top to bottom. The diagram shows some arrows pointing upwards and backwards. This indicates that a later stage may reveal the need for some extra work at an earlier stage, but this should definitely be the exception rather the rule. After all, the flow of a waterfall should be downwards with the possibility of just a little splashing back! The limited scope for iteration is in fact one of the strengths of this process model. With a large project you want to avoid having to go back and rework tasks that you thought had been completed. For a start, having to reopen what was previously thought to be a completed activity plays havoc with promised completion dates.

We contend that there is nothing intrinsically wrong with the waterfall approach, even though more recent writers have suggested different models. It is the ideal that the project manager strives for. The waterfall approach allows project completion times to be forecast with more confidence than may be the case with some more iterative approaches and this allows projects to be controlled effectively. However where there is uncertainty about how a system is

The first description of this approach is said to be that of H. D. Bennington in 'Production of Large Computer Programs' in 1956. This was reprinted in 1983 in *Annals of the History of Computing* 5(4).

to be implemented, and unfortunately there very often is, a more flexible, iterative, approach may be required.

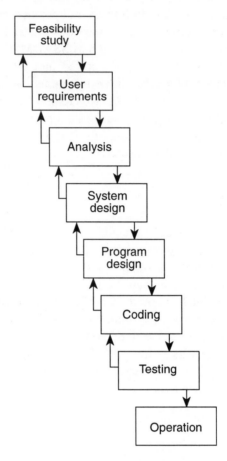

Figure 4.2 *The waterfall model.*

The V-process model

Figure 4.3 gives a diagrammatic representation of this model. This is an elaboration of the waterfall model and stresses the necessity for validation activities that match the activities that create things.

The V-process model can be seen as expanding the activity **testing** in the waterfall model. Each step has a matching validation process which may, where defects are found, cause a loop back to the corresponding development stage and a reworking of the following steps. Ideally this feeding back should only occur where a discrepancy has been found between what was specified by a particular activity and what was actually implemented in the next lower activity on the descent of the V loop. For example, the system designer may have written that a calculation be carried out in a certain way. The person who structured the program which fulfilled this design may have misunderstood what was required. At system testing stage, the system designer would carry out checks which ensure that the programs are doing what was specified in the design document and would discover the program designer's misreading of that document. Only corrections should be fed back, not the system designer's second thoughts, otherwise the project would be slipping into an 'evolutionary prototyping' approach.

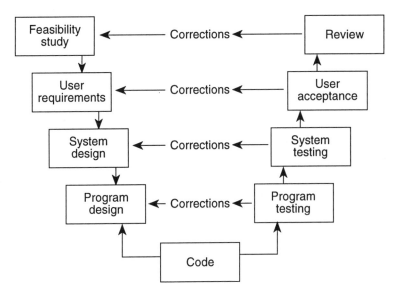

Figure 4.3 *The V-process model.*

Figure 4.3 shows the V-process model. The review that is held after the system has been implemented is shown as possibly feeding corrections back to the feasibility study which may have been conducted months or years before. How would this work in practice?

Exercise 4.4

The spiral model

It could be argued that this is another way of looking at the basic waterfall model. In the waterfall model, there is a possible escape at the end of any of the activities in the sequence. A feasibility study may decide that the implementation of a proposed system would be beneficial. The management therefore authorize work on the detailed collection and analysis of user requirements. Some analysis, for instance the interviewing of users, may already have taken place at the feasibility stage, but a more thorough investigation is now launched. This may

The original ideas behind the spiral model can be found in B. W. Boehm's 1988 paper 'A spiral model of software development and enhancement' in *IEEE Computer* 21(5).

reveal that in fact the costs of implementing the system would be higher than originally estimated and lead managers to decide to abandon the project.

A greater level of detail is considered at each stage of the project and a greater degree of confidence about the probability of success for the project should be justified. This can be portrayed as a loop or a spiral where the system to be implemented is considered in more and more detail in each sweep and an evaluation process is undertaken before the next iteration is embarked upon. Figure 4.4 illustrates how SSADM can be interpreted in such a way.

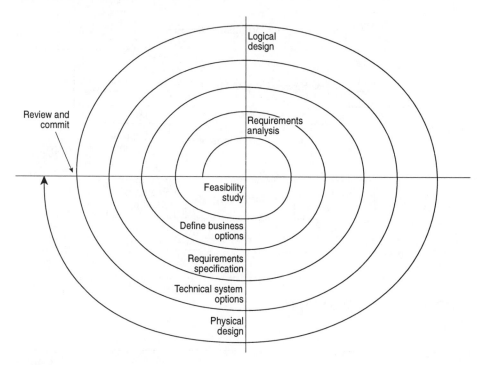

Figure 4.4 *The application of the spiral model to SSADM version 4.*

Software prototyping

Much of the material on prototyping is based on the survey by D. Ince and S. Hekmatpour in 'Rapid Software Prototyping' in *Oxford Survey of Information Technology* 3 (1983).

A prototype is a working model of one or more aspects of the projected system. It is constructed and tested quickly and inexpensively in order to test out assumptions.

Prototypes can be classified as throw-away, evolutionary or incremental.

- **Throw-away prototypes** – here the prototype is used only to test out some ideas and is then discarded when the development of the operational system is commenced. The prototype could be developed using a different software environment (e.g. a 4GL as opposed to a 3GL for the final system where machine efficiency may be important) or even on a different kind of hardware platform.

- **Evolutionary prototypes** – the prototype is developed and modified until it is finally in a state where it can become the operational system. In this case the standards that are used to develop the software have to be carefully considered.
- **Incremental prototypes** – it could be argued that this is strictly speaking not prototyping. The operational system is developed and implemented in small stages so that the feed-back from the earlier stages can influence the development of the later stages.

Some of the reasons that have been put forward for prototyping are the following.

A good book on the general topic of prototyping is R. Vonk's *Prototyping: the effective use of CASE Technology*, Prentice Hall, 1990.

- **Learning by doing** – when we have just done something for the first time we can usually look back and see where we have made mistakes.
- **Improved communication** – users are often reluctant to read the massive documents produced by structured methods. Even if they do read this documentation, they do not get a feel for how the system is likely to work in practice.
- **Improved user involvement** – the users may be more actively involved in design decisions about the new system.
- **Clarification of partially-known requirements** – where there is no existing system to mimic, users can often get a better idea of what might be useful to them in a potential system by trying out prototypes.
- **Demonstration of the consistency and completeness of a specification** – any mechanism that attempts to implement a specification on a computer is likely to uncover ambiguities and omissions.
- **Reduced need for documentation** – because a working prototype can be examined there is less need for detailed documentation. Some may argue, however, that this is a very dangerous suggestion.
- **Reduced maintenance costs (i.e. changes after the system goes live)** – if the user is unable to suggest modifications at the prototyping stage the chances are that they will ask for the changes as modifications to the operational system. This reduction of maintenance costs is the main plank in the financial case for creating prototypes.
- **Production of expected results** – the problem with creating test runs is generally not the creation of the test data but the accurate calculation of the expected results. A prototype may be of some assistance here.

The most important justification for a prototype is the need to reduce uncertainty by conducting an experiment.

Software prototyping is not without its drawbacks and dangers, however.

- **Users may misunderstand the role of the prototype** – for example, they may expect the prototype to be as robust as an operational system when incorrect data is entered or they may expect the prototype to have as fast a response as the operational system although this was not the intention.
- **Lack of project standards possible** – evolutionary prototyping could just be an excuse for a sloppy 'hack it out and see what happens' approach.

- **Lack of control** – it may be difficult to control the prototyping cycle as the driving force may be the users' propensity to try out new things.
- **Additional expense** – building and exercising a prototype will incur additional expenses. The additional expense may not be quite as much as might be feared as many analysis and design tasks would have to be undertaken anyway. Some research suggests that typically there is a 10% extra cost to produce a prototype.
- **Machine efficiency** – a system built through prototyping, while sensitive to the users' needs, may not be as efficient in machine terms as one developed using more conventional methods.
- **Close proximity of developers** – prototyping may mean that code developers may have to be sited close to the users. One trend has been for organizations in developed countries to get program coding done cheaply in Third World countries such as India. Prototyping may not allow this.

Other ways of categorizing prototypes

What is being learnt?

The most important reason for having a prototype is that there is a need to learn about an area of uncertainty. For any prototype it is essential that the project managers define at the outset what it is intended to learn from the prototype.

This has a particular relevance to student projects. Students often realize that the software that they are to write as part of their project could not safely be used by real users. They therefore call the software a 'prototype'. However, if it is a real prototype then they must:

- specify what they hope to learn from the prototype
- plan how the prototype is to be evaluated
- report on what has actually been learnt.

Prototypes may be used to find out how a new development technique can be used. This would be the case where a new methodology is being used in a pilot scheme. Alternatively, the development methods may be well-known, but the nature of the application may be uncertain.

Different projects will have uncertainties at different stages. Prototypes may therefore be used at different stages. A prototype might be used, for instance at the requirements gathering stage to pin down those requirements that seem blurred and shifting. A prototype might, on the other hand, be used at the design stage to test out the users' ability to navigate through a sequence of input screens.

To what extent is the prototyping to be done?

It would be unusual for the whole of the application to be prototyped. The prototyping might take one of the following forms.

- **Mock-ups** – for example, copies of the screens that the system is to use are shown to the users on a terminal, but the screens cannot be actually used.
- **Simulated interaction** – for example, the user can type in a request to access a record and the system will respond by showing the details of a record, but the details shown are always the same and no access is made to a data base.
- **Partial working model:**
  vertical – some features are prototyped fully
  horizontal – all features are prototyped but not in detail (e.g. perhaps there is not full validation of input).

What is being prototyped?

- **The human–computer interface** – with information systems, what the system is to do has usually been established and agreed by management at a fairly early stage in the development of the system. Prototyping tends to be confined to establishing the precise way in which the operators are to interact with the system. In this case it is important that the physical vehicle for the prototype be as similar as possible to the operational system.
- **The functionality of the system** – in other cases the precise way that the system should operate may not be known. This may particularly be the case where a computer model of some real-world phenomenon is being developed. The algorithms used may need to be repeatedly adjusted until they approximately imitate the behaviour they should be modelling.

Exercise 4.5

At what stage of a system development project (e.g. feasibility study, requirements analysis etc.) would a prototype be useful as a means of reducing the following uncertainties.

(a) There is a proposal that the senior managers of an insurance company have personal access to management information through an executive information system installed on personal computers located on their desks. Such a system would be costly to set up and there is some doubt about whether the managers would actually use the system.

(b) A computer system is to support sales office staff taking phone calls from members of the public enquiring about motor insurance and giving quotations over the phone.

(c) The insurance company is considering implementing the telephone sales system using the system development features supplied by the 4GL Ingres/Vision. They are not sure, at the moment, that it can provide the kind of interface that would be needed and are also concerned about the possible response times of a system developed using Ingres/Vision.

Tools

Special tools are not essential for prototyping but some have made it more practicable.

Fourth generation languages (4GLs)

These have many features which allow simple computer-based information systems to be set up quickly so that they can be demonstrated to the staff who will use them. Making lots of changes to an application written in a 3GL rapidly makes the software more difficult to alter safely while 4GL applications such as those implemented using Ingres/Vision tend to be more flexible.

It is suggested that the ease of use of some 4GL application builders and the increasing IT awareness of end-users may allow end users to create their own prototypes.

System tools

These days there are many useful software tools which are either part of an operating system or are closely related to it. Transaction processing monitors, screen handlers, and general purpose query languages may be included in this category. These tools may be very powerful and may be used as the means of creating at least part of a prototype. An example of this is the UNIX facility YACC ('yet another compiler compiler') which can be used as a programming language translator.

Very high level languages

An example of this would be APL. These are extremely powerful languages, but usually need very skilled programmers to use them effectively

Specification animators

See D. Rann, J. Turner and J. Whitworth *Z: A Beginner's Guide* in this series.

If a system is written in a formal notation such as Z or VDM, then it is possible for the design notation to be converted into an executable version. This might be used to generate example test cases for scrutiny by the potential users.

Configuration management

Chapter 9 explores configuration management further.

Where a prototype is being constantly tested by the users and modified by the developers there is a need to be able to control the different versions being produced and where necessary to back-track to previous versions.

A prototyping example

The use of prototyping on the COMET Commercial Estimating System project at the Royal Dockyards was the subject of a study, information about which has been published. The Royal Dockyards had been transferred to a system of 'commercial management' where they had to produce estimates of the cost of doing tasks that could then be compared against the cost of contracting the work out. Staff at the dockyards were inexperienced with this method of working.

It was decided to implement a computer system to support the estimating process and it was realized that the human–computer interface would be important. For this reason, the software house implementing the system suggested a prototyping approach

Among the questions that had to be decided was who should be present at evaluation sessions. If managers were there, would they dominate the proceedings at the expense of those who would actually use the system? Furthermore, if the designers were present they might well feel defensive about the system presented and try and argue against changes suggested.

Details of the study can be found in Mayhew, P. J., Worseley, C. J. & Dearnley, P. A. 'Control of Software Prototyping Process: Change Classification Approach'. *Information and Systems Technology* 13(2) 59-66 published in 1989.

The results of the prototype

The impact of prototyping may be judged by the fact that although the preliminary design had been done using SSADM, as a result of the evaluation of the prototype the number of screens in the system was doubled.

A major problem was that of controlling changes to the prototype. In order to record and control the changes suggested by users, the changes were categorized into three types.

- **Cosmetic** (about 35% of changes)
  These were simply changes to the layout of the screen. They were:
    (a) implemented
    (b) recorded.

- **Local** (about 60% of changes)
  These involved changes to the way that the screen was processed but did not affect other parts of the system. They were:
    (a) implemented
    (b) recorded
    (c) backed-up so that they could removed at a later stage if necessary
    (d) inspected retrospectively.

Inspections are discussed in Chapter 11.

- **Global** (about 5% of changes)
  These were changes that affected more than one part of the processing. All changes here had to be the subject of a design review before they could be implemented.

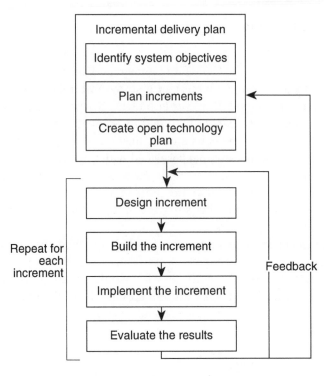

Figure 4.5 *Intentional incremental delivery.*

Incremental delivery

Principles of Software Engineering Management by Tom Gilb, published by Addison-Wesley in 1988 argues strongly in favour of this approach.

This is similar to the 'incremental prototyping' approach mentioned above. One of the most prominent advocates of this approach is Tom Gilb. The approach involves breaking the system down into small components which are then implemented and delivered in sequence. Each component that is delivered must actually give some benefit to the user. Figure 4.5 gives a general idea of the approach.

Advantages of this approach

These are some of the justifications given for the approach.

- The feedback from early increments can influence the later stages.
- The possibility of changes in requirements is not so great as with large monolithic projects because of the shorter timespan between the design of a component and its delivery.
- Users get benefits earlier than with a conventional approach.
- Early delivery of some useful components improves cash flow, because you get some return on investment early on.
- Smaller subprojects are easier to control and manage.

- 'Gold-plating', i.e. the requesting of features that are unnecessary and not in fact used, is less as users will know that they get more than one bite of the cherry: if a feature is not in the current increment than it may be included in the next.
- The project can be temporarily abandoned if more urgent work crops up.
- Job satisfaction is increased for developers who see their labours bearing fruit at regular, short, intervals.

Disadvantages

On the other hand these disadvantages have been put forward.

- 'Software breakage', i.e. later increments may require the earlier increments to be modified.
- Programmers may be more productive working on one large system than on a series of smaller ones.

The incremental delivery plan

The content of each increment and the order the increments are to be delivered to the users of the system have to be planned at the outset.

Basically the same process has to be undertaken as in strategic planning but at a more detailed level where the attention is given to increments of a user application rather than whole applications. The elements of the incremental plan are the **system objectives, incremental plan** and the **open technology plan**.

The process of planning the increments of a project as described by Gilb has similarities with strategic planning described in the previous chapter.

Identify system objectives

The purpose is to give an idea of the 'big picture', the overall objectives that the system is to achieve. These can then expanded into more specific functional goals and quality goals.

Functional goals will include:

- objectives it is intended to achieve
- jobs the system is to do
- computer/non-computer functions to achieve them.

In addition, measurable quality characteristics should be defined such as reliability, response and security. This reflects Tom Gilb's concern that system developers always keep sight of the objectives that they are trying to achieve on behalf of their clients. In the quickly changing environment of an application individual requirements may change over the course of the project, but the objectives should not.

Chapter 11 discusses software quality characteristics.

Plan increments

Having defined the overall objectives, the next stage is to plan the increments using the following guidelines:

- steps typically should consist of 1% to 5% of the total project!
- non-computer steps should be included
- ideally, an increment should take one month or less and should not at the outside take more than three months
- each increment should deliver some benefit to the user
- some increments will be physically dependent on others
- value-to-cost ratios may be used to decide priorities (see below).

Very often a new system will be replacing an old computer system and the first increments may use parts of the old system. For example, the data for the data base of the new system may initially be obtained from the old system's standing files.

Which steps should be first? Some steps may be prerequisites because of physical dependencies but others may be in any order. Value-to-cost ratios may be used to establish the order in which increments are to be developed. The customer is asked to rate the value of each increment with a score in the range 1–10 in terms of its value to them. The developers also rate the cost of developing each of the increments with a score in the range 0–10. This may seem a rather crude way of evaluating costs and benefits, but people may be unwilling to be more precise. By then dividing the value rating by the cost rating, a rating which indicates the relative 'value for money' of each increment may be derived.

The value to cost ratio = V/C where V is a score 1–10 representing value to customer and C is a score 0–10 representing cost.

Table 4.1 *Ranking by value to cost ratio*

Step	Value	Cost	Ratio	Rank
Profit reports	9	1	9	(2nd)
Online data base	1	9	0·11	(6th)
Ad hoc enquiry	5	5	1	(4th)
Production sequence plans	2	8	0·25	(5th)
Purchasing profit factors	9	4	2·25	(3rd)
Clerical procedures	0	7	0	(7th)
Profit based pay for managers	9	0	∞	(1st)

Create open technology plan

Note that 'open technology' in this context does not necessarily mean a UNIX™ environment. If the system is to be able to cope with new components being continually added then it has to be built so that it is extendible, portable and maintainable.

As a minimum this will require the use of:

- a standard high level language
- a standard operating system
- small modules
- variable parameters, e.g. items such as organization name, department names, charge rates etc. are held in a parameter file that may be amended without programmer intervention
- standard database management system.

These are all things that might be expected as a matter of course in a modern IS development environment.

An incremental example

Tom Gilb describes a project where a software house negotiated a fixed price contract with a 3-month delivery time with the Swedish Government to supply a system to support map-making. It later became apparent that the original estimate of effort upon which the bid was based was probably about half what the real effort would be.

The project was replanned so that it was divided into ten increments, each supplying something of use to the customer. The final increments were not available until three months after the contract's delivery date. The customer was not in fact unhappy about this as the most important parts of the system had actually been delivered early.

Conclusion

This chapter has stressed the need to examine each project carefully to see if it has characteristics which suggest that a particular approach or process model. These characteristics may also suggest the addition of specific activities to the project plan.

The classic waterfall process model which attempts to minimize iteration should lead to projects that are easy to control. Unfortunately many projects do not lend themselves to this structure. Prototyping may be able to reduce project uncertainties by allowing knowledge to be bought through experimentation. The incremental approach encourages the execution of a series of small, manageable, 'mini-projects' but does have some costs.

Further exercises

1. A building society has a long history of implementing computer-based information systems to support the work of its branches. It uses a proprietary

structured systems analysis and design method. It has been decided to create a computer model of the property market. This would attempt for example to calculate the effect of changes of interest rates on house values. There is some concern that the usual methodology used for IS development would not be appropriate for the new project.

(a) Why might there be this concern and what alternative approaches should be considered?

(b) Outline a plan for the development of the system which illustrates the application of your preferred methodology for this project.

2. A software package is to be designed and built to assist in software cost estimation. It will input certain parameters and produce initial cost estimates to be used at bidding time.

(a) It has been suggested that a software prototype would be of value in these circumstances. Explain why this might be.

(b) Discuss how such prototyping could be controlled to ensure that it is conducted in an orderly and effective way and within a specified time span.

3. An invoicing system is to have the following components: amend invoice, produce invoice, produce monthly statements, record cash payment, clear paid invoices from database, create customer records, delete customer.

(a) What physical dependencies govern the order in which these transactions are implemented?

(b) How could the system be broken down into increments which would be of some value to the users (hint – think about the problems of taking existing details onto a database when a system is first implemented).

4. What are the features of the following that contribute to an open systems architecture as recommended by Tom Gilb:

(a) the UNIX™ operating system

(b) SQL

(c) C++

(d) Jackson Structured Programming.

Chapter 5

Software estimation

OBJECTIVES

When you have completed this chapter you will be able to:

- ☐ avoid the dangers of unrealistic estimates

- ☐ estimate projects using a bottom-up approach

- ☐ apply the basic COCOMO equation

- ☐ count the function points for a system

- ☐ use the most appropriate estimating methods for the systems analysis and programming stages of a project.

Introduction

One definition of a successful project is that the system is delivered 'on time and within budget and with the required quality' which implies that targets are set and the project leader then tries to meet those targets. This assumes that the targets are reasonable – the possibility of a project leader achieving record levels of productivity from their team, but still not meeting a deadline because of incorrect initial estimates is not recognized. Realistic estimates are therefore crucial to the project leader.

What sorts of problems might a project leader such as Amanda, who is in charge of the IOE Maintenance Group Accounts project, encounter when trying to do estimates? Estimating the effort required to implement software is notoriously difficult. Some of the difficulties of estimating are inherent in the very nature of software, especially its complexity and invisibility. In addition the intensely human activities which make up system development cannot be treated in a purely mechanistic way. Other difficulties are outlined in the paragraphs below.

In Chapter 1, the special characteristics of software identified by Brooks i.e. complexity, conformity, changeability and invisibility, were discussed.

- **Novel applications of software** – with traditional engineering projects, it is often the case that a similar artefact to one constructed previously is to be built again but for a different customer or in a different location. The estimates for such a project can therefore be based on previous experience. With software, in most major projects the product is different and will therefore be clouded with doubts and uncertainties.
- **Changing technology** – for example, at IOE the original maintenance billing system may have been written in Cobol, while the new extension for group accounts that Amanda is managing might be developed using a fourth generation environment such as Ingres/Vision.
- **Lack of homogeneity of project experience** – as we will see, effective estimating should be based on information about how projects in the past have performed. It is surprising how many organizations do not make this data available to staff. Amanda might also find that even where the previous project data is available, it may not be that useful.

Table 5.1 is a set of figures recorded for actual projects carried out by the same organization.

Table 5.1 *Some project data – effort in work months (as percentage of total effort in brackets)*

The figures are taken from B. A. Kitchenham and N. R. Taylor 'Software Project Development Cost Estimation' in *Journal of Systems and Software* 1985 (5).

The abbreviation SLOC stands for 'source lines of code'. SLOC is one way of indicating the size of a system.

Project	Design wm	Design (%)	Coding wm	Coding (%)	Testing wm	Testing (%)	Total wm	Total SLOC
a	3·9	(23)	5·3	(32)	7·4	(44)	16·7	6050
b	2·7	(12)	13·4	(59)	6·5	(26)	22·6	8363
c	3·5	(11)	26·8	(83)	1·9	(6)	32·2	13334
d	0·8	(21)	2·4	(62)	0·7	(18)	3·9	5942
e	1·8	(10)	7·7	(44)	7·8	(45)	17·3	3315
f	19·0	(28)	29·7	(44)	19·0	(28)	67·7	38988
g	2·1	(21)	7·4	(74)	0·5	(5)	10·1	38614
h	1·3	(7)	12·7	(66)	5·3	(27)	19·3	12762
i	8·5	(14)	22·7	(38)	28·2	(47)	59·5	26500

Exercise 5.1

Calculate the productivity (i.e. SLOC per work month) of each of the projects in Table 5.1 and also for the organization as a whole. If the project leaders for projects a and d had correctly estimated the source number of lines of code (SLOC) and then used the average productivity of the organization to calculate the effort needed to complete the projects, how far out would their estimates have been from the actual effort?

It would be very difficult on the basis of this information to advise a project manager about what sort of productivity to expect, or about the probable distribution of effort between the phases of design, coding and testing that could be expected from a new project.

There have been some attempts to set up public databases of past projects. However this data seems to be of limited use to estimators. There are uncertainties in the way that various terms can be interpreted. For example, what exactly is meant by the term 'testing'? Does it cover the activity of the programmer when they are debugging their code? Does 'design' include drawing up program structure diagrams or does this come under the heading of 'programming'?

- **Subjective nature of estimating** – some research shows that people tend to underestimate the difficulty of small tasks and overestimate that of large ones. In the world of software development this is perhaps justifiable as large projects are usually disproportionately more complex and more difficult than smaller ones.
- **Political implications** – different groups within an organization have different objectives. The IOE information systems development managers may, for example, want to see as many systems as possible implemented and will therefore put pressure on estimators to reduce cost estimates. As Amanda is responsible for the development of the maintenance group accounts sub-system, she may be concerned that the project does not exceed its budget and is not delivered late as this will reflect badly on herself. She may therefore try to increase the estimates. One suggestion is that all estimates should be carried out within the organization by a specialist estimating group, independent of both the users and the project team. Not all agree with this, as staff involved in a project are more likely to be committed to targets where they have participated in formulating them.

The possibility of the different groups with stakes in a project having different and possibly conflicting objectives was discussed in Chapter 1.

Where are estimates done?

Estimates are carried out at various stages of a software project. At each stage the reasons for the estimate and the methods used will vary.

- **Strategic planning** – the costs of computerizing potential applications as well as the benefits of doing so may need to be estimated to help decide what priority to give to each project. Such estimates may also influence the numbers of various types of development staff to be recruited by the organization.
- **Feasibility study** – this ascertains that the benefits of the potential system will justify the costs.
- **System specification** – most system development methodologies usefully distinguish between the definition of the users' requirements and the design which documents how those requirements are to be fulfilled. The effort needed to implement different design proposals will need to be estimated. Estimates at

Chapter 3 discusses strategic planning in some detail. See also Chris Clare and Gordon Stutely, *Information Systems –Strategy to Design* in this series.

the design stage will also confirm that the feasibility study is still valid, taking into account all that has been learnt during detailed requirements analysis.

The estimate at this stage cannot be based only on the user requirement: some kind of technical plan is also needed – see Chapter 4.

- **Evaluation of suppliers' proposals** – in the case of the IOE maintenance group accounts sub-system, for example, IOE may consider putting the actual system-building out to tender. Staff in the software houses which are considering a bid would need to scrutinize the system specification and produce estimates on which to base a proposal. Amanda may still be required to carry out her own estimate to help judge the bids received. IOE may wish to question a proposal which seems too low: they might wonder, for example, whether the proposer had properly understood the requirements. If, on the other hand, the bids seem too high they may reconsider in-house development.
- **Project planning** – as the planning and implementation of the project progresses to greater levels of detail, more detailed estimates of smaller work components will be made. As well as confirming the earlier and more broad-brush estimates, these will help answer questions about, for example, when staff will be available to start new tasks.

Two general points can be made here:

- as the project proceeds so the accuracy of the estimates should improve as more knowledge about the nature of the project becomes available;
- a conventional wisdom is that at the beginning of the project the user requirement (i.e. a logical model of the required system) is of paramount importance and that premature consideration of the physical implementation is to be avoided. In order to do an estimate, however, the estimator will have to speculate about this physical implementation (e.g. how many programs will have to be written?).

To set estimating into the context of the Step Wise framework (Figure 5.1) presented in Chapter 1, re-estimating may take place at almost any step, but specific provision is made for it at Step 3, 'Analyse project characteristics', where a relatively high-level estimate will be produced, and in Step 5 for each individual activity. As Steps 5–8 are repeated at progressively lower levels, so estimates will be done at a finer degree of detail. As we will see later in this chapter, different methods of estimating are needed at these different planning steps.

Problems with over- and under-estimates

A project leader such as Amanda will need to be aware that the estimate itself, if known to the development team, will influence the time required to implement the system. An over-estimate may cause the project to take longer than it would otherwise. This can be explained by the application of two 'laws'.

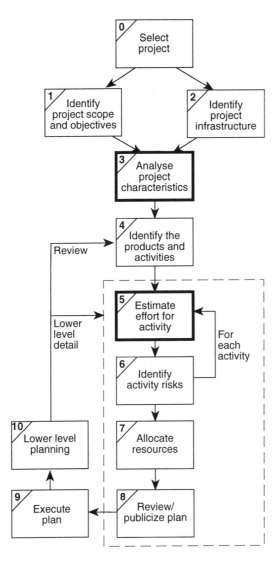

Figure 5.1 *Software estimation takes place in Steps 3 and 5 in particular.*

- **Parkinson's Law** – work expands to fill the time available, i.e. given an easy target staff will work less hard.
- **Brooks' Law** – the effort required to implement a project will go up disproportionately with the number of staff assigned to the project. As the project team grows in size so will the effort that has to go into management, coordination and communication. This has given rise, in extreme cases, to the notion of Brooks' Law: 'putting more people on a late job makes it later'. If there is an over-estimate of the effort required then this may lead to more staff being allocated than are needed and managerial overheads will be increased. This is more likely to be of significance with large projects.

Parkinson's law was originally expounded in C. Northcote Parkinson's tongue-in-cheek book *Parkinson's Law* John Murray, 1957. Brooks' law comes from *The Mythical Man-month* that has been referred to already.

See T. K. Hamid and S. E. Madnick 'Impact of Schedule Estimation on Software Project Behaviour' *IEEE Software* July 1986 3(4) pp 70–75.

Some have suggested that while the under-estimated project may not be completed on time or to cost, it may still be implemented in a shorter time than a project with a more generous estimate. There must, however, be limits to this phenomenon where all the slack in the project is taken up.

The danger with the underestimate is the effect on quality. Staff, particularly those with less experience, may respond to pressing deadlines by producing work which is substandard. Since we are into laws, this may be seen as a manifestation of Weinberg's zeroth law of reliability: 'If a system does not have to be reliable, it can meet any other objective'. In other words, if there is no need for the program to actually work, you can meet any programming deadline that may be set! Substandard work may only become visible at the later, testing, phases of a project which are particularly difficult to control and where extensive rework can have catastrophic consequences for the project completion date.

Because of the possible effects on the behaviour of development staff of the size of estimates, they may be artificially reduced by their managers to increase pressure on staff. This will only work where staff are unaware that this has been done. Research has found that motivation and morale are enhanced where targets are achievable. If, over a period of time, staff become aware that the targets set are unattainable and that projects are routinely not meeting their published targets then this will help to destroy motivation. Furthermore, people like to think of themselves as winners and there is a general tendency to put success down to our own efforts while failure is blamed on the organization.

Barry Boehm devised the COCOMO estimating model which is described later in this chapter.

In the end, an estimate is not really a prediction, it is a **management goal.** Barry Boehm has suggested that if a software development cost is within 20% of the estimated cost estimate for the job then a good manager can turn it into a self-fulfilling prophecy. A project leader like Amanda will work hard to make the actual performance conform to the estimate.

The basis for software estimating

The need for historical data

Nearly all estimating methods need information about how projects have been implemented in the past. However, care needs to be taken in judging the applicability of data to the estimator's own circumstances because of possible differences in environmental factors such as the programming languages used, the software tools available, the standards enforced and the experience of the staff.

Measure of work

SLOC has already been used in Table 5.1.

It is normally not possible to calculate directly the actual cost or time required to implement a project. The time taken to write a program may vary according to the competence or experience of the programmer. Implementation time may also vary because of environmental factors such as the software tools available. The usual practice is therefore to express the work content of the system to be implemented independently of effort using a measure such as source lines of code (SLOC). The reader may also come across the abbreviation KLOC which refers to thousands of lines of code.

As can be imagined, SLOC is a very imprecise measure. Does it include comment lines? Are data declarations to be included? Unfortunately, researchers have not been consistent on these points. The writers' view is that comment lines are excluded, but data declarations are included. The argument for including data declarations is that in Cobol, especially, it is possible to transfer much of the specification of processing to the DATA DIVISION, e.g. by using the report writer facility. Others may argue over this, but the main point is that consistency is essential.

It is difficult to count SLOC in modern fourth generation languages which often use tables or diagrams to record programming rules. Different measures of size are needed such as function points which are explained further on in this chapter.

Complexity

Given that two programs both have 2 KLOC, it does not follow that each would take the same amount of time to write, even if done by the same programmer in the same environment. One program may be more complex. Because of this SLOC estimates have to be modified to take complexity into account. Attempts have been made to find objective measures of complexity, but often it will depend on the subjective judgement of the estimator.

Differences in complexity may be one of the reasons for the inconsistencies in Table 5.1.

Bottom-up estimating

Estimating methods can be generally divided into bottom-up and top-down approaches. With the bottom-up approach the estimator breaks the project into its component tasks and then estimates how much effort will be required to carry out each task. With a large project, the process of breaking down into tasks would be a repetitive one: each task would be analysed into its component subtasks and these in turn would be further analysed. It is suggested that this is repeated until you get to components that can be executed by a single person in about a week or two. The reader may wonder why this is not called a top-down approach: after all you are starting from the top and working down! Although this top-down analysis is an essential precursor to bottom-up estimating, it is really a separate one – that of producing a Work Breakdown Schedule (WBS). The bottom-up part comes in adding up the calculated effort for each activity to get an overall estimate.

The bottom-up approach is most appropriate at the later, more detailed, stages of project planning. If this method is used early on in the project cycle then the estimator will have to make some assumptions about the characteristics of the final system, for example the number and size of program modules. These are just working assumptions and imply no commitment when it comes to the actual design of the system.

Where a project is completely novel or there is no historical data available, the estimator would be well advised to use the bottom-up approach.

Exercise 5.2

Brigette at Brightmouth HE College has been told that there is a requirement, now that the payroll system has been successfully installed, to create a sub-system that analyses the staff costs of each course. Details of the pay that each member of staff receives may be obtained from the payroll standing data. The number of hours that each member of staff spends teaching on each course may be obtained from standing files on a computer-based time-tabling system.

What tasks would have to be undertaken to implement this requirement? Try and identify tasks that would take one person about 1 or 2 weeks.

Which tasks are the ones whose durations are most difficult to estimate?

The top-down approach and parametric models

The top-down approach is normally associated with parametric models. These may be explained using the analogy of estimating the cost of rebuilding a house. This would be of practical concern to a householder because they would need to ensure that they have sufficient insurance cover to allow them to rebuild their property if it were destroyed. Unless they happen to be in the building trade it is unlikely that they are going to be able to work out how many bricklayer-hours, how many carpenter-hours, electrician-hours and so on would be required. Insurance companies, however, produce convenient tables where the house-owner can find an estimate of rebuilding costs based on such **parameters** as the number of storeys and the floor space that a house has. This is a simple parametric model.

The effort needed to implement a project will be related to variables mainly associated with characteristics of the final system. The form of the parametric model will normally be one or more formulae in the form:

$$\text{effort} = (\text{parameter value}) \times \text{constant}$$

For example, a parameter value might be in the form 'thousands of lines of code' (KLOC) and the constant 25 days. The values to be used will often be matters of subjective judgement.

Having calculated the overall effort required, the problem is then to allocate proportions of that effort to the various activities within that project.

The top-down and bottom-up approaches are not mutually exclusive. Project managers will probably try to get a number of different estimates from different people using different methods. Some parts of an overall estimate could be derived using a top-down approach while other parts could be calculated using a bottom-up method.

At the earlier stages of a project, top-down approach would tend to be used, while at later stages the bottom-up approach might be preferred.

Students on a course are required to produce a written report on an IT-related topic each term. If you wanted to create a model to estimate how long it should take a student to complete such an assignment, what measure of work content would you use? Some reports might be more difficult to produce than others: what factors might affect the degree of difficulty?

Exercise 5.3

The classic example of a parametric model is COCOMO which we will now discuss.

COCOMO: a parametric model

Boehm's COCOMO (COnstructive COst MOdel) is often referred to in the literature on software project management and particularly in connection with software estimating.

Boehm originally based the model on a study of 63 projects. Of these only seven were business systems and so it is applicable to applications other than information systems. The basic model is built around the equation

$$(mm) = c(kdsi)^k$$

where *mm* is the number of 'man-months' i.e. units of 152 working hours, *kdsi* is thousands of delivered source code instructions, and *c* and *k* are constants.

The first step is to derive an estimate of the system size in terms of *kdsi*. The constants, *c* and *k* (see Table 5.2), depend on whether the system under scrutiny can be classified, in Boehm's terms, as organic, semi-detached or embedded. These relate to the technical nature of the system and the development environment.

Boehm described the principles of the COCOMO models in *Software Engineering Economics*, Prentice-Hall, 1981.

You may prefer *wm* (for 'work month') to *mm* and *kloc* to *kdsi*. We have used the same terms as Boehm to avoid confusion when referencing *Software Engineering Economics*.

- **Organic mode** – this would typically be the case when relatively small teams develop software in a highly familiar in-house environment and when the system being developed is small and the interface requirements are flexible.
- **Embedded mode** – this means the product being developed has to operate within very tight constraints and changes to the system are very costly.

Generally, information systems would tend to be regarded as organic while industrial systems would be embedded.

• **Semi-detached mode** – this combines elements of the organic and the embedded modes or has characteristics which come between the two.

Table 5.2 *COCOMO constants*

System type	c	k
Organic	2·4	1·05
Semi-detached	3·0	1·12
Embedded	3·6	1·20

Exercise 5.4

Apply the basic COCOMO model to the lines of code figures in Table 5.1 to generate estimated work-months of effort, assuming a semi-detached mode. Compare the calculated figures with the actuals.

As well as the intermediate model, a further, detailed, COCOMO model attempts to allocate effort to individual project phases.

Boehm in fact found this to be a poor predictor of the effort required and so went on to develop the intermediate version of COCOMO which takes into account 15 cost drivers. In the intermediate model, a nominal effort estimate, (mm_{nom}) is derived in a similar way as for the basic model.

The nominal estimate is then adjusted by a development effort multiplier (*dem*):

$$(mm_{est}) = (mm_{nom}) \times (dem)$$

where *(dem)* is calculated by taking into account multipliers based on the following cost drivers:

• required software reliability
• data base size
• product complexity
• execution time constraints
• main storage constraints
• virtual machine volatility
• computer turn around time
• analyst capability
• application experience
• programmer capability
• virtual machine experience
• programming language experience
• use of modern programming practices
• use of software tools
• required development schedule.

These multipliers take into account such influences on productivity as Boehm's finding that having a programming team fully conversant with the programming language to be used could reduce the effort required to implement the project by up to 20% compared to a team with a very low or initially non-existent familiarity with the programming language. In fact, the biggest influence on productivity according to Boehm is the capability of the implementation team.

Does COCOMO actually work? The evidence seems mixed. Some research in the United Kingdom looked at figures for project developed by ICL and British Telecom and found that COCOMO would be a poor estimator. Others must have clearly found it useful as there have been numerous refinements and extensions to the method such as Ada COCOMO. Currently (1995), a COCOMO 2.0 is being developed which, it is hoped, will address a wider range of software environments and the newer methods and practices in software development.

We are now going to look at some alternative estimating methods in further detail.

Expert judgement

This is asking someone who is knowledgeable about either the application area or the development environment to give an estimate of the effort needed to carry out a task. This method will most likely be used when estimating the effort needed to change an existing piece of software. The estimator would have carry out some kind of impact analysis in order to judge the proportion of code that will be affected and from that derive an estimate. Someone already familiar with the software will be in the best position to do this.

'Price to win' and 'design to cost'

With 'price to win', the estimator guesses what the potential client is likely to be willing to pay and then quotes a price to win the business regardless of the actual project content. Most writers on the topic warn against this approach!

It is, however, close to a more respectable engineering practice, 'design to cost'. In many situations the resources available for computer development are pretty well fixed. In this case, rather than designing the system and then costing it, the system has to be planned and designed with the firm idea that the cost is fixed. This may mean reducing the functionality of the proposed system to keep within these resource constraints. In these circumstances, estimating is not an isolated activity but is woven into the very fabric of systems development.

Estimating by analogy

In this case, when the estimator is sizing a new project they seek out previous projects that have similar characteristics and for which accurate size and effort data is held. Having found a previous project that fits, the estimator tries to

identify the differences between the current project and the previous one and
make adjustments to produce the estimate for the new system.

This may be a good approach where you have information about some
previous projects but not enough to draw generalized conclusions about what
variables might make good size parameters

A problem here is how you actually identify the similarities and differences
between the different systems.

Albrecht function point analysis

See A. J. Albrecht and J.
E. Gaffney Jr., 'Software
Function, Source Lines of
Code, and Development
Effort Prediction: A
Software Science
Validation' in *IEEE
Transactions on Software
Engineering*, November
1983 SE-9(6) pp 639–
648.

Approaches to estimating such as COCOMO are based on SLOC which assumes
the use of a selected third generation language. Function point analysis attempts
to get away from this limitation. This method is a top down method that was
devised by Allan Albrecht when he worked for IBM. Albrecht was investigating
programming productivity and needed some way to quantify the underlying
functions of programs independently of the programming languages in which
they had been coded. He developed the idea of function points.

The basis of function point analysis is that computer-based information
systems comprise five major components, or 'external user types' in Albrecht's
terminology, that are of benefit to the users:

- **External input types** are input transactions which update internal computer
  files.
- **External output types** are transactions where data is output to the user.
  Typically these would be printed reports as VDU displays would come under
  external enquiry types (see below).
- **Logical internal file types** are the standing files used by the system (file types
  really refers to record types). For example on a serially organized personnel
  records file, records for employees may be grouped into departments each
  headed by a department record. This would count as two internal file types.

Albrecht also dictates that
output external interface
files should be double
counted as logical internal
file types as well.

- **External interface file types** allow for output and input that may pass to and
  from other computer applications. Examples of this would be the transmission
  of accounting data from an order processing system to the main ledger system
  or the production of a file of direct debit details on a magnetic medium to be
  passed to BACS. Files shared between applications would also be counted
  here.
- **External enquiry types** are transactions initiated by the user which provide
  information but do not update the internal files.

The analyst has to identify each instance of each external user type in the
projected system. They then have to classify the complexity of each component
as either simple, average or complex. The counts of each external user type in
each complexity band are multiplied by suitable factors (see Table 5.3) to get
function point scores which are summed to obtain an overall function point count
which indicates the information processing size.

Table 5.3 *Albrecht complexity multipliers*

External user type	Multiplier		
	Simple	*Average*	*Complex*
External input type	3	4	6
External output type	4	5	7
Logical internal file type	7	10	15
External interface file type	5	7	10
External enquiry file type	3	4	6

The Albrecht method has been elaborated over the years so that there are now rules to guide the estimator about how user types are to be rated.

Exercise 5.5

The task for which Brigette has been made responsible in Exercise 5.2 needs a program which will extract yearly salaries from the payroll file, and hours taught on each course by each member of staff and the details of courses from two files maintained by the time-tabling system. The program will calculate the staff costs for each course and put the results into a computer file which will then be read by the main accounting system. The program will also produce a report showing for each course the hours taught by each member of staff and the cost of those hours.

Using the method described above, calculate the Albrecht function points for this subsystem assuming that the report is complex, but that all the other elements are of average difficulty.

Function point analysis now goes on to take into account the fact that the effort required to implement a computer-based information system will relate not just to the number and complexity of the features to be provided but also to the environment in which the system is to operate.

Function point analysis identifies 14 factors which can influence the degree of difficulty associated with implementing a system. The list that Albrecht produced related particularly to the concerns of information system developers in the late 1970s and early 1980s. Some technology which was then new and relatively threatening is now well established.

The technical complexity adjustment (TCA) calculation has lots of problems. Some have even found that it produces less accurate estimates than using the unadjusted function point count. Because of these difficulties, we are going to leave further discussion of the TCA.

Tables have been calculated to convert the function points to lines of code for various languages. For example, it is suggested that 106 lines of Cobol are needed on average to implement a function point, while for C the figure is 150 and for Basic 64.

Further details on TCA can be found in the Albrecht and Gaffney paper.
Some of these conversion factors do not seem to be very convincing (e.g. 6 SLOC per function point for spreadsheets).

Exercise 5.6

In the case of the subsystem described in Exercise 5.5 for which Brigette is responsible at Brightmouth HE College, how many lines of Cobol code should be needed to implement this subsystem, according to the standard conversion?

Function points Mark II

This method has came into the public domain with the publication of the book by Charles R. Symons *Software Sizing and Estimating – Mark II FPA,* John Wiley and Sons, 1991.

The Mark II method has been recommended by CCTA (Central Computer and Telecommunications Agency) which lays down standards for UK government projects. At one time this Mark II approach seemed to be a good method to use with SSADM but some difficulties are now apparent. The 'Mark II' implies an improvement and replacement of the Albrecht method. The Albrecht method, however, has had many refinements made to it and FPA Mark II remains a minority method used mainly in the UK.

The underlying formula is basically the same as for the Albrecht method:

function points = (information processing size) × (technical complexity adjustment)

As with Albrecht, the information processing size is measured in unadjusted function points (UFPs). The assumption here is that an information system comprises transactions which have the basic structure shown in Figure 5.2.

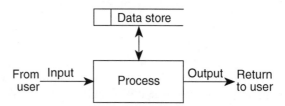

Figure 5.2 *Model of a transaction.*

For each transaction the UFPs are calculated:

W_i × (number of input data element types) +
W_e × (number of entity types referenced) +
W_o × (number of output data element types)

Here, W_i, W_e, and W_o are weightings that may be derived by asking developers what proportion of effort has been spent in previous projects developing those parts of the software that deal with processing inputs, accessing and modifying stored data and processing outputs. From this it should be possible to work out the average hours of work generated by instances of each type of element.

The weightings are then normalized into ratios which add up to 2·5. If this way of getting hold of the weightings seems too time-consuming then some industry averages are available which are currently (i.e. in 1995) 0·58 for W_i, 1·66 for W_e and 0·26 for W_o.

The only reason why 2·5 has been adopted here is to facilitate comparison with Albrecht function points.

A cash receipt transaction in the IOE maintenance accounts system accesses two entity types – INVOICE and CASH-RECEIPT.

Example 5.1

The data elements that are input are:

> Invoice number
> Date received
> Cash received

If an INVOICE record is not found for the invoice number then an error message is issued. If the invoice number is found then a CASH-RECEIPT record is created.

The error message constitutes the only output data element that the transaction has to cater for.

The unadjusted function points, using the industry average weightings, for this transaction would therefore be:

$$(0·58 \times 3) + (1·66 \times 2) + (0·26 \times 1) = 5·32$$

One of the transactions that will be part of the IOE maintenance group accounts subsystem for which Amanda is responsible will be used to set up details of new group account customers.

Exercise 5.7

The operator will input:

> Customer account number
> Customer name
> Address
> Postcode
> Customer type
> Statement production date

All this information will be set up in a CUSTOMER record on the system's database. If a CUSTOMER account already exists for the account number that has been input, an error message will be displayed to the operator.

Calculate the number of unadjusted Mark II function points for this transaction, using the industry average weightings.

FPA Mark II follows the Albrecht method in recognizing that one system delivering the same functionality as another may be more difficult to implement (but also more valuable to the users) because of additional technical requirements. For example, the incorporation of additional security measures would increase the amount of effort to deliver the system. The original Albrecht FPA method identified 14 factors – FPA Mark II identifies five more factors:

- interfaces to other applications
- special security features
- direct access for third parties
- user training features
- documentation requirements.

Symons encourages the addition of other factors to suit local circumstances.

This simplified approach assumes rather unrealistically that the factors affecting productivity are the same for each project.

With both the Albrecht and Symons methods, the function points can be counted for previous projects where actual effort is known. If you have figures for the effort expended on past projects (in work-days for instance) and also the system sizes in function points, you should be able to work out a productivity rate, i.e.

$$\text{productivity} = \text{size/effort}$$

For new projects, the function points can be counted and then the effort can be projected using the productivity rate derived above:

$$\text{effort} = \text{size/productivity}$$

Symons is very much against the idea of using function points to estimate SLOC rather than effort. One finding by Symons is that productivity, i.e. the effort per function point to implement a system, is influenced very much by the size of the project.

A systems analysis-oriented approach

SSADM (Structured Systems Analysis and Design Method) is the structured method originally developed as a standard for the United Kingdom government.

Because function point analysis is a top-down method, it produces overall estimates for the whole project. When we plan a project in more detail, we want to estimate the effort that will be needed for individual activities and the function point approach is of limited help.

We are now going to look at two estimating approaches which would help us to estimate the effort needed for individual activities. The first is suitable for the systems analysis stage, the second for programming activities.

We discussed the need for parameters when describing top-down estimating.

The first, systems analysis oriented, approach is to identify the factors that influence the effort needed for each separate stage or step of a methodology such as SSADM. The parameters will not be based on characteristics of the final system but on attributes of the intermediate products of SSADM, e.g. data flow diagrams.

SSADM looks at systems from three main points of view.

- **Data structures** – the entities about which data is to be held, the attributes of each type of entity and the relationships between different types of entity are all investigated. The major vehicle for documenting the findings is the logical data structure (LDS).
- **Processes** – the way that data flows through the system and is used and modified by various processes which may store and retrieve data in data stores is analysed and recorded in data flow diagrams (DFDs) with their supporting documentation. This is an iterative representation so that a process identified at a high level may further analysed to see what data flows, processes and data stores it has within its boundaries. Hence reference is made to first level DFDs, second level DFDs and so on.
- **Transformations** – the ways that the attributes of each type of entity are modified during its lifetime are analysed taking particular account of the sequence in which these changes take place and their preconditions. These are documented in entity life histories (ELHs).

For a detailed explanation see M. Prior and B. Robinson, *Systems Analysis Techniques*, in this series.

At the initial stages of SSADM the attention is focused on data structures and processes. A general guideline for estimating is that the more entities and processes there are in a system the longer it will take to go through the stages of SSADM.

Examples of the parameters that could be used to estimate the effort to carry out activities in SSADM include

A_1	the number of top level DFD processes
A_2	the number of entities on the overview LDS
A_3	the number of major documents in the existing system
A_4	the number of user areas affected by the project.

At first, many parameter values that are important for later activities will not be known for certain. Instead estimated parameter values will have to be calculated using rules of thumb such as

A_5	the number of key interviews	$A_4 \times 2$
A_6	the number of support interviews	$A_5 \times 0.5$
A_7	the number of second level DFD processes	$A_1 \times 2.5$
A_8	the number of third level DFD processes	$A_7 \times 0.75$
A_9	the number of entries on LDS	$A_2 \times 1.5$

As the project progresses, these estimated parameter values will be replaced by the actual ones.

SSADM is divided into a number of component **stages** which are further sub-divided into **steps**. The effort for each task within a step can be estimated by the formula

effort = (parameter value) × (days per parameter unit)

Example 5.2 – different versions of SSADM have different requirements: here we assume that all documents have to be analysed

Relational data analysis is the process of putting the data found on various documents into third normal form. This may be done for each document used by the existing system and past experience may show that about half a day is needed to analyse each document. The effort to do this could therefore be calculated as:

$$A_3 \times 0.5 \text{ days}$$
$$B_3 \times 0.5 \text{ days}$$

A_3, you may remember, is the number of major documents in the system. Each of these documents will need to be analysed. There may be other flows of information which are not in document form which will need to be analysed as well. This is catered for by B_3, a parameter which represents the number of data flows from external entities. We may not know this when we do the estimate and so a rule of thumb is used which assumes that, on average, each top-level process has two flows of data from outside the system:

$$2 \times (A_1 + B_1)$$

B_1 is the number of new processes that have been added to the original DFD to take into account new user requirements – it's assumed that we do know this.

Exercise 5.8

An elementary process description (EPD) is produced for each process that appears on a data flow diagram and which is not further expanded as a data flow diagram at a lower level. An EPD is a textual description of what a process does and it is estimated that 0·25 of a day is needed to create each one of them. The top level DFD is found to have six processes. All these processes have been broken down into second level DFDs. Half the second level DFDs are broken down into third level DFDs. Estimate the amount of effort needed to produce EPD's for the system.

(Hint – you are not given the number of processes on second and third level DFDs, but this can be estimated using rules of thumb shown earlier.)

A program-oriented approach

The previous approach would be useful at the analysis and design stage of a project, but what about the programming stage? An approach might be based on the following steps.

(a) Envisage the number and type of programs in the final system

This is easiest where the system is of a conventional and well understood nature. Most information systems are built from a small set of system operations e.g.

Insert, Amend, Update, Display, Delete, Print. The same principle should equally apply to embedded systems albeit with a different set of primitive functions.

(b) Estimate the SLOC of each identified program

The estimator must have a particular implementation language in mind for this step.

One way to judge the number of instructions likely to be in a program is to draw up a program structure diagram and to visualize how many instructions would be needed to implement each identified procedure. The estimator may look at existing programs which have a similar functional description to assist them in this process.

Where programs for an information system are similar (e.g. they are data validation programs) then the number of data item types processed by each program is likely to be the major influence on size.

Function point analysis Mark II is also based on the idea that the number of data item types processed influences program size.

(c) Estimate the work content taking into account complexity and technical difficulty

The practice is to multiply the SLOC estimate by a factor for complexity and technical difficulty. This factor will depend largely on the subjective judgement of the estimator. For example, the requirement to meet particular highly constrained performance targets can greatly increase programming effort.

A weighting may be given when there is uncertainty, for example about a new technique used in particular module, but this should not be excessive. Where there is a large amount of uncertainty then specific measures should be taken to reduce this, e.g. by the use of exploratory prototypes.

See Chapter 4 for a discussion of prototypes.

(d) Calculate the work-days effort

Historical data can be used to provide ratios to convert weighted SLOC to effort. These conversion factors are often based on the productivity of a 'standard programmer' of about 15–18 months of experience. In installations where the rate of turnover is lower and the average programmer experience is higher this may be reflected in the conversion rate employed.

Draw up an outline program structure diagram for a program to do the processing described in Exercise 5.7 which sets up CUSTOMER records. For each box on your diagram estimate the number of lines of code needed to implement the routine in a third generation language such as Cobol.

Exercise 5.9

Conclusion

To summarize some key points:

- estimates are really management targets
- collect as much information about previous projects as possible
- use more than one method of estimating
- top-down approaches will be used at the earlier stages of project planning while bottom-up approaches will be more prominent later on
- seek a range of opinions
- document your method of doing estimates and record all your assumptions.

Chapter 6

Activity planning

OBJECTIVES

When you have completed this chapter you will be able to:

☐   produce an activity plan for a project

☐   estimate the overall duration of a project

☐   create a critical path and a precedence network for a project

☐   identify a project's critical path.

Introduction

In earlier chapters we looked at methods for forecasting the effort required for a project – both for the project as a whole and for individual activities. A detailed plan for the project must include a schedule indicating the start and completion times for each activity and thus when cash flows are expected to take place. This will enable us to:

- ensure that the appropriate resources will be available precisely when required
- avoid different activities competing for the same resources at the same time
- produce a detailed schedule of which staff carry out each activity
- produce a detailed plan against which actual achievement may be measured
- produce a cash flow forecast
- replan the project during its life to correct drift from the target.

To be effective, a plan must be stated as a set of targets, the achievement of which can be unambiguously measured. The activity plan does this by providing a target start and completion date for each activity (or a window within which each activity may be carried out). The starts and completions of activities must be clearly visible and this is one of the reasons why it is advisable to ensure that each and every project activity produces some tangible product or 'deliverable'.

Project monitoring is discussed in more detail in Chapter 9.

Monitoring the project's progress is then, at least in part, a case of ensuring that the products of each activity are delivered on time.

As a project progresses it is unlikely that everything will go according to plan. Much of the job of project management concerns recognizing when something has gone wrong, identifying its causes and revising the plan to mitigate its effects. The activity plan should provide a means of evaluating the consequences of not meeting any of the activity target dates and guidance as to how the plan might most effectively be modified to bring the project back to target. We shall see that the activity plan may well also offer guidance as to which components of a project should be most closely monitored.

The objectives of activity planning

In addition to providing project and resource schedules, activity planning aims to achieve a number of other objectives which may be summarized as follows.

- **Feasibility assessment** – is the project possible within required timescales and resource constraints? It is not until we have constructed a detailed plan that we can forecast a completion date with any reasonable knowledge of its achievability. The fact that a project may have been estimated as requiring 2 work-years effort may not mean that it would be feasible to complete it within, say, 3 months were 8 people to work on it – that will depend upon the availability of staff and the degree to which activities may be undertaken in parallel.

- **Resource allocation** – what are the most effective ways of allocating resources to the project and when should they be available? The project plan allows us to investigate the relationship between timescales and resource availability (in general allocating additional resources to a project shortens its duration) and the efficacy of additional spending on resource procurement.

- **Detailed costing** – how much will the project cost and when is that expenditure likely to take place? After producing an activity plan and allocating specific resources we can obtain more detailed estimates of costs and their timing.

Chapter 10 discusses motivation in more detail.

- **Motivation** – providing targets and being seen to monitor achievement against targets is an effective way of motivating staff, particularly where they have been involved in setting those targets in the first place.

- **Coordination** – when do the staff in different departments need to be available to work on a particular project and when do staff need to be transferred between projects? The project plan, particularly with large projects involving more than a single project team, provides an effective vehicle for communication and co-ordination between teams. In situations where staff may need to be transferred between project teams (or work concurrently on more than one project), a set of integrated project schedules should ensure that such staff are available when required and do not suffer periods of enforced idleness.

Activity planning and scheduling techniques place an emphasis on the timescale and the allocation of resources. In doing so they treat as a priority the objective of completing the project in a minimum time at an acceptable cost or, alternatively, meeting an arbitrarily set target date at minimum cost. These are not, in themselves, concerned with meeting quality targets which generally impose constraints on the scheduling process.

In Chapter 2 we saw that Amanda's wish to check that four module specifications were correct, while increasing the likely quality of the product, created a constraint that could potentially delay the next stage of the project.

One effective way of shortening project durations is to carry out activities in parallel. Clearly we cannot undertake all the activities at the same time – some require the completion of others before they can start and there are likely to be resource constraints limiting how much may be done simultaneously. Activity scheduling will, however, give us an indication of the cost of these constraints in terms of lengthening timescales and provide us with an indication of how timescales may be shortened by relaxing those constraints. It is up to us, if we try relaxing precedence constraints by for example allowing a program coding task to commence before the design has been completed, to ensure that we are clear about the potential effects on product quality

When to plan

Planning is an ongoing process of refinement – each iteration becoming more detailed and more accurate than the last. Over successive iterations the emphasis and purpose of planning will shift.

During the feasibility study, the main purpose of planning will be to estimate timescales and the risks of not achieving target completion dates or keeping within budget. As the project proceeds beyond the feasibility study, the emphasis will be placed upon the production of activity plans for ensuring resource availability and cash flow control.

The four plan levels specified in PRINCE are described in Appendix A.

Throughout the project, until the final deliverable has reached the customer, monitoring and replanning must continue to correct any drift that might prevent meeting time or cost targets.

Project schedules

Before work commences on a project, or possibly a stage of a larger project, the project plan must be developed to the level of showing dates when each activity should start and finish and when and how much of each resource will be required. Once the plan has been refined to this level of detail we call it a project schedule. Creating a project schedule comprises four main stages.

The first step in producing the plan is to decide what activities need to be carried out and in what order they are to be done. From this we can construct an **ideal activity plan** – that is, a plan of when each activity would ideally be undertaken were resources not a constraint. It is the creation of the ideal activity plan that we shall discuss in this chapter. This activity plan is generated by Steps 4 and 5 of Step Wise (Figure 6.1).

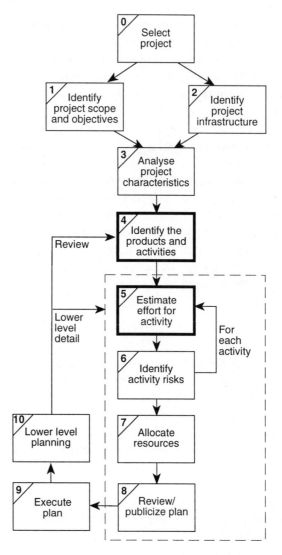

Figure 6.1 *Activity planning is carried out in Steps 4 and 5.*

The ideal activity plan will then be the subject of an **activity risk analysis**, aimed at identifying potential problems. This may suggest alterations to the ideal activity plan and will almost certainly have implications for resource allocation. Activity risk analysis is the subject of Chapter 7.

The third step is **resource allocation**. The expected availability of resources may place constraints on when certain activities may be carried out and our ideal plan may need to be adapted to take account of this. Resource allocation is covered in Chapter 8.

The final step is **schedule production.** Once resources have been allocated to each activity we will be in a position to draw up and publish a project schedule, i.e. a schedule which indicates planned start and completion dates and a resource requirements statement for each activity. Chapter 9 discusses how this is done and the role of the schedule in managing a project.

Projects and activities

Defining activities

Before we try to identify the activities that make up a project it is worth reviewing what we mean by a project and its activities and adding some assumptions that are relevant when we start to produce an activity plan.

- A project is composed of a number of inter-related activities.
- A project may start when at least one of its activities is ready to start.
- A project will be completed when all of the activities comprising it have been completed.
- An activity must have a clearly defined start and a clearly defined end-point, normally marked by the production of a tangible deliverable.
- If an activity requires a resource (as most do) then that resource requirement must be forecastable and is assumed to be required at a constant level throughout the duration of the activity.
- The duration of an activity must be forecastable – assuming normal circumstances, and the reasonable availability of resources.
- Some activities may require that others are completed before they can begin (these are known as **precedence requirements**).

Activities must be defined so that they meet these criteria. Any activity that does not meet these criteria must be redefined.

Identifying activities

Essentially there are two approaches to identifying the activities that make up a project – we shall call them the activity-based approach and the product-based approach.

The activity-based approach consists of writing down a list of all the activities that the project is thought to involve. This may involve a brainstorming session involving the whole project team or it may stem from an analysis of similar past projects. Either way, the objective is to construct a comprehensive list of activities which may then be ordered according to their precedence requirements. When listing activities, particularly for a large project, it may be helpful to subdivide the project into the main life-cycle stages and consider each of these separately.

The product-based approach, used in PRINCE and Step Wise, has already been described in Chapter 2. It consists of producing a Product Breakdown Structure and a Product Flow Diagram and then deriving an ordered list of activities by identifying the transformations that turn some products into others. An advantage of this approach is that it is less likely that a product will be left out of a Project Breakdown Structure than that an activity might be omitted from an unstructured activity list. This is particularly true if using a methodology such as SSADM which clearly specifies each of the products required and the activities required to produce it.

Sequencing and scheduling activities

Throughout the project we will require a schedule that clearly indicates when each of the project's activities are planned to occur and what resources they will need. We shall be considering scheduling in more detail in Chapter 9, but let us consider in outline how we might present a schedule for a small project. One way of presenting such a plan is to use a bar chart as shown in Figure 6.2.

The chart shown has been drawn up taking account of the nature of the development process (i.e. certain tasks must be completed before others may start) and the resources that are available (e.g. activity C follows activity B because Andy cannot work on both tasks at the same time). In drawing up the chart we have therefore done two things – we have sequenced the tasks (i.e. identified the dependencies between activities dictated by the development process) and scheduled them (i.e. specified when they should take place). The scheduling has had to take account the availability of staff and the ways in which the activities have been allocated to them. The schedule might look quite different were there a different number of staff or were we to allocate the activities differently.

In the case of small projects this combined sequencing–scheduling approach might be quite suitable, particularly where we wish to allocate individuals to particular tasks at an early planning stage. However, on larger projects it is better to separate out these two activities: to sequence the task according to their logical relationships and then to schedule them taking into account resources and other factors.

Separating the logical sequencing from the scheduling may be likened to the principle used in SSADM of separating the logical system from its physical implementation.

The bar chart does not show why certain decisions have been made. It is not clear, for example, why activity H is not scheduled to start until week 9. It could be that it cannot start until activity F has been completed or it might be because Charlie is going to be on holiday during week 8.

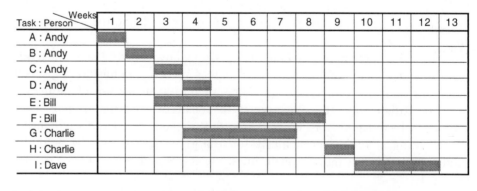

Activity key:
- A: Overall design
- B: Specify module 1
- C: Specify module 2
- D: Specify module 3
- E: Code module 1
- F: Code module 3
- G: Code module 2
- H: Integration testing
- I: System testing

Figure 6.2 *A project plan as a bar chart.*

Approaches to scheduling that achieve this separation between the **logical** and the **physical** use networks to model the project and it is these approaches that we will consider in subsequent sections of this chapter.

Network planning models

These project scheduling techniques model the project's activities and their relationships as a network. In the network time flows from left to right. These techniques were originally developed in the 1950s – the two best known being CPM (critical path method) and PERT (program evaluation review technique). More recently a variation on these techniques, called precedence networks, has become popular and it is this method that is adopted in the majority of computer packages currently available. All three methods are very similar and it must be admitted that many people use the same name (particularly CPM) indiscriminately to refer to any or all of the methods.

In the following sections of this chapter we will look at the critical path method and precedence networks – a discussion of PERT will be reserved for Chapter 7 when we look at risk analysis.

> CPM was developed by the Du Pont Chemical Company who published the method in 1958, claiming that it had saved them $1 million in its first year of use.

Formulating a network model

The first stage in creating a network model is to represent the activities and their interrelationships as a graph. In CPM we do this by representing activities as links (arrowed lines) in the graph – the nodes (circles) representing the events of activities starting and finishing.

In Chapter 2 we saw how Amanda used her Product Breakdown to obtain an activity network. Figure 6.3 shows the fragment of her network that was discussed in that chapter and Figure 6.4 shows how this network would look represented as a critical path network.

Case Study Example

Constructing CPM networks

Before we look at how CPM networks are used it is worth spending a few moments considering the rules for their construction.

> CPM networks are examples of directed graphs.

A project network may only have one start node. The start node (node 1 in Figure 6.4) designates the point at which the project may start. All activities coming from that node may start immediately resources are available – that is, they do not have to wait for any other activities to be completed.

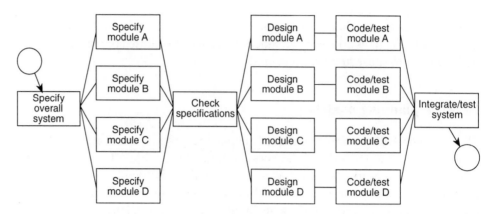

Figure 6.3 *The IOE maintenance group accounts project activity network fragment with a checkpoint activity added.*

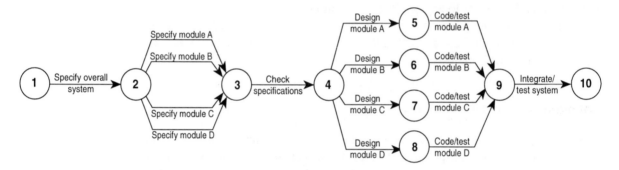

Figure 6.4 *The IOE maintenance group accounts project activity network fragment represented as a CPM network.*

A project network may have only one end node. The end node designates the completion of the project and a project may only finish once! The end node for the project fragment shown in Figure 6.4 is the one numbered 10.

A link has duration. A link represents an activity and, in general, activities take time to execute. Notice, however, that the network in Figure 6.4 does not contain any reference to durations. The links are not drawn in any way to represent the activity durations.

The network drawing merely represents the logic of the project – the rules governing the order in which activities are to be carried out.

Nodes have no duration. Nodes are events and, as such, are instantaneous points in time. The source node is the event of the project becoming ready to start and the sink node is the event of the project becoming completed. Intermediate nodes represent two simultaneous events – the event of all activities leading in to a node having been completed and the event of all activities leading out of that node being in a position to be started.

In Figure 6.5 node 3 is the event that both coding and data take-on have been completed and activity program testing is free to start. Installation may be started only when event 4 has been achieved, i.e. as soon as program testing has been completed.

Figure 6.5 *Fragment of a CPM network.*

Time moves from left to right. In general, if at all possible, networks are drawn so that time moves from left to right. It is rare that this convention needs to be flouted but, in any case, the arrows on the activity lines give a strong visual indication of the time flow of the project.

Nodes are numbered sequentially. There are no precise rules about node numbering but nodes should be numbered so that head nodes (those at the 'arrow' end of an activity) always have a higher number than tail events (those at the 'non-arrow' end of an activity. This convention makes it easy to spot loops.

A network may not contain loops. Figure 6.6 demonstrates a loop in a CPM network. A loop is an error in that it represents a situation that cannot occur in practice. While loops, in the sense of iteration, may occur in practice, they cannot be directly represented in a project network. Note that the logic of Figure 6.6 suggests that program testing cannot start until the errors have been corrected.

If we know the number of times we expect to go round, say, a test–diagnose– correct loop then we can draw the activities as a straight sequence. If we do not know how many times the loop is going to be executed then we cannot calculate the duration of the project.

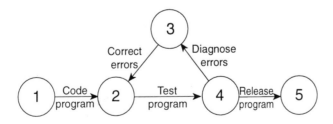

Figure 6.6 *A loop.*

A network may not contain dangles. A dangling activity such as *Write user manual* in Figure 6.7 cannot exist as it would suggest there are two completion points for the project. If, in Figure 6.7 node 5 represents the true project completion point and there are no activities dependent on activity *Write user* *manual*, then the network should be redrawn so that activity *Write user manual* starts at node *2* and terminates at node *5*. In other words, all events, except the first and the last, must have at least one activity entering them and at least one activity leaving them and all activities must start and end with an event.

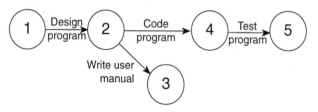

Figure 6.7 *A dangle.*

Precedents are the immediate preceding activities. In Figure 6.5 activity *Program test* cannot start until both *Code* and *Data take-on* have been completed and activity *Install* cannot start until *Program test* has finished. *Code* and *Data take-on* can therefore be said to be precedents of *Program test*, and *Program test* is a precedent of *Install*. Note that we do not speak of *Code* and *Data take-on* as precedents of *Install* – that relationship is implicit in the previous statement.

Exercise 6.1

Take a look at the networks in Figure 6.8. State what is wrong with each of them and where possible redraw them correctly.

Using dummy activities

When two paths within a network have a common event although they are, in other respects independent, a logical error such as that illustrated in Figure 6.9 may occur.

Suppose that, in a particular project, it is necessary to specify a certain piece of hardware before placing an order for it and before coding the software. Before coding the software it is also necessary to specify the appropriate data structures, although clearly we do not need to wait for this to be done before the hardware may be ordered.

Figure 6.9 is an attempt to model the situation described above, although it is incorrect in that it requires both hardware specification and data structure design to be completed before either an order may be placed or software coding may commence.

We can resolve this problem by separating the two (more or less) independent paths and introducing a dummy activity to link the completion of data structure design to the start of the activity placing an order. This effectively breaks the link between data structure design and placing the order and is shown in Figure 6.10.

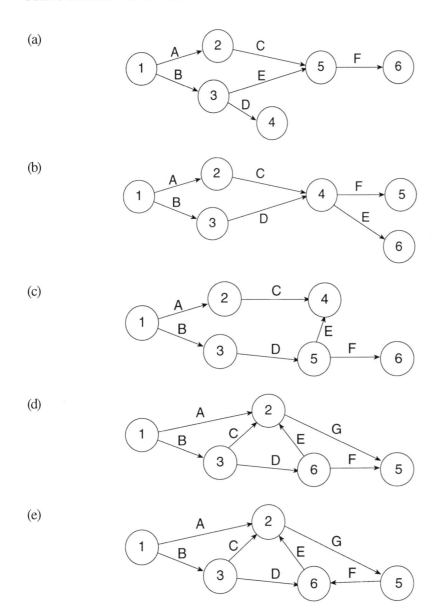

Figure 6.8 *Some activity networks.*

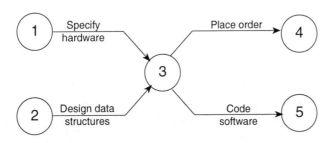

Figure 6.9 *Two paths with a common node.*

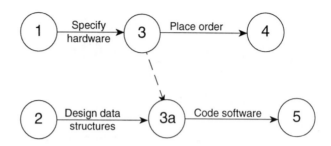

Figure 6.10 *Two paths linked by a dummy activity.*

Dummy activities, shown as dotted lines an the network diagram, have a zero duration and use no resources. They are often used to aid in the layout of network drawings as in Figure 6.11.

The use of a dummy activity where two activities share the same start and end nodes makes it easier to distinguish the activity end-points.

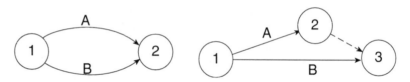

Figure 6.11 *Another use of a dummy activity.*

Exercise 6.2

Take another look at Brigette's HE College payroll activity network fragment shown in Figure 2.6. Redraw this as a CPM network.

Representing lagged activities

We may come across situations where we wish to undertake two activities in parallel so long as there is a lag between the two. We might wish to document amendments to a program as it was being tested – particularly if evaluating a prototype. In such a case we could designate an activity 'test and document amendments'. This would, however, make it impossible to show amendment recording starting after testing has begun and finishing a little after the completion of testing.

Where activities may occur in parallel with a time lag between them we represent these with pairs of dummy activities as shown in Figure 6.12. Where the activities are lagged because a stage in one activity must be completed before the other may proceed, it is likely to be better to show each stage as a separate activity.

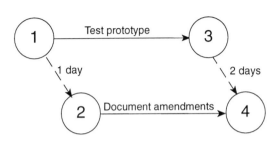

Figure 6.12 *Using the ladder technique to show lags.*

Where parallel activities have a time lag we may show this as a 'ladder' of activities. In this case documentation may proceed alongside prototype testing so long as it starts at least a day later. It will finish two days after the completion of prototype testing.

Adding the time dimension

Having created the logical network model indicating what needs to be done and the interrelationships between those activities, we are now ready to start thinking about when each activity should be undertaken.

The critical path method is concerned with two primary objectives: planning the project in such a way that it is completed as quickly as possible; and identifying those activities where a delay in their execution is likely to affect the overall end date of the project or later activities' start dates.

The method requires that for each activity we have an estimate of its duration. The network is then analysed by carrying out a **forward pass**, to calculate the earliest dates at which activities may commence and the project be completed, and a **backward pass**, to calculate the latest start dates for activities and the **critical path**.

In practice we would use a computer package to carry out these calculations for anything but the smallest of projects. It is important, though, that we understand how the calculations are carried out in order to interpret the results correctly and understand the limitations of the method.

The description and example that follow use the small example project outlined in Table 6.1 – a project composed of eight activities whose durations have been estimated as shown in the table.

CPM conventions

There are a number of differing conventions that have been adopted for entering information on a CPM network. Typically the diagram is used to record information about the events rather than the activities – activity-based information (other than labels or descriptions) is generally held on a separate activity table.

Standard event labelling conventions are adopted to show the earliest and latest dates at which an event may occur.

One of the more common conventions for labelling nodes, and the one adopted here, is to divide the node circle into quadrants and use those quadrants to show the event number, the latest and earliest dates by which the event should occur, and the event slack (which will be explained later).

Table 6.1 *A example project specification with estimated activity durations and precedence requirements*

Activity		Duration (weeks)	Precedents
A	Hardware selection	6	
B	Software design	4	
C	Install hardware	3	A
D	Code software	4	B
E	File take-on	3	B
F	Write user manuals	10	
G	User training	3	E, F
H	Install & test system	2	C, D

Exercise 6.3

Draw an activity network using CPM conventions for the project specified in Table 6.1.

When you have completed it, compare your result with that shown in Figure 6.13.

The forward pass

The forward pass is carried out to calculate the earliest date on which each event may be achieved and the earliest date on which each activity may be started and completed. The earliest date for an event is the earliest date by which all activities upon which it depends can be completed.

Figure 6.13 illustrates the network for the project specified in Table 6.1.

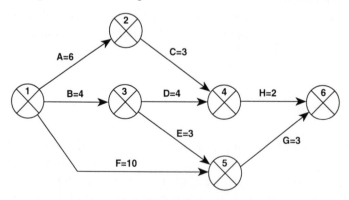

Figure 6.13 *The CPM network for the example project.*

By convention, dates indicate the end of the a period and the project is therefore shown as starting in week zero (or the beginning of week 1).

The forward pass and the calculation of earliest start dates is calculated according to the following reasoning.

During the forward pass, earliest dates are recorded as they are calculated. For events they are recorded on the network diagram and for activities they are recorded on the activity table.

- Activities A, B and F may start immediately so the earliest date for event 1 is zero and the earliest start date for these three activities also zero.
- Activity A will take 6 weeks, so the earliest it can finish is week 6 (recorded in the activity table). Therefore the earliest we can achieve event 2 is week 6.
- Activity B will take 4 weeks, so the earliest it can finish and the earliest we can achieve event 3 is week 4.
- Activity F will take 10 weeks, so the earliest it can finish is week 10 – we cannot, however, tell whether or not this is also the earliest date that we can achieve event 5 since we have not, as yet, calculated when activity E will finish.
- Activity E can start as early as week 4 (the earliest date for event 3) and, since it is forecasted to take 3 weeks will be completed, at the earliest, at the end of week 7.
- Event 5 may be achieved when both E and F have been completed, i.e. week 10 (the later of 7 and 10).
- Similarly we can reason that event 4 will have an earliest date of week 9 – the later of 8 (the earliest finish for activity D) and 9 (the earliest finish for activity C).
- The earliest date for the completion of the project, event 6, is therefore the end of week 13 – the later of 11 (the earliest finish for H) and 13 (the earliest finish for G).

The results of the forward pass are shown in Figure 6.14 and Table 6.2.

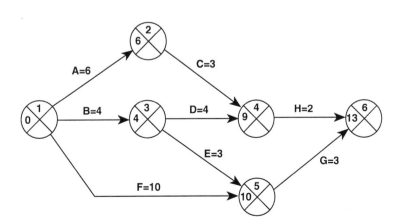

The forward pass rule: the earliest date for an event is the earliest finish date for all the activities terminating at that event. Where more than one activity terminates at a common event we take the latest of the earliest finish dates for those activities.

Figure 6.14 *A CPM network after the forward pass.*

Table 6.2 *The activity table after the forward pass*

Activity	Duration (weeks)	Earliest start date	Latest start date	Earliest finish fate	Latest finish date	Total float
A	6	0		6		
B	4	0		4		
C	3	6		9		
D	4	4		8		
E	3	4		7		
F	10	0		10		
G	3	10		13		
H	2	9		11		

The backward pass

The second stage is to carry out a backward pass to calculate the latest date at which each event may be achieved, and each activity started and finished, without delaying the end date of the project. The latest date for an event is the latest date by which all following activities must be started for the project to be completed on time. In calculating the latest dates we assume that the latest finish date for the project is the same as the earliest finish date – i.e. we wish to complete the project as early as possible.

Figure 6.15 illustrates our network and Table 6.3 the activity table after carrying out the backward pass – as with the forward pass, event dates are recorded on the diagram and activity dates on the activity table.

The latest event dates are calculated as follows.

- The latest date for node 6 is assumed to be week 13, the same as the earliest date.
- The latest date for event 5 is week 10, since activity G will take 3 weeks and must be completed by week 13 if the project end date is not to be exceeded.
- The latest date for event 4 is week 11 since activity H does not need to be started until week 11 if it takes 2 weeks and does not need to be completed until week 13.
- The latest date for event 3 is the latest date by which we must be in a position to start both activities D and E. Activity E need not finish until week 10 and need not therefore start until week 7. Activity D need not finish until week 11 and, having a duration of 4 weeks, need not start until week 7. The latest date for event 3 is therefore week 7.
- The latest date for event 2 is week 8 since C, which takes 3 weeks, need not be finished until week 11.

• The latest date for event 1 is the latest by which we must be in a position to start activity A (which must start by week 2), activity B (which must start by week 3) and activity F (which must start by week 0). This event's latest date is therefore zero. This is, of course, not very surprising since it tells us that if the project does not start on time it won't finish on time.

The earliest and latest dates for the start event must always be the same unless an arithmetic error has occurred.

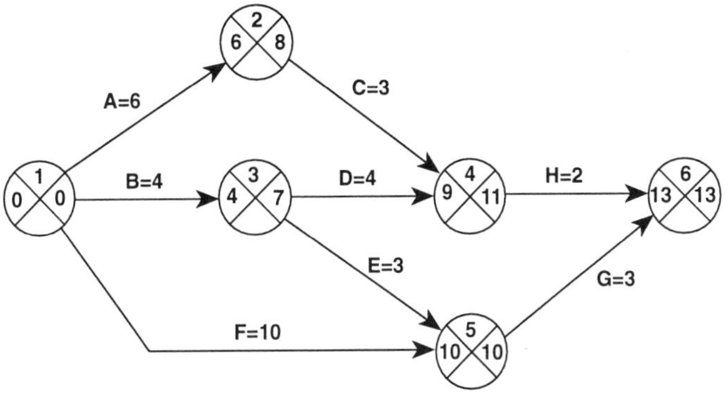

Figure 6.15 *The CPM network after the backward pass.*

The backward pass rule: the latest date for an event is the latest start date for all the activities that may commence from that event. Where more than one activity commences at a common event we take the earliest of the latest start dates for those activities.

Table 6.3 *The activity table following the backward pass*

Activity	Duration (weeks)	Earliest start date	Latest start date	Earliest finish fate	Latest finish date	Total float
A	6	0	2	6	8	
B	4	0	3	4	7	
C	3	6	8	9	11	
D	4	4	7	8	11	
E	3	4	7	7	10	
F	10	0	0	10	10	
G	3	10	10	13	13	
H	2	9	11	11	13	

Identifying the critical path

The difference between the earliest date and the latest date for an event is known as the **slack** – it is a measure of how late an event may be without affecting the end date of the project. Any event with a slack of zero is critical in the sense that any delay in achieving that event will delay the completion date of the project as a whole. There will always be at least one path through the network joining those critical events – this path is known as the **critical path** (Figure 6.16).

The significance of the critical path is two-fold.

Any delay on the critical path will delay the project.

- In managing the project we must pay particular attention to monitoring activities on the critical path so that the effects of any delay or resource unavailability are detected and corrected at the earliest opportunity.
- In planning the project it is the critical path that we must shorten if we are to reduce the overall duration of the project.

The critical path is the longest path through the network.

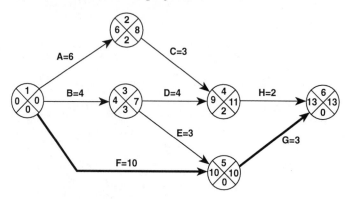

Figure 6.16 *The critical path.*

Activity float

Whereas events have **slack**, activities posses **float**. The total float shown in Table 6.4 is the difference between the earliest start date of an activity and its latest start (or the difference between its earliest finish and its latest finish). It tells us by how long the activity's start or completion may be delayed without affecting the end date of the project.

Table 6.4 *The activity schedule showing total float for each activity*

Activity	Duration (weeks)	Earliest start date	Latest start date	Earliest finish fate	Latest finish date	Total float
A	6	0	2	6	8	2
B	4	0	3	4	7	3
C	3	6	8	9	11	2
D	4	4	7	8	11	3
E	3	4	7	7	10	3
F	10	0	0	10	10	0
G	3	10	10	13	13	0
H	2	9	11	11	13	2

Total float may only be used once.

Although the total float is shown for each activity, it really 'belongs' to a path through the network. Activities A and C each have 2 weeks total float. If, however, activity A uses up its float (i.e. it is not completed until week 8) then activity B will have zero float (it will have become critical). In such circumstances it may be misleading and detrimental to the project's success to publicize total float!

There are a number of other measures of activity float, including the following.

- **Free float** – the time by which an activity may be delayed without affecting any subsequent activity. This might be considered a more satisfactory measure of float for publicizing to the staff involved in undertaking the activities.
- **Interfering float** – the difference between total float and free float. This is quite commonly used, particularly in association with the free float. Once the free float has been used (or if it is zero), the interfering float tells us by how much the activity may be delayed without delaying the project end date – even though it will delay the start of subsequent activities.

Calculate the free float and interfering float for each of the activities shown in the activity network (Table 6.4). **Exercise 6.4**

Shortening project durations

If we wish to shorten the overall duration of a project we would normally consider attempting to reduce activity durations. In many cases this may be done by applying more resources to the task – working overtime or procuring additional staff, for example. The critical path indicates where we must look to save time – if we are trying to bring forward the end date of the project there is clearly no point in attempting to shorten non-critical activities. Referring to Figure 6.16 it can be seen that we could complete the project in week 12 by reducing the duration of activity F by one week (to 9 weeks).

Referring to Figure 6.16, suppose that the duration for activity F is shortened to 8 weeks. Calculate the end date for the project. **Exercise 6.5**

What would the end date for the project be if activity F were shortened to 7 weeks? Why?

As we reduce activity times along the critical path we must continually check for any new critical path emerging and redirect our attention where necessary.

There will come a point when we can no longer safely, or cost-effectively, reduce critical activity durations in an attempt to bring forward the project end date. Further savings, if needed, must be sought in a consideration of our work methods and by questioning the logical sequencing of activities. Generally, time savings are to be found by increasing the amount of parallelism in the network and the removal of bottlenecks (subject always, of course, to resource and quality constraints).

Identifying critical activities

For a more in-depth discussion of the role of the critical path in project monitoring see Chapter 9.

The critical path identifies those activities which are critical to the end date of the project; however, activities that are not on the critical path may become critical. As the project proceeds, activities will invariably use up some of their float and this will require a periodic recalculation of the network. As soon as the activities along a particular path use up their total float then that path will become the critical path and a number of hitherto non-critical activities will suddenly become critical.

It is therefore common practice to identify 'near-critical' paths – those whose lengths are within, say, 10–20% of the duration of the critical path or those with a total float of less than, say, 10% of the project's uncompleted duration.

The importance of identifying critical and near-critical activities is that it is they that are most likely to be the cause of delays in completing the project. We shall see, in the next three chapters, that identifying these activities is an important step in risk analysis, resource allocation and project monitoring.

Precedence networks

Where CPM networks use links to represent activities and nodes to represent events, precedence networks use boxes (nodes) to represent activities (sometimes known as work items) and links to represent dependencies. The boxes may carry task descriptions and duration estimates and the links may contain a duration denoting a lag between the completion of one task and the start of the next.

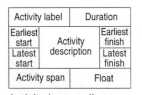

Activity boxes allow substantial detail to be recorded on a precedence network.

In the notation we use here, the items indicated in the boxes are the same as those shown on the CPM network and activity table with the addition of **activity span**. Activity span is the difference between the earliest start date and the latest finish date and is a measure of the maximum time allowable for the activity.

Proponents of precedence networks claim that they are easier to draw neatly, dummy activities are virtually redundant and that it is easier for people to interpret them. Figure 6.17 shows the example project in Figure 6.16 drawn as a precedence network. As you can see, it contains much more information that the CPM network and we do not need to keep a separate activity table. The critical path through activities F and G is shown as a heavy line.

A further advantage of precedence networks is that they can represent parallel lagged activities. The example shown in Figure 6.12 which required the use of dummy activities in a CPM network may be represented much more elegantly in a precedence network as shown in Figure 6.18.

Analysis of precedence networks proceeds in exactly the same ways as discussed above – we carry out a forward and backward pass to calculate earliest and latest start and finish dates and identify the critical path.

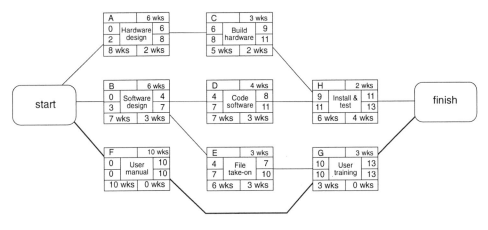

Figure 6.17 *A precedence network.*

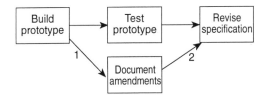

Documenting amendments may take place alongside prototype testing so long as it starts at least one day later and finishes two days later.

Figure 6.18 *Parallel lagged activities in a precedence network.*

Exercise 6.6

Refer back to Amanda's CPM network illustrated in Figure 6.4 and redraw it as a precedence network.

Using the activity durations given in Table 6.5, calculate the earliest completion date for the project and identify the critical path on your network.

Table 6.5 *Estimated activity durations for Amanda's network*

Activity	Estimated duration (days)	Activity	Estimated duration (days)
Specify overall	34	Design module C	4
Specify module A	20	Design module D	4
Specify module B	15	Code/test module A	30
Specify module C	25	Code/test module B	28
Specify module D	15	Code/test module C	15
Check specification	2	Code/test module D	25
Design module A	7	System integration	6
Design module B	6		

Conclusion

In this chapter we have discussed the use of the critical path method and precedence networks to obtain an ideal activity plan. This plan tells us in which order we should execute activities and the earliest and latest we can start and finish them.

These techniques help us to identify which activities are critical to meeting a target completion date.

In order to manage the project we need to turn the activity plan into a schedule which will specify precisely when each activity is scheduled to start and finish. Before we can do this we must consider what resources will be required and whether or not they will be available at appropriate times. As we shall see, the allocation of resources to an activity may be affected by how we view the importance of the task and the risks associated with it. In the next two chapters we look at these aspects of project planning before we consider how we might publish a schedule for the project.

Further exercises

1. Draw an activity network using either CPM or precedence network conventions for each of the following projects:
   - getting married
   - choosing and purchasing a desktop computer
   - organizing and carrying out a survey of users' opinions of an information system.

2. If you have access to a project planning package, use it to produce a project plan for the IOE maintenance group accounts project. Base your plan on that used for Exercise 6.6 and verify that your package reports the same information as you calculated manually when you did the exercise.

3. Based on your answer to Exercise 6.6 discuss what options Amanda might consider if she found it necessary to complete the project earlier than day 104?

Chapter 7

Risk management

OBJECTIVES

After completing this chapter you will be able to:

☐ identify the factors putting a project at risk

☐ categorize and prioritize action for risk elimination or containment

☐ quantify the likely effects of risk on project time-scales.

Introduction

In Chapter 3 we considered project evaluation including assessment of the risk of the project not delivering the expected benefits. In this chapter we are concerned with the risk of the development project not proceeding according to plan. We are primarily concerned with the risks of the project running late or over budget and with the identification of the steps that may be taken to avoid or minimize those risks.

Some risks are more important than others. Whether or not a particular risk is important depends on the nature of the risk, its likely effects on a particular activity and the criticality of the activity. High risk activities on a project's critical path are a cause for concern.

To reduce these dangers we must ensure that risks are minimized or, at least, distributed over the project and, ideally, removed from critical path activities.

The risk of an activity running over time is likely to depend, at least in part, on who is doing or managing it. The evaluation of risk and the allocation of staff and other resources are therefore closely connected.

The allocation of resources is discussed in the next chapter.

The nature of risk

For the purpose of identifying and managing those risks that may cause a project to overrun its time-scale or budget, it is convenient to identify three types of risk:

• those caused by the inherent difficulties of estimation

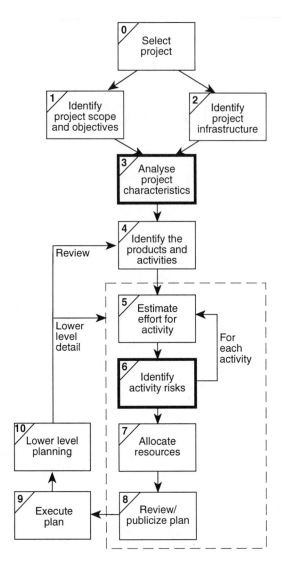

Figure 7.1 *Risk analysis is carried out in Steps 3 and 6.*

- those due to assumptions made during the planning process
- those of unforeseen (or at least unplanned for) events occurring.

Estimation errors

Improved quality control should make it easier to predict the time required for program and system testing.

Some tasks are harder to estimate than others because of the lack of experience of similar tasks or because of the nature of a task. Producing a set of user manuals is reasonably straightforward and, given that we have carried out similar tasks previously, we should be able to estimate how long it will take and how much it will cost with some degree of accuracy. On the other hand, the time required for program testing and debugging, may be difficult to predict with a similar degree of accuracy – even if we have written similar programs in the past.

Estimation may be improved by analysing historic data for similar activities and similar systems. Keeping records comparing our original estimates with the final outcome will reveal the type of tasks that are difficult to estimate correctly.

See Chapter 5 for methods of estimation.

Planning assumptions

At every stage during planning, assumptions are made which, if not valid, may put the plan at risk. Our activity network, for example, is likely to be built on the assumption of using a particular design methodology – which may be subsequently changed. We generally assume that, following coding, a module will be tested and then integrated with others – we may not plan for module testing showing up the need for changes in the original design.

At each stage in the planning process it is important to list explicitly all of the assumptions that have been made and identify what effects they may have on the plan if they are inappropriate.

Eventualities

Some eventualities may never be foreseen and we can only resign ourselves to the fact that unimaginable things do, sometimes, happen. They are, however, very rare. The majority of unexpected events can, in fact, be identified – the requirements specification might be altered after some of the modules have been coded, the senior programmer might take maternity leave, the required hardware might not be delivered on time. Identifying these possible eventualities is one of the first steps in any risk assessment and risk management exercise.

Managing risk

The objective of risk management is to avoid or minimize the adverse effects of unforeseen events by avoiding the risks or drawing up contingency plans for dealing with them. Before we can do so, however, we need to identify the risks and prioritize them. Risk management consists of the following five activities.

- **Hazard identification** – This consists of listing all of the hazards that may adversely affect the successful execution of the project.
- **Risk analysis** – This consists of assessing the likelihood and impact of each hazard.
- **Risk prioritization** – avoiding or minimizing risks takes an effort and may incur costs. It is therefore necessary to prioritize the risks in some way before drawing up plans for their avoidance or containment.
- **Risk reduction** – this involves removing the risk or drawing up plans for reducing its effects.

Risk monitoring is
discussed in Chapter 9.

- **Risk monitoring** – the importance and likelihood of particular risks may change as the project proceeds. Risks must therefore be monitored throughout the life of the project.

Hazard identification

The first stage in any risk assessment exercise is to identify the hazards that might affect the duration or resource costs of the project. It is common to use a questionnaire listing the possible hazards and factors that influence them. Typical questionnaires may list many, even hundreds, of factors and there are, today, a number of expert system-based computer packages available which assist in this analysis.

The categories of factors that need to be considered include the following.

Some of these issues
have been addressed in
Chapter 4.

Application factors. The nature of the application – whether it is a simple data processing package, a safety-critical system or a large distributed system with real-time elements – is likely to be a critical factor. The expected size of the application is also important – the larger the system, the greater is the likelihood of errors and communication and management problems.

Avoiding some of the risks
associated with staff
factors is discussed in
Chapter 10.

Staff factors. The experience and skills of the staff involved are clearly major factors – an experienced programmer is, one would hope, less likely to make errors than one with little experience. We must, however, also consider the appropriateness of the experience – experience in coding small data processing modules in Cobol may be of little value if we are developing a complex real-time control system using C++.

Such factors as the level of staff satisfaction and the staff turn-over rates are also important to the success of any project – demotivated staff or key personnel leaving unexpectedly has caused many a project to fail.

Project methods. Using well specified and structured methods (such as PRINCE and SSADM) for project management and system development may decrease the risk of delivering an unsatisfactory system late. Using such methods for the first time, though, may cause problems and delays – it is only with experience that the benefits accrue.

Hardware/software factors. A project that requires new hardware for development is likely to pose a higher risk than one where the software can be developed on existing (and familiar) hardware. Where a system is developed on one type of hardware or software platform to be used on another there may be additional (and high) risks at installation.

Changeover factors. The need for an 'all-in-one' changeover to the new system may pose particular risks. Incremental or gradual changeover may minimize the risks involved but may not be practical for some applications. Parallel running may provide a safety net but may be impossible or too costly.

Supplier factors. The extent to which a project relies on external organizations which cannot be directly controlled may well influence the project's success. Delays in, for example, the installation of telephone lines or delivery of equipment may be difficult to avoid – particularly if the project is of little consequence to the external supplier.

Environment factors. Changes in the environment may also affect a project's success. A significant change in the taxation regulations could, for example, have serious consequences for the development of a payroll package.

Brigette finds that Brightmouth HE College does not have a project hazard checklist or questionnaire and decides to produce her own for the payroll project. List at least one question that she might include under each of the above headings.

Exercise 7.1

Although some factors may influence the project as a whole it is necessary to consider them individually for each activity – a key member of staff being ill during fact-finding may, for example, be far less serious than a similar absence during user training. Within a PRINCE environment it may be appropriate to list the factors for each of the products identified in the product breakdown structure.

Risk analysis

Having identified the hazards that may affect our project we need some way of assessing their importance. Some risks may be relatively unimportant (e.g. the risk that some of the documentation is delivered a day late), whereas some may be of major significance (e.g. the risk that the software is delivered late). Some may be quite likely to occur (e.g. a programmer may take a few days sick leave), whereas others are relatively unlikely (e.g. hardware failure causing loss of completed code). The importance of a risk, known as the **risk value** or **risk exposure**, depends upon the **likelihood** of the hazard occurring and its potential effect or cost or **impact**.

Ideally the potential cost of a risk would be estimated in monetary terms and the likelihood assessed as a probability. We could then multiply the two together to obtain an expected cost which could be compared to the cost of taking avoidance action. Estimation of these costs and probabilities is likely to be difficult, time-consuming and costly.

Expected costs and benefits were used in cost–benefit analysis in Chapter 3.

In any case, it is important to obtain some quantitative measure of each of the two factors because, without this, it would be difficult to compare or rank risks in a meaningful way. Moreover, the effort put into obtaining a good quantitative estimate is likely to provide a deeper and valuable understanding of the problem.

A simple scoring method provides quantitative measure for assessing each risk. Likelihood and impact are each scored on, say, a scale of 1 to 10 and the risk value obtained by multiplying these two scores together.

Likelihood measures are assigned so that the hazard that is most likely to occur receives a score of 10 and the least likely a score of 1. Impact measures must take into account the total risk to the project. This must include the following potential costs:

- the cost of delays to scheduled dates for deliverables
- cost overruns caused by using additional or more expensive resources
- the costs incurred or implicit in any compromise to the system's quality or functionality.

Table 7.1 illustrates part of Amanda's risk value assessment. Notice that the hazard with the highest risk value may not be the one that is most likely nor the one with the greatest potential impact.

Table 7.1 *Part of Amanda's risk value assessment*

Hazard	Likelihood	Impact	Risk Value
Changes to requirements specification during coding	2	8	16
Specification takes longer than expected	3	7	21
Staff sickness affecting critical path activities	5	7	35
Staff sickness affecting non-critical activities	7	3	21
Module coding takes longer than expected	5	5	25
Module testing demonstrates errors or deficiencies in design	1	10	10

Prioritizing the risks

Risk values may be reduced by reducing the likelihood of the hazard or its impact. Any attempt to reduce a risk value will, however, have a cost associated with it and it is therefore important to ensure that this effort is applied in the most effective way. We therefore need a way of prioritizing the risks so that the more important ones can receive the greatest attention.

We could prioritize the risks solely according to their risk value but, in practice, there are other factors that must be taken into account.

- **Confidence of the risk assessment** – some of our risk value assessments may be relatively poor. Where this is the case there may be the need for further investigation before action may be planned.
- **Compound risks** – some risks may be dependant on others. Where this is the case they should be treated together as a single risk.
- **The number of risks** – there is a limit to the number of risks that may be effectively considered and acted on by a project manager. We may therefore wish to limit the size of the prioritized list.
- **Cost of action** – some risks, once recognized, may be reduced or avoided immediately with very little cost or effort and it may be sensible to take action on these regardless of their risk value. For other risks we need to compare the costs of taking action with the benefits of reducing the risk. One method for doing this is to calculate the risk reduction leverage (RRL) using the equation

The RRL may be used as a factor in prioritizing risks and for evaluating alternative courses of action in dealing with a particular risk.

$$RRL = \frac{RV_{before} - RV_{after}}{\text{risk reduction cost}}$$

where RV_{before} is the original risk value and RV_{after} is the expected risk value after taking action. Risk reduction costs must be expressed in the same units as risk values – that is, expected monetary values or score values.

Reducing the risks

There are four strategies for risk reduction.

- **Hazard prevention** – some hazards may be prevented from occurring or their likelihood reduced to insignificant levels. The risk of key staff being unavailable for meetings may be minimized by early scheduling.
- **Likelihood reduction** – some risks, while they cannot be prevented, may have their likelihoods reduced by prior planning. The risk of late changes to a requirements specification may, for example, be reduced by prototyping. Prototyping will not eliminate the risk of late changes and would need to be supplemented by contingency planning.
- **Risk avoidance** – a project may, for example, be protected from the risk of overrunning the schedule by increasing duration estimates or reducing functionality.
- **Risk transfer** – the impact of some risks may be transferred away from the project by, for example, contracting out or taking out insurance.
- **Contingency planning** – some risks may not be preventable and contingency plans will need to be drawn up to reduce the impact should the hazard occur. A project manager may well draw up contingency plans for using agency programmers to minimize the impact of any unplanned absence of programming staff.

Some risks are specific to a project, whereas others generic in that they are likely to affect all software projects to a greater or lesser degree. There are a number of checklists listing common generic risks and typical actions for risk reduction – that in Table 7.2 is based upon a list produce by Barry Boehm.

Table 7.2 *Software projects risks and strategies for risk reduction.*

This top ten list of software risks is based on one presented by Barry Boehm in his *Tutorial on Software Risk Management*, IEEE Computer Society, 1989.

Risk	Risk reduction techniques
Personnel shortfalls	staffing with top talent; job matching; team building; training and career development; early scheduling of key personnel
Unrealistic time and cost estimates	multiple estimation techniques; design to cost; incremental development; recording and analysis of past projects; standardization of methods
Developing the wrong software functions	improved project evaluation; formal specification methods; user surveys; prototyping; early users' manuals
Developing the wrong user interface	prototyping; task analysis; user involvement
Gold plating	requirements scrubbing; prototyping; cost–benefit analysis; design to cost
Late changes to requirements	stringent change control procedures; high change threshold; incremental prototyping; incremental development (defer changes)
Shortfalls in external supplied components	benchmarking; inspections; formal specifications; contractual agreements; quality assurance procedures and certification
Shortfalls in externally performed tasks	quality assurance procedures; competitive design or prototyping; teambuilding; contract incentives
Real-time performance shortfalls	simulation; benchmarking; prototyping; tuning; technical analysis
Development technically too difficult	technical analysis; cost–benefit analysis; prototyping; staff training and development.

Exercise 7.2

For each of the risks listed in Table 7.1 identify actions that Amanda might take to reduce their likelihood or impact.

Evaluating risks to the schedule

We have seen that not all risks can be eliminated – even those that may be classified as avoidable or manageable may, in the event, still cause problems affecting activity durations. By identifying and categorizing those risks, and in particular, their likely effects on the duration of planned activities, we can assess what impact they are likely to have on our activity plan.

We will now take a look at two methods for assessing the effects of these uncertainties on the project schedule.

Using PERT to evaluate the effects of uncertainty

PERT was developed to take account of the uncertainty surrounding estimates of task durations. It was developed in an environment of expensive, high-risk and state-of-the-art projects – not that dissimilar to many of today's large software projects.

The method is very similar to the CPM technique (indeed many practitioners use the terms PERT and CPM interchangeably) but, instead of using a single estimate for the duration of each task, PERT requires three estimates.

PERT (program evaluation and review technique) was published in the same year as CPM. Developed for the Fleet Ballistic Missiles Program it is said to have saved considerable time in development of the Polaris missile.

- **Most likely time** – the time we would expect the task to take under normal circumstances. We shall denote this by the letter m.
- **Optimistic time** – the shortest time in which we could expect to complete the activity barring outright miracles. We shall use the letter a to denote this.
- **Pessimistic time** – the worst possible time allowing for all reasonable eventualities but excluding 'acts of God and warfare' (as they say in most insurance exclusion clauses). We shall denote this by b.

PERT then combines these three estimates to form a single expected duration, t_e, using the formula

$$t_e = \frac{a + 4m + b}{6}$$

Table 7.3 provides additional activity duration estimates for the network shown in Figure 6.14. There are new estimates for a and b and the original activity duration estimates have been used as the most likely times, m. Calculate the expected duration, t_e, for each activity.

Exercise 7.3

Using expected durations

The expected durations are used to carry out a forward pass through a network in using the same method as the CPM technique. In this case, however, the calculated event dates are not the earliest possible dates but are the dates by which we expect to achieve those events.

Table 7.3 *PERT activity time estimates*

	Activity durations (weeks)		
Activity	*Optimistic (a)*	*Most likely (m)*	*Pessimistic (b)*
A	5	6	8
B	3	4	5
C	2	3	3
D	3·5	4	5
E	1	3	4
F	8	10	15
G	2	3	4
H	2	2	2·5

Exercise 7.4

Before reading further, use your calculated expected activity durations to carry out a forward pass through the network (Figure 6.14) and verify that the project duration is 13·5 weeks.

What does an expected duration of 13·5 weeks mean in terms of the completion date for the project?

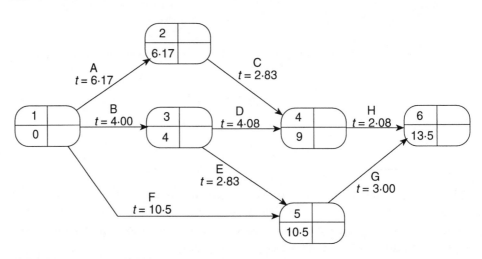

Event number	Target date
Expected date	Standard deviation

The PERT event labelling convention adopted here indicates event number and its target date along with the calculated values for expected time and standard deviation.

Figure 7.2 *The PERT network after the forward pass.*

The PERT network illustrated in Figure 7.2 indicates that we expect the project to take 13·5 weeks – unlike CPM this does not indicate the earliest date by which we could complete the project but the expected (or most likely) date. An advantage of this approach is that it places an emphasis on the uncertainty of the real world. Rather than being tempted to say 'the completion date for the project is …' we are lead to say 'we expect to complete the project by …'.

It also focuses attention on the uncertainty of the estimation of activity durations. Requesting three estimates for each activity emphasizes the fact that we are not certain what will happen – we are forced to take into account the fact that estimates are approximate.

Activity standard deviations

A quantitative measure of the degree of uncertainty of an activity duration estimate may be obtained by calculating the standard deviation s of an activity time using the formula

$$s = \frac{b - a}{6}$$

The activity standard deviation is proportional to the difference between the optimistic and pessimistic estimates and may be used as a ranking measure of the degree of uncertainty or risk for each activity. The activity expected durations and standard deviations for our sample project are shown in Table 7.4.

This standard deviation formula is based on the rationale that there are approximately six standard deviations between the extreme tails of many statistical distributions.

Table 7.4 *Expected times and standard deviations*

| Activity | Activity durations (weeks) | | | | |
	Optimistic (a)	Most likely (m)	Pessimistic (b)	Expected (t_e)	Standard deviation (s)
A	5	6	8	6·17	0·50
B	3	4	5	4·00	0·33
C	2	3	3	2·83	0·17
D	3·5	4	5	4·08	0·25
E	1	3	4	2·83	0·50
F	8	10	15	10·50	1·17
G	2	3	4	3·00	0·33
H	2	2	2·5	2·08	0·08

The likelihood of meeting targets

The main advantage of the PERT technique is that it provides a method for estimating the probability of meeting or missing target dates. There may only be a single target date – the project completion – but we may wish to set additional intermediate targets.

Suppose that we must complete the project within 15 weeks at the outside. We expect it will take 13·5 weeks but it could take more or, perhaps, less. In addition, suppose that activity C must be completed by week 10 as it is to be carried out by a member of staff who is scheduled to be working on another project and that event 5 represents the delivery of intermediate products to the customer. These three target dates are shown on the PERT network in Figure 7.3.

The PERT technique uses the following three-step method for calculating the probability of meeting or missing a target date

- calculate the standard deviation of each project event
- calculate the z value for each event that has a target date
- convert z values to a probabilities.

Calculating the standard deviation of each project event

The square of the standard deviation is known as the variance. Standard deviations may not be added together but variances may.

Standard deviations for the project events may be calculated by carrying out a forward pass using the activity standard deviations in a manner similar to that used with expected durations. There is, however, one small difference – to add two standard deviations we must add their squares and then find the square root of the sum. Exercise 7.5 illustrates the technique.

Exercise 7.5

The standard deviation for event 3 depends solely on that of activity B. The standard deviation for event 3 is therefore 0·33.

For event 5 there are two possible paths, B + E or F. The total standard deviation for path B + E is $\sqrt{(0.33^2 + 0.50^2)} = 0.6$ and that for path F is 1·17; the standard deviation for event 5 is therefore the greater of the two, 1·17.

Verify that the standard deviations for each of the other events in the project are as shown in Figure 7.3.

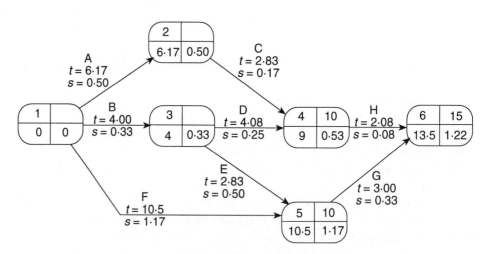

Figure 7.3 *The PERT network with three target dates and calculated event standard deviations.*

Calculating the z values

The z value is calculated for each node that has a target date. It is equivalent to the number of standard deviations between its expected and target dates. It is calculated using the formula

$$z = \frac{T - t_e}{s}$$

where t_e is the expected date and T the target date.

The z value for event 4 is $(10 - 9{\cdot}00)/0{\cdot}53 = 1{\cdot}8867$.

    Calculate the z values for the other events with target dates in the network shown in Figure 7.3.

Exercise 7.6

Converting z values to probabilities

A z value may be converted to the probability of not meeting the target date by using the graph in Figure 7.4.

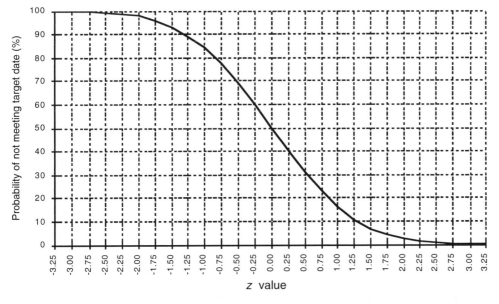

This graph is the equivalent of tables of z values, also known as standard normal deviates, which may be found in most statistics text books.

Figure 7.4 *The probability of obtaining a value within z standard deviations of the mean for a normal distribution.*

Exercise 7.7

The z value for the project completion (event 6) is 1·23. Using Figure 7.4 we can see that this equates to a probability of approximately 11%, i.e. there is an 11% risk of not meeting the target date of the end of week 15.

Find the probabilities of not achieving events 4 or 5 by their target dates of the end of week 10.

What is the likelihood of completing the project by week 14?

The advantages of PERT

We have seen that by requesting multivalued activity duration estimates and calculating expected dates PERT focuses attention on the uncertainty of forecasting. We can use the technique to calculate the standard deviation for each task and use this to rank them according to their degree of risk. Using this ranking, we can see, for example, that activity F is the one over which we have greatest uncertainty, whereas activity C should, in principle, give us relatively little cause for concern.

If we use the expected times and standard deviations for forward passes through the network we can, for any event or activity completion, estimate the probability of meeting any set target. In particular, by setting target dates along the critical path, we can focus on those activities posing the greatest risk to the project's schedule.

Monte Carlo simulation

As an alternative to the PERT technique, and to provide a greater degree of flexibility in specifying likely activity durations, we can use Monte Carlo simulation techniques to evaluate the risks of not achieving deadlines. The basis of this technique is the calculation of event times for a project network a large number of times, each time selecting activity times randomly from a set of alternatives. The results are then be tabulated, summarized or displayed as a graph such as that shown in Figure 7.5.

Activity duration estimates may be specified in a variety of forms depending upon the information available. If for example, we have historic data available about the durations of similar activities, we may be able to specify durations as a probability distribution. With less information available we may, at least, be able to provide three time estimates as used by PERT.

The calculation required is extensive and is not practical without the aid of a computer. Fortunately, there are a number of packages available for carrying out Monte Carlo simulation. Some will exchange data with project scheduling packages and some interface to standard spreadsheet software. The majority of these packages will apply Monte Carlo risk analysis to cost and resource as well as duration estimates.

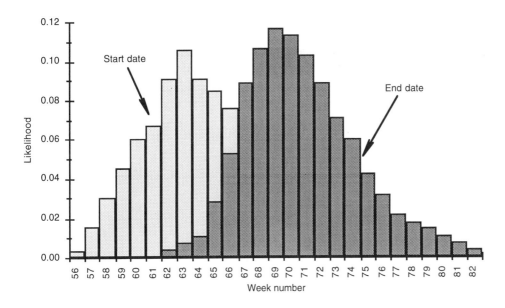

Figure 7.5 *Risk profile for an activity generated using Monte Carlo simulation.*

Conclusions

In this chapter we have seen how to identify and manage the risks that might affect the success of a project. Risk management is concerned with assessing and prioritizing risks and drawing up plans for addressing those risks before they become problems.

This chapter has also described techniques for estimating the effect of risk on the project's activity network and schedule.

Many of the risks affecting software projects may be reduced by allocating more experienced staff to those activities that may be affected. In the next chapter we consider the allocation of staff to activities in more detail.

Further exercises

1. Identify five risks than may affect the success of the Brightmouth College payroll project and suggest strategies that Brigette might consider for dealing with each of them.

2. The list of risks and risk reduction strategies in Table 7.2 is concerned with generic risks for software projects. What additional risks can you identify that would be specific to Amanda's IOE accounts project?

3. List the major risks that might affect your next programming assignment and identify strategies for minimizing each of those risks.

4. If you have access to a project planning computer package find out whether or not it supports the PERT methods described in this chapter.

Chapter 8

Resource allocation

OBJECTIVES

After completing this chapter you will be able to:

☐ identify the resources required for a project

☐ make the demand for resources more even throughout the life of a project

☐ produce a work plan and resource schedule.

Introduction

In Chapter 6 we saw how to use activity network analysis techniques to plan when activities should take place. The *when* was calculated as a time-span during which an activity should take place – bounded by the earliest start and latest finish dates. In Chapter 7 we used the PERT technique to forecast a range of expected dates by which activities would be completed. In both cases these plans took no account the availability of resources.

In this chapter we shall see how to match the activity plan to available resources and, where necessary, assess the efficacy of changing the plan to fit the resources. Figure 8.1 shows where resource allocation is applied in Step Wise.

In general, the allocation of resources to activities will lead us to review and modify the ideal activity plan. It may cause us to revise stage or project completion dates. In any event, it is likely to lead to a narrowing of the time-spans within which activities may be scheduled.

The final result of resource allocation will normally be a number of schedules including:

- **activity schedule** – indicating the planned start and completion dates for each activity
- **resource schedule** – showing the dates on which each resource will be required and the level of that requirement
- **cost schedule** – showing the planned cumulative expenditure incurred by the use of resources over time.

These schedules will provide the basis for the day-to-day control and management of the project which are described in Chapter 9.

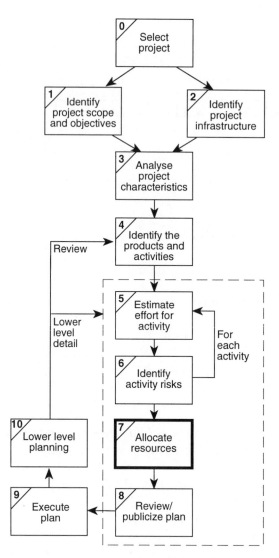

Figure 8.1 *Resource allocation is carried out as Step 7.*

The nature of resources

A resource is any item or person required for the execution of the project. This covers many things – from paper clips to key personnel – and it is unlikely we would wish to itemize every resource required, let alone draw up a schedule for their use! Stationery and other standard office supplies, for example, need not normally be the concern of the project manager – ensuring there is always an adequate supply is the role of the office manager. The project manager must concentrate on those resources where there is a possibility that, without planning, they may not be sufficiently available when required.

Some resources, such as a project manager, will be required for the duration of the project whereas others, such as a specific programmer, may be required for a single activity. The former, while vital to the success of the project, may not require the same level of scheduling as the latter. Individual programmers, for example, may be committed to working on a number of projects and it may be important to book their time well in advance.

In general, resources will fall into one of seven categories.

- **Labour** – the main items in this category will be members of the development project team such as the project manager, systems analysts and programmers. Equally important will be the quality assurance team and other support staff and any employees of the client organization who might be required to undertake or participate in specific activities.
- **Equipment** – obvious items will include workstations and other computing and office equipment. We must not forget that staff also need basic equipment such as desks and chairs which may need to be obtained if we are recruiting or relocating staff.
- **Materials** – materials are items that are consumed rather than equipment which is used. They are of little consequence in most software projects but may be important for some – software which is to be widely distributed may, for example, require supplies of floppy disks to be specially obtained.
- **Space** – for projects that are undertaken with existing staff, space is normally readily available. If any additional staff (recruited or contracted) are needed then office space will need to be found.
- **Services** – some projects may require procurement of specialist services – development of a wide area distributed system, for example, may require scheduling of telecommunications services.
- **Time** – time is the resource that is being offset against the other primary resources – project time-scales may be reduced by increasing other resources and will almost certainly be extended if they are unexpectedly reduced.
- **Money** – money is a secondary resource – it may be used to buy other resources and will be consumed as other resources are used. It is similar to other resources in that it is available at a cost – in this case interest charges.

The cost of money as a resource is a factor taken into account in DCF evaluation.

Identifying resource requirements

The first step in producing a resource allocation plan is to list the resources that will be required along with the expected level of demand.

Amanda has produced a precedence network for the IOE project (Figure 8.2) and used this as a basis for a resource requirements list part of which is shown in Table 8.1. Notice that, at this stage, she has not allocated individuals to tasks but

Case study example

has decided on the type of staff that will be required. The activity durations assume that they will be carried out by 'standard' analysts or programmers.

At this stage, it is better that the resource requirements list should include something that may later be deleted as unnecessary than to omit something essential. Amanda has therefore included additional office space as a possible requirement, should contract programming staff be recruited.

Having produced the resource requirements list the next stage is to map this onto the activity plan to assess the distribution of resources required over the duration of the project. This is best done by representing the activity plan as a bar chart and using this to produce a resource histogram for each resource.

Figure 8.3 illustrates Amanda's activity plan as a bar chart and a resource histogram for analyst/designers. Each activity has been scheduled to start at its earliest start date – a sensible initial strategy since we would, other things being equal, wish to save any float to allow for contingencies. Earliest start date scheduling, as is the case with Amanda's project, frequently creates resource histograms that start with a peak and then tail off.

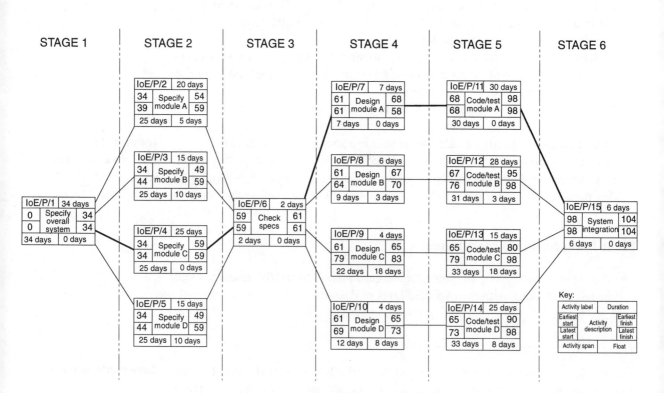

Figure 8.2 *The IOE precedence network.*

Stage	Activity	Resource	Days & level	Notes
ALL		Project manager	104 F/T	
1	All	Workstation	34	Check software availability
	IoE/P/1	Senior analysts	34 F/T	
2	All	Workstation	3	1 per person would be ideal
	IoE/P/2	Analyst/designer	20 F/T	
	IoE/P/3	Analyst/designer	15 F/T	
	IoE/P/4	Analyst/designer	25 F/T	
	IoE/P/5	Analyst/designer	15 F/T	Could use analyst/programmer
3	All	Workstation	2 F/T	
	IoE/P/6	Senior analyst	2 F/T	
4	All	Workstation	3	As stage 2
	IoE/P/7	Analyst/designer	7 F/T	
	IoE/P/8	Analyst/designer	6 F/T	
	IoE/P/9	Analyst/designer	4 F/T	
	IoE/P/10	Analyst/designer	4 F/T	
5	All	Workstation	4	1 per programmer
	All	Office space		If contract programmers used
	IoE/P/11	Programmer	30 F/T	
	IoE/P/12	Programmer	28 F/T	
	IoE/P/13	Programmer	15 F/T	
	IoE/P/14	Programmer	25 F/T	
6	All	Full m/c access		Approx. 16 h for full system test
	IoE/P/15	Analyst/designer	6 F/T	

Table 8.1 *Part of Amanda's resource requirements list.*

Changing the level of resources on a project over time, particularly personnel, generally adds to the cost of a project. Recruiting staff has costs and even where staff are transferred internally time will be needed for familiarization with the new project environment.

The resource histogram in Figure 8.3 poses particular problems in that it calls for two analyst designers to be idle for eleven days, one for six days and one for two days between the specification and design stage. It is unlikely that IOE would have another project requiring their skills for exactly those periods of time and this raises the question as to whether this idle time should be charged to Amanda's project.

White rectangles indicate when an activity is scheduled and shaded rectangles the total float.

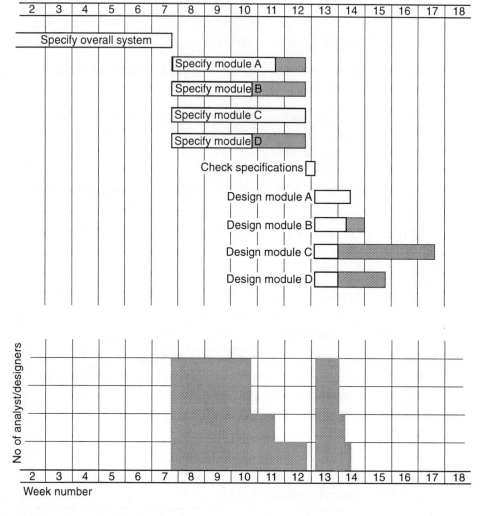

Figure 8.3 *Part of Amanda's bar chart and resource histogram for analyst/designers.*

The ideal resource histogram will be smooth with, perhaps an initial build-up and a staged run-down. An additional problem with an uneven resource histogram is that it is more likely to call for levels of resource beyond those available. Figure 8.4 illustrates a how, by adjusting the start date of some activities and splitting others, a resource histogram may, subject to constraints such as precedence requirements, be smoothed to contain resource demand at available levels. The different letters represent staff working on each task, i.e. one person working on A, two on B and C etc.

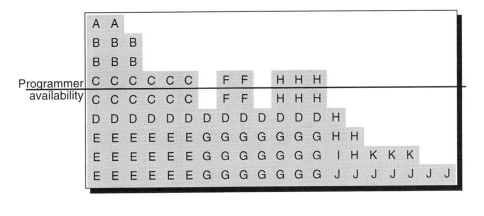

The majority of project planning software packages will produce resource histograms based on earliest activity start dates.

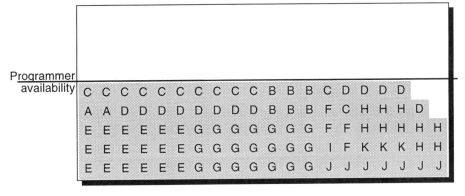

Some project planning packages will carry out resource smoothing automatically although they are unlikely to take into account all the factors that could be used by a project manager.

Figure 8.4 *A resource histogram showing demand for staff before and after smoothing.*

In Figure 8.4 the original histogram was created by scheduling a set of activities at their earliest start dates. The resource histogram shows the typical peaked shape caused by earliest start date scheduling and calls for a total of nine staff where only five are available for the project.

By delaying the start of some of the activities it has been possible to smooth the histogram and reduce the maximum level of demand for the resource. Notice that some activities, such as C and D, have been split. Where non-critical activities can be split they may provide a useful way of filling troughs in the demand for a resource but in software projects it is difficult to split tasks without increasing the time they take.

Some of the activities call for more than one unit of the resource at a time – activity F, for example, requires two programmers each working for two weeks. It might be possible to reschedule this activity to use one programmer over four weeks although that has not been considered in this case.

Exercise 8.1

Amanda has already decided to use only three analyst/designers on the project in order to reduce costs. Her current resource histogram, however, calls for four during both stage 2 and stage 4. Suggest what she might do to smooth the histogram and reduce the number of analyst/designers required to three.

It is helpful to prioritize activities so that resources may be allocated to competing activities in some rational order. The priority is always to allocate resources to critical path activities and then to those activities that are most likely to affect others. Of the various ways of prioritizing activities two are described below.

- **Total float priority** – activities are ordered according to their total float, those with the smallest total float having the highest priority. In the simplest application of this method activities are allocated resources in ascending order of total float. However, as scheduling proceeds, activities will be delayed (if resources are not available at their earliest start dates) and total floats will be reduced. It is therefore desirable to recalculate floats (and hence reorder the activities) each time an activity is delayed.
- **Ordered list priority** – with this method activities which may proceed at the same time are ordered according to a set of simple criteria. An example of this is Burman's priority list which takes into account activity duration as well as total float:

P J Burman, *Precedence Networks for Planning and Control*, McGraw-Hill, 1972.

1. shortest critical activity
2. critical activities
3. shortest non-critical activity
4. non-critical activity with least float
5. non-critical activities.

Unfortunately, resource smoothing, or even containment of resource demand to available levels is not always possible within planned time-scales – deferring activities to smooth out resource peaks may put back project completion. Where that is the case we may need to consider ways of increasing the available resource levels or altering working methods.

Exercise 8.2

Amanda finds that, with only three analyst/designers the specification of module D (see Figure 8.3) will have to be deferred until after the specification of module B and this will add five days to the overall project duration (making 109 in total). She had hoped to have the project completed within 100 days and this is a further disappointment. She therefore decides to have another look at her activity plan.

You will remember that early on she decided that she should check all of the specifications together (activity IoE/P/6) before allowing design to start. It is now apparent that this is causing a significant bottleneck and delaying module D will only exacerbate the problem. She therefore decides on a compromise – she will

check the specifications for modules A, B and D together but will then go ahead
with their design without waiting for the module C specification. This will be
checked against the others when it is complete.

She redraws her precedence network to reflect this inserting the new activity of
checking the module C specification against the others (activity IoE/P/6a). This is
shown in Figure 8.5. Draw a new resource histogram to reflect this change.

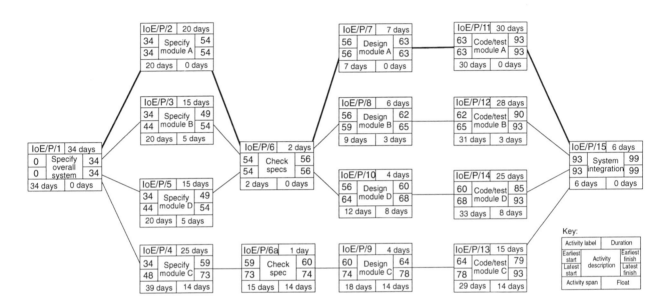

Figure 8.5 *Amanda's revised precedence network.*

Creating critical paths

Scheduling resources may create new critical paths. Delaying the start of an
activity because of lack of resources will cause that activity to become critical if
this uses up its float. Furthermore, a delay in completing one activity may delay
the availability of a resource required for a later activity. If the later one is already
critical then the earlier one may now have been made critical by linking their
resources.

Amanda's revised schedule, which still calls for four analysts designers but
only for a single day is illustrated in the solution to Exercise 8.2 (check it in the
back of the book if you have not done so already). Notice that in rescheduling
some of the activities she has introduced additional critical activities. Delaying
the specification of module C has used up all of its float – and that of the
subsequent activities along that path! Amanda now has two critical paths – the
one shown on the precedence network and the new one.

In a large project resource linking criticalities may be quite complex – a hint of the potential problems may be appreciated by looking at the next exercise.

<table>
<tr><td>Exercise 8.3</td><td>Amanda decides to delay the specification of module C for a further day to ensure that only three analyst/designers will be required. The relevant part of her revised bar chart and resource histogram are shown in Figure 8.6.

Which activities will now be critical?</td></tr>
</table>

Counting the cost

The discussion so far has concentrated on trying to complete the project by the earliest completion date with the minimum number of staff. We have seen that doing this places constraints on when activities may be carried out and increases the risk of not meeting target dates.

Alternatively, Amanda could have considered using additional staff or lengthening the overall duration of the project. The additional costs of employing extra staff would need to be compared to the costs of delayed delivery and the increased risk of not meeting the scheduled date. The relationship between these factors is discussed later in this chapter.

Being specific

Allocating resources and smoothing resource histograms is relatively straightforward where all resources of a given type can be considered more or less equivalent. When allocating labourers to activities in a large building project we need not distinguish between individuals – there are likely to be many labourers and they may be treated as equals so far as skills and productivity are concerned.

This is seldom the case with software projects. We saw in Chapter 5 that, because of the nature of software development, skill and experience play a significant part in determining the time taken and, potentially, the quality of the final product. With the exception of extremely large projects it makes sense to allocate individual members of staff to activities as early as possible, as this may lead us to revise our estimate of its duration.

In allocating individuals to tasks a number of factors need to be taken into account.

- **Availability** – we need to know whether a particular individual will be available when required. Reference to the departmental work plan may determine this but the wise project manager will always investigate the risks that might be involved – earlier projects might, for example, over-run and affect the availability of an individual.

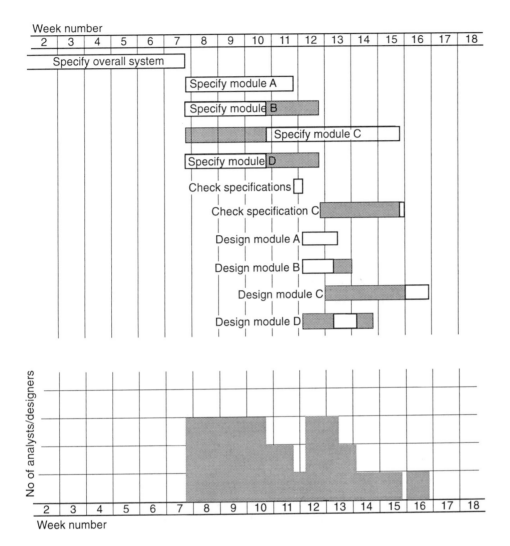

Figure 8.6 *Amanda's project scheduled to require three analyst/designers.*

- **Criticality** – allocation of more experienced personnel to activities on the critical path may help in shortening project durations or at least reduce the risk of overrun.
- **Risk** – we saw how to undertake activity risk assessment in the previous chapter. Identifying those activities posing the greatest risk, and knowing the factors influencing them, helps to allocate staff. Allocating the most experienced staff to the highest risk activities is likely to have the greatest effect in reducing overall project uncertainties. More experienced staff are, however, likely to be more expensive.
- **Training** – it will benefit the organization if positive steps are taken to allocate junior staff to appropriate non-critical activities where there will be sufficient

Reappraisal of the critical path and PERT or Monte Carlo risk analysis may need to be carried out in parallel with staff allocation.

slack for them to train and develop skills. There may even be direct benefits to the particular project since some costs may be allocated to the training budget.

- **Team Building** – the selection of individuals must also take account of the final shape of the project team and the way they will work together. This and additional aspects of personnel management are discussed in Chapter 10.

Exercise 8.4

Amanda has decided that, where possible, whoever writes the specification for a module should also produce the design as she believes this will improve the commitment and motivation of the three analyst/designers, Belinda, Tom and Daisy.

She has decided that she will use Tom, a trainee analyst/designer, for the specification and design of module D as both of these activities have a large float compared to their activity span ($6/21$ and $9/13$ of their span respectively). Since the specification and design of module C are on the critical path she decides to allocate both of these tasks to Belinda, a particularly experienced and capable member of staff.

Having made these decisions she has almost no flexibility in how she assigns the other specification and design activities. Work out from the activity bar chart produced as part of the solution to Exercise 8.2 (shown in Figure 8.6) who she assigns to which of the remaining specification and design activities.

Publishing the resource schedule

In allocating and scheduling resources we have used the activity plan (a precedence network in the case of the examples in this chapter), activity bar charts and resource histograms. Although good as planning tools they are not the best way of publishing and communicating project schedules. For this we need some form of work plan. Work plans are commonly published either as lists or charts such as that illustrated in Figure 8.7. In this case Amanda has chosen not to include activity floats (which could be indicated by shaded bars) as she fears that one or two members of the team may work with less urgency if they are aware that their activities are not critical.

Notice that, somewhat unusually, it is assumed there are no Bank Holidays or other non-productive periods during the 100 days of the project and that none of the team have holidays for the periods they are shown as working.

Amanda has also made no explicit allowance for staff taking sick leave.

Amanda now transfers some of the information from the work schedule to her precedence network. In particular she amends the earliest start dates for activities and any other constraints (such as revised latest finish dates where resources need to be made available) that have been introduced. A copy of her revised precedence network is shown in Figure 8.8 – notice that she has highlighted all critical activities and paths.

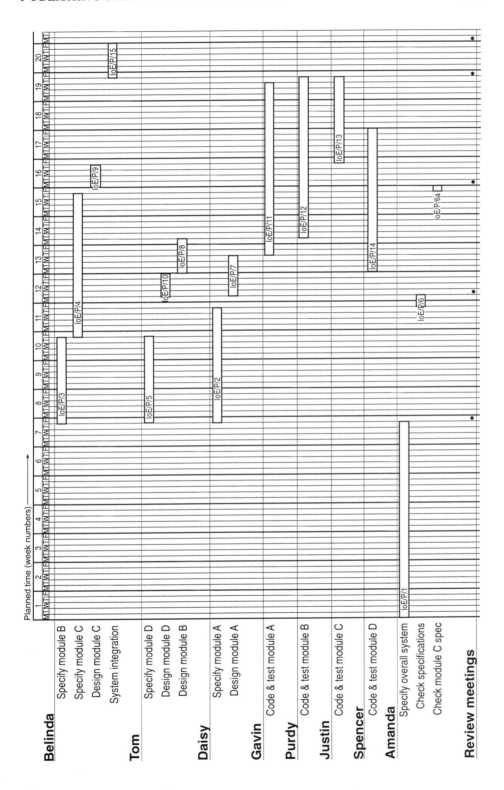

Figure 8.7 *Amanda's work schedule.*

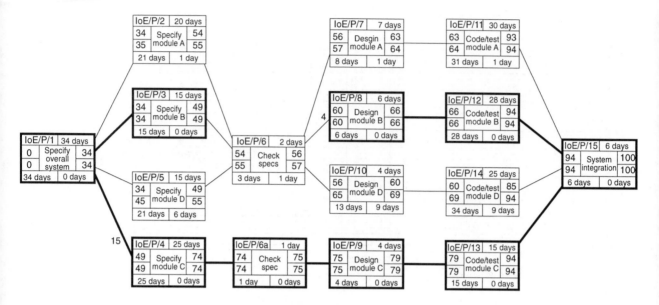

Figure 8.8 *Amanda's revised precedence network showing scheduled start and completion dates.*

Cost schedules

It is now time to produce a detailed cost schedule showing weekly or monthly costs over the life of the project. This will provide a more detailed and accurate estimate of costs and will serve as a plan against which project progress may be monitored.

Calculating cost is straightforward where the organization has standard cost figures for staff and other resources. Where this is not the case, then the project manager will have to calculate the costs.

In general, costs may be categorized as follows.

- **Staff costs** – these will include staff salaries as well as the other direct costs of employment such as the employer's contribution to National Insurance, pension scheme contributions, holiday pay and sickness benefit. These are commonly charged to projects at hourly rates based on weekly work records completed by staff. Note that contract staff may be charged by the week or month – even when they are idle.
- **Overheads** – overheads represent expenditure that an organization incurs that cannot be directly related to individual projects or jobs including space rental, interest charges and the costs of service departments (such as personnel). Overhead costs may be recovered by making a fixed charge on development departments (in which case they may appear as a weekly or monthly charge for a project), or by an additional percentage charge on direct staff employment

costs, These additional charges or oncosts can easily equal or exceed the direct employment costs.
• **Usage charges** – in some organizations projects may be charged directly for use of resources such as computer time (rather than their cost being recovered as an overhead). This will normally be on an 'as used' basis.

Exercise 8.5

Amanda finds that IOE recovers some overheads as oncosts on direct staff costs although others are recovered by charging a fixed £200 per day against projects. Staff costs (including overheads) are as shown in Table 8.2. In addition to the commitments in the work plan (Figure 8.7) Amanda estimates that, in total, she will have spent an additional 10 days planning the project and carrying out the post-project review.

Calculate the total cost for Amanda's project on this basis. How is the expenditure spread over the life of the project?

Table 8.2 *Staff costs (including oncosts) for Amanda's project team*

Staff member	Daily cost (£)
Amanda	300
Belinda	250
Tom	175
Daisy	225
Gavin	150
Purdy	150
Justin	150
Spencer	150

Figure 8.9 shows the weekly costs over the 20 weeks that she expects the project to take. This is a typical cost profile – building up slowly to a peak and then tailing off quite rapidly at the end of the project. Figure 8.10 illustrates the cumulative cost of the project and it is generally this that would be used for cost control purposes.

The scheduling sequence

Going from an ideal activity plan to a costed schedule can be represented as a sequence of steps rather like the classic waterfall life-cycle model. In the ideal world we would start with the activity plan and use this as the basis for our risk assessment. The activity plan and risk assessment would provide the basis for our resource allocation and schedule from which we would produce cost schedules.

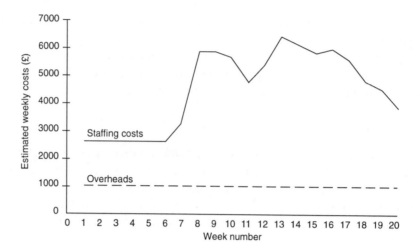

Figure 8.9 *Weekly project costs for the IOE project.*

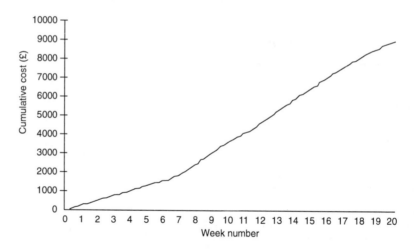

Figure 8.10 *Cumulative project costs for the IOE project.*

In practice, as we have seen by looking at Amanda's project, a successful resource allocation may necessitate revisions to the activity plan which, in turn, will affect our risk assessment. Similarly, the cost schedule may indicate the need or desirability to reallocate resources or revise activity plans – particularly where that schedule indicates a higher overall project cost than originally anticipated.

The interplay between the plans and schedules is complex – any change to any one will affect each of the others. Some factors may be directly compared in terms of money – the cost of hiring additional staff may be balanced against the costs of delaying the project's end date. Some factors, however, are difficult to express in money terms (the cost of an increased risk, for example) and will include an element of subjectivity.

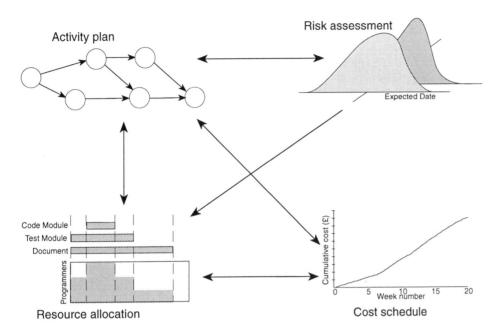

Figure 8.11 *Successful project scheduling is not a simple sequence.*

While a good computer-based project planning package will assist greatly in demonstrating the consequences of change and keeping the planning synchronized, successful project scheduling is largely dependant upon the skill and experience of the project manager in juggling the many factors involved.

Conclusion

In this chapter we have discussed the problems of allocating resources to project activities and the conversion of an activity plan to a work schedule. In particular, we have seen the importance of the following.

- identifying all the resources needed
- arranging activity starts to minimize variations in resource levels over the level of the project
- allocating resources to competing activities in a rational order of priority
- taking care in allocating the right staff to critical activities.

Further exercises

1. Burman's priority ordering for allocating resources to activities takes into account the activity duration as well as its total float. Why do you think this is advantageous?

2. If you have access to a project planning package use it to produce an activity plan for Amanda's project and include the staff resource requirements for each activity. Explore the facilities of your package and answer the following questions.

    •   Can you set up resource types and ask the package to allocate individuals to tasks?

    •   Will your package allow you to specify productivity factors for individual members of staff so that the duration of an activity depends upon who is carrying it out?

    •   Will your package carry out resource smoothing or provide a minimum cost solution?

    •   Can you replicate Amanda's resource schedule (see Figure 8.7) – or produce a better one?

3. On a large project it may be the responsibility of a team leader to allocate tasks to individuals. Why might it be unsatisfactory to leave such allocations entirely to the discretion of the team leader?

4. In scheduling her project, Amanda ignored the risks of absence due to staff sickness. What might she have done to estimate the likelihood of this occurring and how might she have taken account of the risk when scheduling the project?

Chapter 9

Monitoring and control

OBJECTIVES

In this chapter you will learn how to:

- ☐ monitor the progress of projects

- ☐ assess the risk of slippage

- ☐ visualize and assess the state of a project

- ☐ revise targets to correct or counteract drift

- ☐ control changes to a project's requirements.

Introduction

Once work schedules have been published and the project is under way, attention must be focused on ensuring progress. This requires monitoring of what is happening, comparison of actual achievement against the schedule and, where necessary, revision of plans and schedules to bring the project as far as possible back on target.

In earlier chapters we have stressed the importance of producing plans that can be monitored – for example, ensuring that activities have clearly defined and visible completion points. We are going to discuss how information about project progress may be gathered. We consider actions that may be taken to ensure a project meets its targets.

The final part of this chapter discusses how we can deal with changes that are imposed from outside – namely changes in requirements.

Monitoring and control

Exercising control over a project and ensuring that targets are met is a matter of regular monitoring, finding out what is happening, and comparing it with current targets. If there is a mismatch between the planned outcomes and the actual ones then either replanning is needed to bring the project back on target or the target will have to be revised. Figure 9.1 illustrates the project control cycle that we met first in Chapter 1.

In practice we are normally concerned with departures from the plan in four dimensions – delays in meeting target dates, shortfalls in quality or functionality, and costs going over target. In this chapter we are mainly concerned with the first and last of these.

See Chapter 11 for a discussion of software quality.

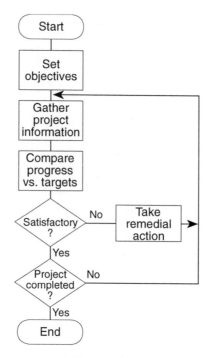

Figure 9.1 *The project control cycle.*

Responsibility

The overall responsibility for ensuring satisfactory progress on a project is often the role of the **project steering committee** or **Project Board**. Day-to-day responsibility will rest with the project manager and, in all but the smallest of projects, aspects of this may be delegated to team leaders.

The concept of a reporting hierarchy was introduced in Chapter 1.

Figure 9.2 illustrates the typical reporting structure found with medium and large projects. With small projects (employing around half a dozen or fewer staff) individual team members may report directly to the project manager but in most cases team leaders will collate reports on their section's progress and forward summaries to the project manager. These, in turn, will be incorporated into project-level reports for the steering committee and, via them or directly, progress reports for the client.

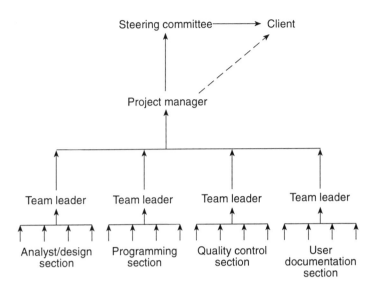

In a PRINCE environment, the project manager will report to the Project Board and may delegate day-to-day responsibility for stages to Stage Managers. Stage Managers may themselves be team leaders.

Figure 9.2 *Project reporting structures.*

Reporting may be verbal or written, formal or informal, regular or ad-hoc and some examples of each type are given in table 9.1. While any effective team leader or project manager will be in touch with team members and available to discuss problems, any such informal reporting of project progress must be complemented by formal reporting procedures – and it is those we are concerned with in this chapter.

Table 9.1 *Categories of reporting*

Report type	Examples	Comment
Verbal formal regular	weekly or monthly progress meetings	while reports may be verbal formal written minutes should be kept
Verbal formal ad-hoc	end-of-stage review meetings	while largely verbal, likely to receive written reports
Written formal regular	job sheets, progress reports	normally weekly using forms
Written formal ad-hoc	exception reports, change reports	
Verbal informal ad-hoc	canteen discussion, social interaction	often provides early warning, must be backed up by formal reporting

Assessing progress

Progress assessment will normally be made on the basis of information collected and collated at regular intervals or when specific events occur. Wherever possible this information will be objective and tangible – whether or not a particular report has been delivered, for example. However, such end-of-activity deliverables may not occur sufficiently frequently throughout the life of the project. Here progress assessment will have to rely on the judgement of the team members who are carrying out the project activities.

Setting checkpoints

The PRINCE standard described in Appendix A has its own terminology.

It is essential to set a series of checkpoints in the initial activity plan. Checkpoints may be:

- regular (monthly, for example)
- tied to specific events such as the production of a report or other deliverable.

Taking snap-shots

The frequency with which the a manager needs to receive information about progress will depend upon the size and degree of risk of the project or that part of the project under their control. Team leaders, for example, may need to assess progress daily (particularly when employing inexperienced staff) whereas stage managers may find weekly or monthly reporting appropriate. In general, the higher the level, the less frequent and less detailed the reporting needs to be.

Short, Monday morning team progress meetings are a common way of motivating staff to meet short term targets.

There are, however, strong arguments in favour of formal weekly collection of information from staff carrying out activities. Collecting data at the end of each week ensures that information is provided while memories are still relatively fresh and provides a mechanism for individuals to review and reflect upon their progress during the past few days.

Major, or project-level, progress reviews will generally take place at particular points during the life of a project – commonly known as review points or control points. PRINCE, for example, designates a series of control points, from the **Project Initiation** to the **Project Closure**, where an assessment of the project and consideration of its future is undertaken.

Collecting the data

As a rule managers will try to break down long activities into more controllable tasks of one or two weeks duration. However, it may still be necessary to gather information about partially completed activities and, in particular, forecasts of how much work is left to be completed. It can be difficult to make such forecasts accurately.

A programmer working on Amanda's project has written the first 250 lines of a Cobol program that is estimated to require 500 lines of code. Explain why it would be unreasonable to assume that the programming task is 50% complete.

Can you make any estimate of how complete it might be?

Where there is a series of products partial completion of activities is easier to estimate. Counting the number of record specifications or screen layouts produced, for example, may provide a reasonable measure of progress.

In some cases intermediate products can be used as in-activity milestones. The first successful compilation of a Cobol program, for example, might be considered a milestone even though it is not the final product of the activity code and test.

Partial completion reporting

Many organizations use standard accounting systems with weekly time sheets to charge staff time to individual jobs. The staff time booked to a project indicates the charges to the project and the work carried out. It does not tell the project manager what has been produced or whether tasks are on schedule.

It is common to adapt or enhance existing accounting systems to meet the needs of project control. Weekly time sheets, for example, are frequently adapted by breaking jobs down to activity level and requiring information about work done in addition to time spent. Figure 9.3 shows a typical example of such a report form, in this case requesting information about likely slippage of completion dates as well as estimates of completeness.

Asking for estimated completion times is can be criticized on the grounds that frequent invitations to reconsider completion dates deflects attention away from the importance of the originally scheduled targets.

Risk reporting

One way of overcoming the objections to partial completion reporting is to avoid asking for estimated completion dates, but rather ask for the team members' estimates of the likelihood of meeting the planned target date.

One way of doing this is the traffic-light method. This consists of the following steps:

- identify the key (first level) elements for assessment in a piece of work
- break these key elements into constituent elements (second level)
- assess each of the second level elements on the scale **green** on target, **amber** not on target but recoverable, and **red** not on target and recoverable only with difficulty
- review all the second level assessments to arrive at first level assessments
- review first and second level assessments to produce an overall assessment.

There are a number of variations on the traffic-light technique. The version described here is in use in IBM and is described in Down, Coleman and Absolon, *Risk Management for Software Projects*, McGraw-Hill, 1994

Weekly time-sheets are a valuable source of information about resources used.

They are often used to provide information about what has been achieved. However, requesting partial completion estimates where they cannot be obtained from objective measures encourages the 99% complete syndrome – tasks are reported as on time until 99% complete, and then stay at 99% complete until finished.

Time Sheet

Staff   John Smith   **Week ending**   24/2/95

Rechargeable hours

Project	Activity code	Description	Hours this week	% Complete	Scheduled completion	Projected completion
P21	A243	Code mod A3	12	30	24/3/95	24/3/95
P34	B771	Document take-on	20	90	3/3/95	10/2/95

Total recharged hours	32

Non-rechargeable hours

Code	Description	Hours	Comment & authorization
Z99	Day in lieu	8	Authorised by RB

Total non-rechargeable hours	8

Figure 9.3 *A weekly time sheet and progress review form.*

For example, Amanda decides to use a version of the traffic-light method for reviewing activities on the IOE project. She breaks each activity into a number of component parts (deciding that further breakdown into constituent parts is unnecessary) and gets the team members to complete a return at the end of each week. Figure 9.4 illustrates Justin's completed assessment at the end of week 16.

Traffic-light assessment only highlights risk of non-achievement, it is not an attempt to estimate work done or quantify expected delays.

Following completion of assessment forms for all activities, the project manager may use these as a basis for evaluating the overall status of the project. Any critical activity classified as amber or red will require further consideration and may lead to a revision of the project schedule. Non-critical activities are only likely to be a problem if they are classified as red.

Staff: Justin								
Ref: IoE/P/13	**Activity: Code & test module C**							
Week number	13	14	15	16	17	18		
Activity summary	G	A	A	R				
Component							*Comments*	
Environment division	G	A	G	G				
Screen handling procedures	G	A	A	G				
File update procedures	G	G	R	A				
Housekeeping procedures	G	G	G	A				
Compilation	G	G	G	R				
Test data runs	G	G	G	A				
Program documentation	G	G	A	R				

Figure 9.4 *A traffic-light assessment of IoE/P/13.*

Note that this form only refers to uncompleted activities. Justin would still need to report activity completions and the time spent on activities.

Visualizing progress

Having collected data about project progress, a manager needs some way of presenting that data to greatest effect. In this section we look at some methods of presenting a picture of the project and its future. Some of these methods (such as Gantt charts) provide a static picture, a single snap-shot, whereas others (such as time-line charts) try to show how the project has progressed and changed through time.

The Gantt chart

One of the simplest and oldest techniques for tracking project progress is the Gantt chart. This is essentially an activity bar chart indicating scheduled activity dates and durations frequently augmented with activity floats. Reported progress is recorded on the chart (normally by shading activity bars) and a 'today cursor' provides an immediate visual indication of which activities are ahead or behind schedule. Figure 9.5 shows part of Amanda's Gantt chart as at the end of Tuesday of week 17. *Code & test module D* has been completed ahead of schedule and *code & test module A* appears also to be ahead of schedule. The coding and testing of the other two modules is behind schedule.

Henry Gantt (1861–1919) was an industrial engineer interested in the efficient organization of work.

The slip chart

A slip chart (Figure 9.6) is very similar alternative favoured by some project managers who believe it provides a more striking visual indication of those activities that are not progressing to schedule – the more the slip line bends the greater the variation from the plan. Additional slip lines may be added at intervals and, as they build up, the project manager will gain an idea as to whether the project is improving (subsequent slip lines bend less) or not. A very jagged slip line indicates a need for rescheduling.

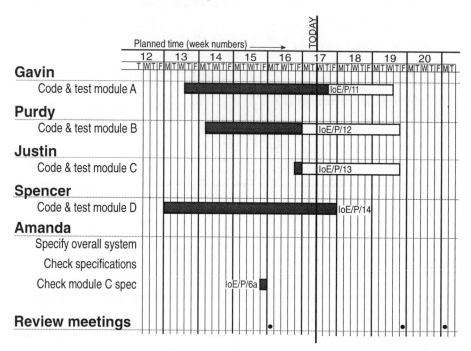

Figure 9.5 *Part of Amanda's Gantt chart showing the 'today cursor' in week 17.*

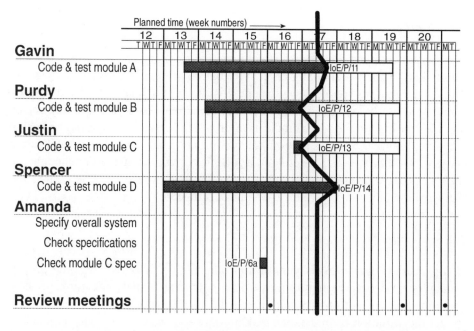

Figure 9.6 *The slip chart emphasizes the relative position of each activity.*

Ball charts

A somewhat more striking way of showing whether or not targets have been met is to use a Ball Chart as in Figure 9.7. In this version of the ball chart the circles indicate start and completion points for activities. The circles initially contain the original scheduled dates. Whenever revisions are produced these are added as second dates in the appropriate circle until an activity is actually started or completed when the relevant date replaces the revised estimate (in bold italic in Figure 9.7). Circles will therefore contain only two dates, the original and most recent target dates, or the original and actual dates.

Where the actual start or finish date for an activity is later than the target date, the circle is coloured red (dark grey in Figure 9.7) – where an actual date is on time or earlier than the target then the circle is coloured green (light grey in Figure 9.7).

Such charts are frequently placed in a prominent position and the colour coded balls provide a constant reminder to the project team and may where more than one team is working, encourage a competitiveness between teams.

Another advantage of ball charts over Gantt and slip charts is that they are relatively easy to keep up to date – only the dates and possibly colours need to be changed, whereas the others need to be redrawn each time target dates are revised.

> David Youll in *Making Software Development Visible*, John Wiley & Sons, 1990, describes a version of the ball chart using three sets of dates and part-coloured balls.

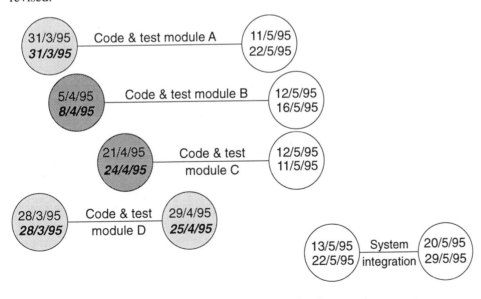

Figure 9.7 *The ball wall chart provides an incentive for meeting targets.*

The timeline

One disadvantage of the charts described so far is that they do not show clearly the slippage of the project completion date through the life of the project. Knowing the current state of a project may help in revising plans to bring it back on target, but analysing and understanding trends may help to avoid slippage in future projects.

The timeline chart is a method of recording and displaying the way in which targets have changed throughout the duration of the project.

Figure 9.8 shows a timeline chart for Brigette's project at the end of the sixth week. Planned time is plotted along the horizontal axis and elapsed time down the vertical axis. The lines meandering down the chart represent scheduled activity completion dates – at the start of the project *analyse existing system* is scheduled to be completed by the Tuesday of week 3, *obtain user requirements* by Thursday of week 5, *issue tender*, the final activity, by Tuesday of week 9, and so on.

Brigette's timeline chart contains only the critical activities for her project; ● indicates actual completion of an activity.

For the sake of clarity, the number of activities on a timeline chart must be limited. Using colour helps to distinguish activities, particularly where lines cross.

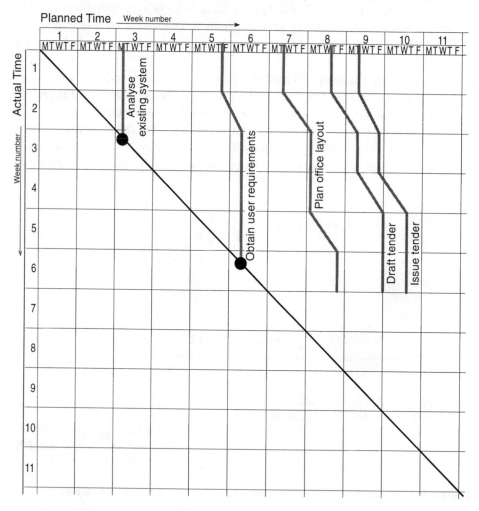

Figure 9.8 *Brigette's timeline chart at the end of week six.*

At the end of the first week Brigette reviews these target dates and leaves them as they are – lines are therefore drawn vertically downwards from the target dates to the end of week one on the actual time axis.

At the end of week two, Brigette decides that *obtain user requirements* will not be completed until Tuesday of week six – she therefore extends that activity line diagonally to reflect this. The other activity completion targets are also delayed correspondingly.

By the Tuesday of week three *analyse existing system* is completed and Brigette puts a blob on the diagonal timeline to indicate that this has happened. At the end of week three she decides to keep to the existing targets.

At the end of week four she adds another three days to *draft tender* and *issue tender*.

Note that, by the end of week six, two activities have been completed and three are still unfinished. Up to this point she has revised target dates on three occasions and the project as a whole is running seven days late.

By the end of week 8 Brigette has completed planning the office layout but finds **Exercise 9.2** that drafting the tender is going to take one week longer that originally anticipated.

What will Brigette's timeline chart look like at the end of week 8?

If the rest of the project goes according to plan, what will Brigette's timeline chart look like when the project is completed?

The timeline chart is useful both during the execution of a project and as part of the post-implementation review. Analysis of the timeline chart, and the reasons for the changes, may well indicate failures in the estimation process or other errors that might, with that knowledge, be avoided in future.

Cost monitoring

Expenditure monitoring is an important component of project control. Not only in itself, but also because it provides an indication of effort that has gone into (or at least been charged to) a project. A project may be on time but only because more money has been spent on activities than originally budgeted. A cumulative expenditure chart such as that shown in Figure 9.9 provides a simple method of comparing actual and planned expenditure. By itself it is not particularly meaningful – Figure 9.9 could, for example, illustrate a project that is running late or one that is on time but has shown substantial costs savings! We need to take account of the current status of the project activities before attempting to interpret the meaning of recorded expenditure.

Cost charts become much more useful if we add projected future costs calculated by adding the estimated costs of uncompleted work to the costs already incurred. Where a computer-based planning tool is used, revision of cost schedules is generally provided automatically once actual expenditure has been recorded. Figure 9.10 illustrates the additional information available once the revised cost schedule is included – in this case it is apparent that the project is behind schedule and over budget.

Project costs may be monitored by a company's accounting system. By themselves, they provide little information about project status.

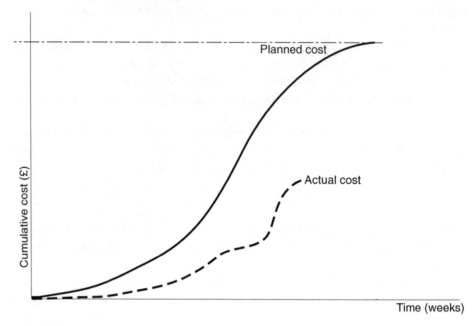

Figure 9.9 *Tracking cumulative expenditure.*

Project costs augmented by project monitoring may be used to generate forecasts of future costs.

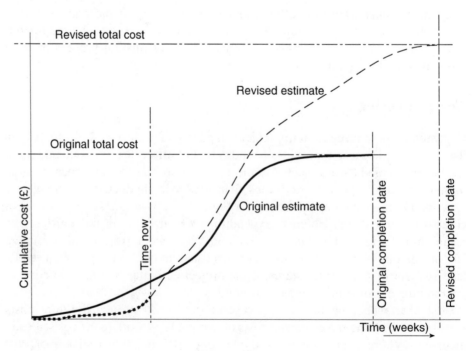

Figure 9.10 *The cumulative expenditure chart may also show revised estimates of cost and completion date.*

Prioritizing monitoring

So far we have assumed that all aspects of a project will receive equal treatment in terms of the degree of monitoring applied. We must not forget, however, that monitoring takes time and uses resources that might sometimes be put to better use!

In this section we list the priorities we might apply in deciding levels of monitoring.

- **Critical path activities** – any delay in an activity on the critical path will cause a delay in the completion date for the project. Critical path activities are therefore likely to have a very high priority for close monitoring.

- **Activities with no free float** – a delay in any activity with no free float will delay at least some subsequent activities even though, if the delay is less than the total float, it may not delay the project completion date. These subsequent delays may have serious effects on our resource schedule as a delay in a subsequent activity may mean that the resource will become unavailable before that activity is completed.

  > Free float is the amount of time an activity may be delayed without affecting any subsequent activity.

- **Activities with less than a specified float** – if any activity has very little float it may use up this float before the regular activity monitoring brings the problem to the project manager's attention. It is common practice to closely monitor those activities with less than, say, one week free float.

- **High risk activities** – a set of high risk activities may have been identified as part of the initial risk profiling exercise. If we are using the PERT three-estimate approach we may designate activities as high risk which have a high estimated duration variance. These activities will be given close attention because they are most likely to overrun or overspend.

  > PERT and the significance of activity duration variance was described in Chapter 7.

- **Activities using critical resources** – activities may be critical because they are very expensive (as in the case of specialized contract programmers). Staff or other resources may only be available for a limited period, especially if they are controlled outside the project team. In any event, an activity that demands a critical resource requires a high level of monitoring.

Getting the project back to target

Almost any project will, at one time or another, be subject to delays and unexpected events. One of the tasks of the project manager is to recognize when this is happening (or, if possible, about to happen) and, with the minimum delay and disruption to the project team, attempt to mitigate the effects of the problem. In most cases the project manager tries to ensure that the scheduled project end date remains unaffected. This may be done by shortening remaining activity durations or shortening the overall duration of the remaining project in the ways described in the next section

The schedule is not sacrosanct – it is a plan that should be adhered to so long as it is relevant and cost-effective.

It should be remembered, however, that this might not always be the most appropriate response to disruptions to a plan. There is little point in spending considerable sums in overtime payments in order to speed up a project if the customer is not overly concerned with the delivery date and there is no other valuable work for the team members once this project is completed.

There are two main strategies to consider when drawing up plans to bring a project back on target – shortening the critical path or altering the activity precedence requirements.

Shorten the critical path

The overall duration of a project is determined by the current critical path so speeding up non critical path activities will not bring forward a project completion date.

Extolling staff to 'work harder' may have some effect although frequently a more positive form of action is required such as the resources for some critical activity. Fact-finding, for example, might be speeded up by allocating an additional analyst to interviewing users. It is unlikely, however, that the coding of a small module would be shortened by allocating an additional programmer – indeed, it might be counterproductive because of the additional time needed organizing and allocating tasks and communicating.

Resource levels may be increased by making them available for longer. Thus, staff may be asked to work overtime for the duration of an activity and computing resources might be made available at times (such as evenings and week-ends) when they might otherwise be inaccessible.

Time/cost trade-off: there is a general rule that timescales may be shortened by buying more (or more expensive) resources; sometimes this is true.

Where these do not provide a sufficient solution, the project manager might consider allocating more efficient resources to activities on the critical path or swapping resources between critical and non-critical activities. This may be particularly appropriate with staff – an experienced programmer may be significantly more productive than a more junior member of the team.

By such means we can attempt to shorten the timescale for critical activities until such time as either we have brought the project back to schedule or further efforts prove unproductive or non cost-effective.

Reconsider the precedence requirements

If attempting to shorten critical activities proves insufficient the next step is to consider the constraints on which some activities have to be deferred pending completion of others. The original project network would most probably have been drawn up assuming 'ideal' conditions and 'normal' working practices. It may be that, to avoid the project delivering late, it is now worth questioning whether as yet unstarted activities really do have to await the completion of others. It may, in a particular organization, be 'normal' to complete system testing before commencing user training. In order to avoid late completion of a project it may, however, be considered acceptable to alter 'normal' practice and start training earlier.

One way to overcome precedence constraints is to subdivide activities into a component which can start immediately and one which is still constrained as before. For example, a user handbook can be drawn up in a draft form from the system specification and then be revised later to take account of subsequent changes.

If we do decide to alter the precedence requirements in such a way it is clearly important to be aware that quality may be compromised and to make a considered decision to compromise quality where needed. It is equally important to assess the degree to which changes in work practices increase risk. It is possible to start coding a module before its design has been completed. It would normally, however, be considered foolhardy to do so since, as well as compromising quality, it would increase the risk of having to redo some of the coding once the final design had been completed and thus delay the project even further.

Change control

So far in this chapter we have assumed that the nature of the tasks to be carried out has not changed. A project leader like Amanda or Brigette may find, however, that requirements are modified because of changing circumstances or because the users get a clearer idea of what is really needed. The payroll system that Brigette is implementing may, for instance, need to be adjusted if the staffing structure at the college is reorganized.

Other, internal, changes will crop up. Amanda may find that there are inconsistencies in the program specifications that only become apparent when the programs are coded and these would result in amendments to the specifications.

Careful control of these changes is needed because an alteration in one document may imply changes to other documents and the system products based on that document. The Product Flow Diagrams that have been explained in an earlier chapter indicate relationships between the products of a project where this may be the case.

A change in a program specification will normally be carried through into changes to the program design and then changed code. What other products may need to be modified?

Exercise 9.3

Configuration librarian's role

Control of changes and documentation ought to be the responsibility of someone who may variously be named the Configuration Librarian, the Configuration Manager or Project Librarian. Among their duties would be:

BS EN ISO 9001:1994 (formerly BS 5750) requires that a formal change control procedure is in place.

- the identification of all items that are subject to change control
- the establishment and maintenance of a central repository of the master copies of all project documentation and software products
- the setting up and running of a formal set of procedures to deal with changes
- the maintenance of records of who has access to which library items and the status of each library item (e.g. whether under development, under test or released).

It may be recalled that it was suggested that the setting up of change control procedures might be one of the first things the Brigette might want to do at Brightmouth HE College.

Change control procedures

A simple change control procedure for operational systems might have the following steps.

1. One or more users may perceive a need for a modification to a system and ask for a change request to be passed to the development staff.
2. The user management consider the change request and if they approve it pass it to the development management.
3. The development management delegate a member of staff to look at the request and to report on the practicality and cost of carrying out the change. They would, as part of this, assess the products that would be affected by the change.
4. The development management report back to the user management on the findings and the user management decide whether, in view of the cost quoted, they wish to go ahead.
5. One or more developers are authorized to take copies of the master products which are to be modified.
6. The copies are modified. In the case of software components this would involve modifying the code and recompiling and testing it.
7. When the development of new versions of the product has been completed the user management will be notified and copies of the software will be released for user acceptance testing.
8. When the user is satisfied that the products are adequate they will authorize their operational release. The master copies of configuration items will be replaced.

Exercise 9.4

The above steps relate to changes to operational systems. How could they be modified to deal with systems under development?

Changes in scope of a system

A common occurrence with IS development projects is for the size of the system to gradually increase. One cause of this may be changes to requirements that are requested by users.

This is sometimes called scope creep.

Think of other reasons why there is a tendency to scope creep.

Exercise 9.5

The scope of a project needs to be carefully monitored and considered. One way is to re-estimate the system size in terms of SLOC or function points at key milestones.

Conclusions

In this chapter we have discussed the requirements for continual monitoring of projects and the need for making progress visible. Among the important points to emerge were:

- planning is pointless unless the execution of the plan is monitored
- activities that are too long need to be subdivided to make them more controllable
- ideally progress should be measured through the delivery of project products
- progress needs to be shown in a visually striking way such as through ball charts in order to communicate information effectively
- costs need to be monitored as well as elapsed time
- delayed projects can often be brought back on track by shortening activity times on the critical path or by relaxing some of the precedence constraints.

Further exercises

1. Take a look at Amanda's project schedule shown in Figure 8.7. Identify those activities scheduled to last more than three weeks and describe how she might monitor progress on each of them on a fortnightly or weekly basis.

2. Amanda's Gantt chart at the end of week 17 (Figure 9.5) indicates that two activities are running late. What effect might this have on the rest of the project. How might Amanda mitigate the effects of this delay?

3. Describe a set of change control procedures that would be appropriate for Brigette to implement at Brightmouth HE College.

Chapter 10

Managing people and organizing teams

OBJECTIVES

When you have completed this chapter, you will be able to:

- ☐ identify some of the factors that influence people's behaviour in a project environment

- ☐ select the most appropriate people for a project

- ☐ appreciate the role of continuing training and learning

- ☐ increase staff motivation

- ☐ improve group working

- ☐ use the most appropriate leadership styles

- ☐ appreciate the characteristics of the various team structures that can be employed.

Introduction

In this chapter we are going to examine some of the problems that Amanda and Brigette may meet when dealing with the staff who will be working for them. Where possible we will see if the findings of researchers in this area can provide them with any ideas about what to do.

First, we are going to look at some of the background to organizational behaviour (OB) research. This raises three areas of concern: staff selection, staff development and, which we deal with in somewhat more detail, staff motivation.

The successful manager needs to encourage effective group working and decision making but needs to balance this, where needed, by purposeful leadership. We look at how this can be achieved. The final part of the chapter looks at some of the more formal aspects of organizational structures.

The issues raised in this chapter have impacts at all stages of project planning and execution but in particular at the following points (see also Figure 10.1).

- Although the project leader may have little control over organizational structure they need to be aware of its implications (Step 2).
- The scope and nature of activities can be set in a way that will enhance staff motivation (Step 4).
- Many risks to project success relate to staffing (Step 6).
- The qualities of individual members of staff should be taken into account when allocating staff to activities (Step 7).

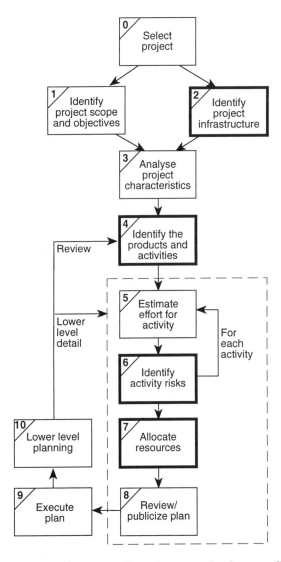

Figure 10.1 *Some places in the Step Wise framework where staffing concerns are important.*

Understanding behaviour

People with practical experience of working on projects invariably identify the handling of people as one of the most important aspects of project management. What people like Amanda and Brigette will want to know is whether the effective and sensitive management of staff can come only from experience or whether guidance can be usefully sought from writers on the topic.

The field of social science known as organizational behaviour (OB) may be of some help. Theories and models have been put forward in order to try to explain people's behaviour. These tend to be structured 'If A is the situation then B is likely to result'. Attempts are then made to observe behaviour or to conduct experiments where variables for A and B are measured and a statistical relationship between the two variables is sought. Unlike physical science it is rarely, if ever, the case that it can be said that B must always follow A – it is a matter of probability.

A major problem with using these findings is that in the real world there is bound to be a very wide range of influences on a situation, many of which will not be apparent to the observer. It is therefore difficult to decide which set of research findings is relevant. A danger is that we end up with a set of maxims which are little better than superstitions. However, it is to hoped that by examining these questions people can become more sensitive and thoughtful about the problems involved with behaviour in organizations.

Charles Handy, *Understanding organisations* 4th edition, Penguin 1993.

In the following discussion we will be making many references to prominent workers in the OB field such as Taylor, Mayo and McGregor. Rather than overwhelming the reader with references, we would recommend the reader who is interested in exploring further what is a fascinating topic to look at Charles Handy's book. Where we have given references these tend to be for works related specifically to an IT environment.

Organizational behaviour: a background

The roots of studies in OB can be traced back to work done in the late 19th and early 20th centuries by Frederick Taylor. By studying the way that manual workers did tasks, he attempted to work out what must be the most productive way of doing these tasks. The workers were then trained to do the work in this way.

Taylor had three basic objectives :

Frederick Winslow Taylor, 1856–1915, is regarded as the father of 'scientific management' of which OB is a part.

- to select the best person for the job
- to instruct them in the best methods
- to give incentives in the form of higher wages to the best workers.

'Taylorism' is often represented as crude and mechanistic these days. Interestingly though, the Taylorist approach is one that is adopted, in part, in modern sports coaching. A coach may attempt to get a javelin thrower, for example, to throw a javelin in a very exact manner in order to get the maximum effect. In the more mundane world of software development, the growth of structured methods is an example of this emphasis on best practice. Both Amanda and Brigette will be concerned that tasks are carried out in the proper way. As we will see, more contentious is Taylor's emphasis on the exclusively financial basis of staff motivation, although Amanda and Brigette will be sure to find many people in their respective environments who hold to Taylor's view on the importance of 'performance-related pay'. One of the practical problems with this is that Amanda and Brigette are likely to have very little control over the financial rewards of their staff. However, they should be encouraged by findings that motivation rests not just on such rewards.

During the 1920s, OB researchers discovered, while carrying out a now famous set of tests on the conditions under which staff worked best, that not only did a group of workers for whom conditions were improved increase their work-rates, but also a control group for whom conditions were unchanged. Simply showing a concern for what workers did increased productivity. This illustrated how the state of mind of the worker influenced their productivity.

> Mayo and his colleagues did this research at the Hawthorne Works of Western Electric in Chicago, hence the 'Hawthorne Effect'.

The original, cash-oriented, view of work that some managers have can be contrasted with a more rounded vision of the person in their place of work. The two attitudes were labelled Theory X and Theory Y by Donald McGregor.

Theory X holds that:

- the average human has an innate dislike of work
- there is a need therefore for coercion, direction and control
- people tend to avoid responsibility.

Theory Y, on the other hand, holds that:

- work is as natural as rest or play
- external control and coercion are not the only ways of bringing about effort directed towards the company's ends
- commitment to objectives is a function of the rewards associated with their achievement
- the average human can learn to accept and further seek responsibility
- the capacity to exercise imagination and other creative qualities is widely distributed.

> A 'reward' does not have to be a financial reward – it could be something like a sense of achievement.

One way of judging whether a manager espouses Theory X or Theory Y is to observe how their place of work reacts when the boss is absent: if there is no discernible change then this is a Theory Y environment; if everyone relaxes and 'messes around', it is a Theory X environment! McGregor's distinction between the two theories also draws attention to the way that expectations influence behaviour. If a manager (or teacher) assumes that you are going to work diligently and do well then you are likely to try and meet their expectations.

Selecting the right person for the job

B. W. Boehm considered the quality of staff the most important influence on productivity when constructing the COCOMO software cost model (Chapter 5).

Taylor stressed the need for the right person for the job. Many factors, such as the use of software tools and methodologies, affect programming productivity. However, one of the biggest differences in software development performance is between individuals. As early as 1968 a comparison of experienced professional programmers working on the same programming task found a ratio, in one case, of 1:25 between the shortest and longest time to code the program and, more significantly perhaps, of 1:28 for the time taken to debug it. Amanda and Brigette should therefore be rightly concerned to get the best possible people working for them.

What sort of characteristics should they be looking for? Should they go, for example, for the experienced programmer or the new graduate with the first class mathematics degree? It is extremely dangerous to generalize but looking specifically at behavioural characteristics the American researcher Cheney found that the most important influence on programmer productivity seemed to be experience. Mathematical aptitude had quite a weak influence in comparison.

P. M. Cheney 'Effects of Individual Characteristics, Organizational Factors and Task Characteristics on Computer Programmer Productivity and Job Satisfaction' in *Information and Management* 7 (1984). J. D. Couger and R. A. Zawacki 'What motivates DP Professionals?' in *Datamation* 24 (1978).

Amanda and Brigette will want staff who can communicate well with each other and, more importantly, with users. They may well have some difficulties here. The American researchers Couger and Zawacki found that computing people would appear to have much weaker 'social needs' than people in other professions. They quote Gerald Weinberg: 'If asked, most programmers probably say they prefer to work alone where they wouldn't be disturbed by other people.' This is reflected in the problem that people who may be attracted to writing software, and are good at it, may not make good managers later in their careers.

The selection process

Although this is an important matter, it has to be stressed that very often the project leader has very little choice about the people who are going to make up their team – they have to make do with the 'materials that are to hand'. Recruitment may very well be regarded as an organizational responsibility: you may be recruiting someone who may, over a period of time, work in many different parts of the same organization.

A general approach might be the following.

- **Create a job specification** Advice may need to be sought here because there may be legal implications in an official document. However, formally or informally, the requirements of the job need to be documented and agreed.
- **Create a job holder profile** Using the job specification, a profile of the sort of person who would be needed to carry out the job is constructed. The qualities, qualifications, education and experience required would be listed.
- **Obtain applicants** Typically, some kind of advertisement would be placed, either within the organization or outside in the trade or local press. The job holder profile would be examined carefully to identify the medium which is

most likely to reach the largest number of potential applicants at least cost. For example, if a specialist of some kind is needed it would make sense to advertise in the relevant specialist journal. The other principle is to give enough information in the advertisement to allow an element of self-elimination. By giving the salary, location, job scope and any essential qualifications, the people applying will be limited to the more realistic candidates.

- **Examine curricula vitae** These should be read carefully and compared to the job holder profile – nothing is more annoying for all concerned than when people whose CVs indicate clearly are not be eligible for the job are called for interview.
- **Interviews etc.** A number of different selection techniques may be tried including aptitude tests, personality tests, and the examination of samples of previous work. All these methods must be related to specific qualities detailed in the job holder profile. Interviews are the most commonly used method. It is better if there is more than one interview session with an applicant and with each session there should not be more than two interviewers as a greater number reduces the possibility of follow-up questions and discussion. Some formal scoring system for the qualities being judged should be devised and interviewers should then decide scores individually which are then compared. An interview may be of a technical nature where the practical expertise of the candidate is assessed, or of a more general nature. In the latter case, a major part of the interview may in fact be evaluating and confirming what was stated in the CV – for example any time gaps in the education and employment history would be investigated, and the precise nature of jobs previously done would need to be explored.
- **Other procedures** References will need to be taken up where necessary, and a medical examination may be needed.

A new analyst/programmer is to be recruited to work in Amanda's team at IOE. The intention is to recruit someone who already has some experience. Make a list of the types of activities that the analyst/programmer should be capable of carrying out that can be used as the basis for a job specification.

Exercise 10.1

Instruction in the best methods

Instruction in the most efficient methods is the second concern that we have taken from Taylor. Obviously, there is a difference between loading pig iron (one of Taylor's studies) and writing C programs, but the principle of having established methods and procedures is, we hope, as well understood in software development as in steel-making.

The need to take into account the time needed to acclimatize new staff was stressed in Chapter 8 on resource allocation.

When a new member of the team is recruited, the team leader will need to plan their induction into the team very carefully. Where a project is already well under way, this may not be very easy to do. However, the effort should be made – it should pay off in the longer run as it will mean that the new recruit will be able to become a fully effective member of the team much more quickly.

The team leader should also be aware of the need to identify the training needs of their team members on a continuing basis. Just as you formulate a user requirement before you consider a new system, and you construct a job holder profile before you recruit a new member of staff, so you should draw up a training needs profile for each of your staff before you consider specific courses. Some training may be of the type provided by commercial training companies. Where money is tight, alternative sources of training need to be considered but training should not be abandoned altogether even if it only consists of a team member being told to find out about a new software tool and then demonstrating it to their colleagues. Of course the nice thing about external courses is that one gets the chance to talk to colleagues from other organizations – but attending meetings of your local branch of the British Computer Society, for example, may serve the same purpose.

The methods learnt need, of course, to be actually applied. Reviews and inspections should help to ensure this.

Motivation

The third concern that we noted from Taylor was that of motivating people to work. We are now going to look at some different models of motivation that have been proposed.

The Taylorist model

Piece-rates are where workers are paid a fixed sum for each item they produce. Day-rates refer to payment for time worked.

Taylor's viewpoint is reflected in the use of piece-rates in manufacturing industry and sales bonuses amongst sales forces. Piece-rates must have some effect because when people are taken off a work-related payment scheme then it is often found that initially productivity will fall. A major problem with piece-rates is that it is difficult to alter the way people work and in software development we are always trying out new methods and tools to improve productivity. In the motor industry, for example, there has been a movement away from piece-rates to day-rates as a precursor to work reorganization.

Group norms are discussed further under group decision making.

Even where work practices are stable and output can be easily related to reward, people paid by the amount they produce will not automatically maximize their output in order to maximize their income. The amount of output will often by constrained by 'group norms', informal, even unspoken, agreements among colleagues about the amount to be produced. There is often a fear that if output is too high management may react by decreasing the amount paid per unit produced.

Rewards have to be related in a simple and direct way to the work produced. Where a computer system is being produced, this may not be easy. It is difficult to isolate and quantify work done, especially as system development is very much a team effort.

A software development department want to improve productivity by encouraging the reuse of existing software components. It has been suggested that this could be encouraged through financial rewards. To what extent do you think this could be done?

Exercise 10.2

Maslow's hierarchy of needs

Different people may be motivated by different things. Clearly money is a very strong motivator when you are broke. However, as the basic need for cash is satisfied, other motivators are likely to emerge. Abraham Maslow, an American psychologist, suggested that there is a hierarchy of needs. As a lower level of needs is satisfied then gradually a higher level of needs emerges. If these are then satisfied then yet another level of will emerge. Basic needs are for things like food and shelter. The highest level need, according to Maslow, is the need for 'self-actualization', the feeling that you are completely fulfilling your potential.

Newspapers often report on the vast sums of money that are paid to the top executives of many companies. Does this mean that these people are at a low level in the Maslow hierarchy of motivation? Do they really need all this money to be motivated? What do you think that the significance of these salaries really is?

Exercise 10.3

Herzberg's two-factor theory

Certain things about a job may make you dissatisfied. If the causes of this dissatisfaction are removed, this does not necessarily make the job more exciting. On the basis of research into job satisfaction that Herzberg and his associates carried out there seemed to be two sets of factors about a job that were of importance.

- **Hygiene or maintenance factors** are the things that can make you dissatisfied if they are not right. They could, for example, be the level of pay or the working conditions.

- **Motivators** are the positive things which make you feel that the job is worthwhile. They are things like the sense of achievement you get or the nature of the work itself.

Brigette, at Brightmouth HE College, may be in an environment where it is difficult to compete with the high level of maintenance factors that can be provided by a large organization like IOE, but the smaller organization with its closer contact with the users may be able to provide better motivators.

Exercise 10.4

Identify three incidents or times when you felt particularly pleased or happy about something to do with your work or study. Identify three occasions when you were particularly dissatisfied with your work or study. Compare your findings with those of your colleagues and try to identify any patterns.

The expectancy theory of motivation

Amanda and Brigette will need to be aware of how the day-to-day ups and downs of project development may affect motivation. A model of motivation developed by someone with the wonderful name of Vroom and his colleagues illustrates this. It identifies three influences on motivation:

- **expectancy** – the belief that working harder will lead to a better performance
- **instrumentality** – the belief that better performance will be rewarded
- **perceived value** – of the resulting reward.

Motivation will be high when all three factors are high. A zero level for any one of the factors can lead to a lack of motivation.

Imagine a situation where you are trying to get a software package supplied by a third party to work. If you come to the conclusion that you cannot get it to work because there is a bug in it, you will give up. No matter how hard you work you will not be able to do any better (zero expectancy).

If you are working on a package for a user and, although you think you can get it to work, you discover that the user has started employing an alternative package and no longer needs this one then you will probably feel you are wasting your time and give up (zero instrumentality).

Given that the users really do want the package, your reward in this set of circumstances may simply be a warm feeling that you have helped your colleagues and that they are grateful to you. If in fact, when the user employs the package all they do is complain and hold you responsible for any shortcomings, then you may avoid getting involved if they later ask for help implementing a different package (low perceived value of reward).

The Oldham–Hackman job characteristics model

Managers should try and group together the elements of the tasks that need to be carried out so that they form meaningful and satisfying assignments. Oldham and Hackman suggest that the satisfaction that a job gives is based on five factors. The first three factors make the job 'meaningful' to the person who is doing it:

- **skill variety** – the number of different skills that the job holder has the opportunity to exercise
- **task identity** – the degree to which your work and its results are identifiable as belonging to you
- **task significance** – the degree to which your job has an influence on others.

The other two factors are:

- **autonomy** – the discretion you have about the way that you do the job
- **feedback** – the information you get back about the results of your work.

Couger and Zawacki found that programmers in general rated their jobs lower on these factors than other professions while systems analysts and analyst-programmers rated them higher. Computer development people experienced about the same level of meaningfulness in their work as other, non-IT professionals, but had lower perceptions of the degree of responsibility and knowledge of results of their work.

Cheney found that in the programming environment, the degree to which programmers got feedback on their work and the degree to which they could contribute to decision making had positive influences on both productivity and job satisfaction, although 'consideration', which was 'the degree to which the leader develops a work climate of psychological support, mutual trust and respect, helpfulness and friendliness' rated as less important.

In practical terms, activities should be designed so that, where possible, staff follow the progress of a particular product and feel personally associated with it.

Methods of improving motivation

- **Setting specific goals** – these goals need to be demanding and yet acceptable to staff. Involving staff in the setting of goals helps to gain acceptance for them.
- **Providing feedback** – not only do goals have to be set but staff have to have regular feedback about how they are progressing.
- **Job design** – jobs can be altered to make them more interesting and give staff more feeling of responsibility.

Two measures are often used to enhance job design – job enlargement and job enrichment.

Job enlargement and job
enrichment are based on
the work of F. Herzberg.

- **Job enlargement** – the scope of the job is increased so that the member of staff carries out a wider range of activities. It is the opposite of increasing specialization. For example, a programmer in a maintenance group might be given responsibility for specifying minor amendments as well as carrying out the actual code changes. It is significant that Couger and Zawacki found that programmer/analysts had a higher degree of job satisfaction than programmers.
- **Job enrichment** – in this case the job is changed so that the holder carries out tasks that are normally done at a higher, managerial, level. Staff might be given responsibility for ordering raw materials, for scheduling their work or for quality control. With a programmer in a maintenance team, they might be given authority to accept requests for changes which involved less than five days' work without the need for their manager's approval.

Working in groups

Having discussed people as individuals, we move on to their place in groups. A key problem with major software projects is that they always involve working in groups, but as we have seen many people attracted to computer development find this difficult.

Formal groups can be subdivided into **command groups** which are the departmental groupings that are seen on organization hierarchy diagrams and which reflect the formal management structure and **task groups** set up to deal with specific tasks. These may call on people from different command groups and would typically be disbanded once the task has been completed.

Becoming a team

Simply throwing people together does not mean that they will immediately be able to work together as a team. Group feelings develop over a period of time. One suggestion is that teams go through five basic stages of development:

This classification is
associated with B. W.
Tuckman and M. A.
Jensen.

- **forming** – the members of the group get to know each other and try to set up some ground rules about behaviour
- **storming** – conflicts arise as various members of the group try to exert leadership and the group's methods of operation are being established
- **norming** – conflicts are largely settled and a feeling of group identity emerges
- **performing** – the emphasis is now on the tasks at hand
- **adjourning** – the group disbands.

Anneka Rice is a late 20th
century television
presenter in the United
Kingdom.

Where people are being put together into a team for the first time, then some specific team-building exercises may be undertaken. Some organizations send their management teams off on outward bound courses! Other organizations have set teams Anneka Rice-type challenges such as redecorating an old people's home. Without going to these lengths, Amanda and Brigette might try and think of some training activity which could assist in team building.

Valuable research has gone into looking at the best mix of personalities in a project team. Belbin studied teams working together on management games using various mixes of people. He initially tried putting all the people who were most able into one group. Surprisingly, these élite teams tended to do very badly – they argued a lot and as a result important tasks were often neglected.

Belbin came to the conclusion that teams needed a balance of different types of people.

R. Meredith Belbin *Management Teams: Why They Succeed or Fail*, Heinemann, 1981, is essential reading for those who have to work in teams.

- **The chair** – not necessarily a brilliant leader but they must be good at running meetings, being calm, strong but tolerant.
- **The plant** – someone who is essentially very good at generating ideas and potential solutions to problems.
- **The monitor-evaluator** – good at evaluating ideas and potential solutions and helping to select the best one.
- **The shaper** – rather a worrier, who helps to direct the team's attention to the important issues.
- **The team worker** – skilled at creating a good working environment, e.g. by 'jollying people along'.
- **The resource investigator** – adept at finding resources in terms of both physical resources and information.
- **The completer-finisher** – good at completing tasks.
- **The company worker** – a good team player who is willing to undertake less attractive tasks if they are needed for team success.

Belbin describes the good chair as: 'someone tolerant enough always to listen to others, but strong enough to reject their advice'.

A person can have elements of more than one type. On the other hand, about 30% of the people examined by Belbin could not be classified at all! To be a good team member you must be able to:

- time your interventions, e.g. not overwhelm the others in the team
- be flexible
- be restrained
- keep the common goals of the team in mind all the time.

Group performance

Are groups more effective than individuals working alone? Given the preference of many people attracted to software development for working on their own, this is an important question. Part of the answer lies in the type of task being undertaken. One way of categorizing group tasks is into:

- additive tasks
- compensatory tasks
- disjunctive tasks
- conjunctive tasks.

Additive tasks are where the efforts of each participant are added together to get the final result, e.g. a gang of people clearing snow. The people involved are interchangeable.

With additive tasks where individual effort is hard to distinguish there is a particular danger of the phenomenon of **social loafing.** Ringleman, a German scientist, noted in experiments involving rope-pulling that the more people working on the task, the less effort each individual is likely to put in.

Exercise 10.5

Social loafing is a problem that students often encounter when carrying out group assignments. What steps can participants in a group take to encourage team members to 'pull their weight' properly?

Code reviews could be seen as an example of a compensatory task.

With **compensatory tasks** the judgements of individual group members are pooled so that errors by some group members are compensated for by the inputs from others. An example of this would be where individual members of a group are asked to provide estimates of the effort needed to produce a piece of software and the results are then averaged. In these circumstances group work is generally more effective than the efforts of individuals.

With **disjunctive tasks** there is only one correct answer. The effectiveness of the group depends on:

- someone coming up with the right answer
- the others recognizing it as being correct.

In general the group can only be as good as its best member and no better. Group working may be justifiable in these circumstances as you do not necessarily know beforehand who the best member is for the problem under consideration. The group may have to deal with, in effect, a series of problems and different team members may have the expertise to deal with different questions.

Another example of a conjunctive task is co-writing a book on software project management.

Conjunctive tasks are where progress is governed by the rate of the slowest performer. Software production where different staff are responsible for different modules seems to be a prime example of this. The overall task is not completed until every participant has completed their part of the work. In this case co-operative attitudes are productive: the team members who are more advanced need to ensure the meeting of group objectives by assisting those who are behind.

Decision making

Before we can look more closely at the effectiveness with which groups can make decisions we need to look in general terms at the decision-making process.

Decisions can be categorized as being:

- **structured** – generally relatively simple, routine decisions where rules can be applied in a fairly straightforward way, or
- **unstructured** – more complex and often requiring a degree of creativity.

Another way of categorizing decisions is by the amount of **risk** and **uncertainty** that is involved.

Yet another distinction is between the rational-economic model and the satisficing model. The **rational-economic** model of decision making is the basis of classical economics. It predicts, for example, that a potential buyer will purchase the goods they require at the lowest possible price. This assumes that the decision maker has a complete knowledge of the state of the market. Imagine that you wanted to buy a personal computer and were determined that you bought it at the lowest possible price. You could spend days, weeks, or months phoning dealers.

Sensible people probably follow a **satisficing** approach and would look at a limited number of representative outlets to get a general idea of prices. Any potential loss of money through having missed an even lower offer would probably be offset by the savings in time, phonecalls, travel and so on. Some research has in fact found that organizations with the most far-reaching and comprehensive solution-seeking techniques are often the poorer financial performers!

Many of the techniques in Chapter 3 are attempts to make decision making more structured.

Many of the techniques in Chapter 3 on project selection are based on the rational-economic model.

Some mental obstacles to good decision making

In this book we have rightly stressed a structured, rational, approach to decision making. Many management decisions in the real world, however, made under pressure and based on incomplete information, are largely intuitive. We may have to accept the role of intuition but be aware that there are some mental obstacles to effective intuitive thinking.

The decision-making process may be influenced by the way that the problem it attempts to solve is **framed**. If the gains to be made by various courses of action are emphasized then the decision makers will tend to go for the least risky course of action. Where the dangers of not taking certain courses of action are emphasized then people will be more prepared to take risks.

Faulty heuristics – heuristics mean rules of thumb. Rules of thumb can be useful but there are dangers:

- they are based only on the information that is to hand which may in fact be misleading
- they are based on stereotypes, such as accepting a Welshman into a male voice choir without an audition because of the 'well-known fact' that the Welsh are a great singing nation.

Escalation of commitment – refers to the way that once you have made a decision it is increasingly difficult to alter it even in the face of evidence that it is wrong.

Information overload – it is actually possible to be presented with too much information so that you 'cannot see the wood for the trees'.

Group decision making

There may be occasions where Amanda at IOE, for instance, may want to consult with her whole project team about some problem. With a project team different specialists and points of view can be brought together. Decisions made by the team as a whole are more likely to be accepted than those that are imposed upon it. A different type of participatory decision-making might occur when end-users are consulted about the way a projected computer system is to operate.

Assuming that the meetings are genuinely collectively responsible and have been properly briefed, research would seem to show that groups are better at solving complex problems where the members of the group have complementary skills and expertise. The meeting allows them to communicate freely and to get ideas accepted.

ETHICS is a participative approach devised by Enid Mumford. See *Designing participatively* Manchester Business School, 1983.

Groups are less effective when dealing with poorly structured problems which need creative solutions. Brainstorming techniques have been developed to help groups in this situation but research seems to show that people often come up with more ideas individually than in a group. Where the aim is to get the involvement of end-users of a computer system, then prototyping and participatory approaches such as ETHICS might be adopted.

Obstacles to good group decision making

Amanda may find that group decision making has some disadvantages: it is time consuming; it can in some cases stir up conflicts within the group; and decisions may be unduly influenced by dominant members of the group.

Once established group norms can survive many changes of membership in the group.

Conflict may, in fact, be less than might be expected. Experiments have shown that people will modify their personal judgements to conform to **group norms**. These are common attitudes that are developed by a group over a period of time.

You might think that this would tend to moderate the more extreme views that some individuals in the group might hold. In fact, people in groups may make decisions that carry more risk than where they have to make the decision on their own. This is known as the **risky shift.**

Measures to reduce the disadvantages of group decision making

One method of making group decision making more efficient and effective is by training members to follow a set procedure. The **Delphi technique** endeavours to collate the judgements of a number of experts without actually bringing them face-to-face. Given a problem, the following procedure is carried out:

- the cooperation of a number of experts is enlisted
- the problem is presented to the experts
- the experts record their recommendations
- these recommendations are collated and reproduced
- the collected responses are recirculated
- the experts comment on the ideas of others and modify their recommendations if so moved
- if the leader detects a consensus then the process is stopped, otherwise the comments are recirculated to the experts.

The big problem with this approach used to be that although the experts could be geographically dispersed the process was time consuming.

What developments in information technology would be of particular assistance to use of the Delphi technique?

Exercise 10.6

Leadership

When Amanda and Brigette first took on project management responsibilities, one of their private anxieties may very well have been a fear that they would not have enough personal authority – that staff would not take them seriously. Leadership is generally taken to mean the ability to influence others in a group to act in a particular way in order to achieve group goals. A leader is not necessarily a good manager or *vice versa* as managers have other roles to play such as those of organizing, planning and controlling.

Authorities on this subject have found it very difficult to agree a list of the common characteristics of good leaders. It would, however, seem safe to say that they seem to have a greater need for power and achievement and have more self-control and more self-confidence than others.

Leadership is based on the idea of some kind of authority or power although leaders do not necessarily have much formal authority. This power may either come from the person's position (**position** power) or from person's individual qualities (**personal** power) or may be a mixture of the two. Position power has been further analyzed into:

- **coercive** power, the ability to force someone to do something by threatening punishment
- **connection** power, which is based on having access to those who have power
- **legitimate** power, which is based on a person's title conferring a special status
- **reward** power, where the holder can confer rewards on those who carry out tasks to their satisfaction.

These ideas are associated with the work of J. R. P. French and B. H. Raven.

Personal power, on the other hand, can be further analysed into:

- **expert** power, which comes from being the person who is able to do a specialized task
- **information** power, where the holder has access to information that others do not
- **referent** power, which is based on the personal attractiveness of the leader.

Exercise 10.7

What kinds of power (as defined above) would the following people have?

(a) An internal auditor looking at the payroll system at Brightmouth HE College.
(b) A consultant who is called in to advise International Office Equipment about ways of improving software development productivity.
(c) The principal of Brightmouth HE College who has told staff that they must accept a new contract or face the sack.
(d) Brigette in respect to the users of the college payroll system.
(e) Amanda in respect of the people in the project team developing the group maintenance accounts application.

Leadership styles

We have already suggested that Amanda and Brigette may be initially concerned about establishing their personal authority. Balanced against this is the need to involve the staff in some of the decision making in order to make the best use of expertise and to gain commitment. Amanda and Brigette will need to judge when they must be authoritative and insist on things and when they must be more flexible and tolerant. Amanda, for example, may decide to be very democratic when formulating plans, but once the plans have been agreed, to insist on a very disciplined execution of the plan. Brigette, on the other hand, may find at Brightmouth HE College that she alone has the technical expertise to make some decisions, but, once she has briefed people on what needs to be done, they expect to be left alone to get on with the job as they best see fit.

Attempts have been made to measure leadership styles on two axes: directive vs. permissive and autocratic vs. democratic:

This approach is associated with Rensis Likert.

- **directive autocrat** – makes decisions alone, close supervision of implementation
- **permissive autocrat** – makes decision alone, subordinates have latitude in implementation
- **directive democrat** – makes decisions participatively, close supervision of implementation
- **permissive democrat** – makes decisions participatively, subordinates have latitude in implementation.

It should be emphasized that there is no one best style of management – it depends on the situation.

Another axis on which there have been attempts to measure management qualities has been on the degree to which a manager is **task-oriented**, that is, the extent to which the execution of the task at hand is paramount, and the degree to which the manager is concerned about the people around them (**people orientation**). It is perhaps not surprising that subordinates appear to perform best with managers who score highly in both respects.

Work environments vary according to the amount of control that can be exerted over the work. Some jobs are routine and predictable (e.g. dealing with batched computer output). Others may be driven by outside factors (e.g. a help-desk) or are situations where future direction is uncertain (e.g. at the early stages of a feasibility study). Where there is a high degree of uncertainty subordinates will seek guidance from above and welcome a task-oriented management style. As control becomes easier, the task-oriented manager is likely to relax and to become more people-oriented and this will have good results. People-oriented managers are better where staff can control the work they do and know what to do without referring matters to their line managers. It is then argued that if control becomes even easier the people-oriented manager will be tempted to get involved in more task-centred questions and that this may have undesirable results.

Research findings also show that where team members are relatively inexperienced a task oriented approach is most effective. As group members mature, consideration for their personal needs and aspirations becomes more valued. Where maturity is very high then there is no need for a strong emphasis on either of these approaches.

What in your view would be the most appropriate management style when dealing with the following subordinates?

Exercise 10.8

(a) At Brightmouth HE College, a former member of the local authority who has dealt with the college payroll for several years and who has been employed by the college to set up and manage the new payroll section.

(b) At International Office Equipment, a new trainee analyst programmer who has just joined Amanda's group.

(c) A very experienced analyst programmer in their 40s, who was recruited into the software development department some time ago from the accounts department and who has been dealing with system support for the old maintenance accounting system that is now being revised.

Organizational structures

Formal versus informal structures

While organizational structures can have an enormous impact on the way a project is conducted, it is something which project leaders such as Amanda at IOE may find they can do little to change.

The formal structure is the one that is expressed in the staff hierarchy chart. It is basically concerned with **authority,** about who has which boss. It is backed by an informal structure of contacts and communication that grows up spontaneously between members of staff during the course of getting on with the job. When the unexpected happens it is often this system that comes into play. Over a period of time the advantages and disadvantages of different organizational structures tend to even out – the informal organization gets built up and staff find unofficial ways of getting around the obstacles posed by the formal structure.

Hierarchical approach

The 'traditional' management structure is based on the concept of the **hierarchy** – each member of staff has only one manager, while a manager will have responsibility for several members of staff. Authority flows from the top down through the structure. A traditional concern has been with the **span of control** – the number of people that a manager can effectively control.

Staff versus line

Staff in organizations can often be divided into **line** workers who actually produce the end product and support **staff** who carry out supporting roles. In some organizations which produce software for the market or as a component of a larger product which is sold, the software specialists might be seen as part of the line. In a financial organization, on the other hand, the information systems department would probably be seen as part of the support staff.

Departmentalization

In drawing up a structure, the question of **differentiation** crops up. This is the question of how the organization is to be departmentalized. This may be based on staff specialisms, product lines, categories of customer or geographical location, for example.

In the case of software development it is usually the case that either a **functional** or a **task-oriented** approach is used. With functional departmentalization, systems analysts may be put in a separate group to the programmers. The programmers would act as a pool from which resources may be drawn for particular tasks. With a task-oriented approach the programmers and systems analysts are grouped together in one project team. The project team may be gathered in order to implement a specific long-term project or may exist on a permanent basis to service the needs of a particular set of users.

One advantage of the functional approach is that it may lead to a more effective use of staff. Programmers can be allocated to jobs on a need basis and be released for other work when a particular task is completed. For instance, in a project team there are bound to be periods of greater and lesser coding activity and a programmer may find there are spells when they are under-utilized. The functional organization will also make it easier for the programmer to have a career which is technically oriented – there will probably be a career structure within the programming department which allows the programmer to rise without having to change their specialism. This type of organization should also encourage the interchange of new technical ideas between technical staff and the promulgation of company wide standards.

A disadvantage is that having two separate departments may lead to communication problems, especially if a programmer is unfamiliar with the application area. There will also be problems with program maintenance – here it is helpful to have programmers who have built up a familiarity with particular parts of the application software. Users may prefer the established project team approach because when they require new software features they will already have a group dedicated to their needs and will not find themselves in the position of always having to fight other departments for development resources. The project team structure tends to favour a pattern of career progression where programmers eventually become systems analysts.

Some organizations have attempted to get the best of both worlds by having a **matrix** structure. In this case the programmer would have two managers: a project leader who would give them day-to-day direction about the work in hand and a programming manager who would be concerned about such things as career development.

Centralized versus decentralized group structures

At the level of a project group a decentralized organization would mean that the group members would tend to make major decisions collectively and that there would be a large degree of free communication between group members. With the centralized approach the group would be broken down into sections, each of which would be directed by a leader who communicates on behalf of the section with other groups.

Decentralized groups, because of the time taken to debate things, tend to work more slowly. They are likely to be affected by the establishment of group norms and the influence of the risky shift which has already been described. However they are better at dealing with complex problems while the centralized group organization deals more effectively with simple problems.

The discussion of centralized versus decentralized groups assumes that software development work has to be done as a group. In fact, given the preference of many software developers for working on their own, an organization where each programmer works in isolation can be envisaged – indeed there are software houses that are based on people working at home.

Egoless programming

G. M. Weinberg *The Psychology of Computer Programming* Van Nostrand Reibold, 1971.

In the early days of computer development managers tended to think of the programmer as communing mysteriously with the machine. The tendency was for programmers to see programs as being an extension of themselves and to feel over-protective towards them. The effects of this on the maintainability of programs can be imagined. Gerald Weinberg made the then revolutionary suggestion that programmers and programming team leaders should read other people's programs. Programs would become in effect the common property of the programming group and programming would become 'egoless'. Peer code reviews are based on this idea Weinberg's ideal programming team was a decentralized group freely communicating within itself.

Chief programmer teams

Brooks' *Mythical Man-Month* has already been referred to. He was in charge of the huge team that created the operating system for the IBM 360 range.

The larger the decentralized group the slower it will get because of the increased communication. On really large time-critical projects a more formalized centralized structure is essential. Brooks pointed out the need for design consistency when producing a large complex system and how this may be difficult when there are a large number of people involved in producing a piece of software. One suggestion was to try and reduce the number of people actually creating software but to make these programmers as productive as possible by giving them as much support as possible.

The result of this train of thought was the **chief programmer** team. The chief programmer is the person who defines the specification, and designs codes, tests and documents the software. They are assisted by a **copilot**, with whom the chief programmer can discuss problems and who writes some code. They are supported by an **editor** to write up the documentation drafted by the chief programmer, a **program clerk** to maintain the actual code, and a **tester.** The general idea is that this team is under the control of a single unifying intellect.

The chief programmer concept was used on the influential *New York Times* data bank project where many aspects of structured programming were tried out. In this case each chief programmer managed a senior level programmer and a program librarian. Additional members could be added to the team on a temporary basis to deal with particular problems or tasks.

The problem with this kind of organization is getting hold of really outstanding programmers to carry out the chief programmer role. There is also the danger of information overload on the chief programmer. There is also the potential problem of staff dissatisfaction among those who are there simply to minister to the needs of the superstar chief programmers.

Controlled decentralized groups

This compromise structure has been suggested and seems to follow common industry practice. A project team is made of groups under the leadership of senior programmers. Within these groups there is free communication and a practice of reviewing each others' work. Communication with other groups is at senior programmer level while a project leader has overall authority.

Conclusion

Some of the important points that have been made in this chapter are:

- people may be motivated by money, but they are motivated by other things as well
- both staff selection and the identification of training needs should be done in an orderly, structured, way where requirements are clearly defined first
- thoughtful job design can increase staff motivation
- consideration should be given, when forming a new project team, to getting the right mix of people and to planning activities which will promote team building
- group working is more effective with some types of activity than others
- different styles of leadership are needed in different situations
- the people who need to communicate most with each other should be grouped together organizationally.

Further exercises

1. An organization has detected low job satisfaction in the following departments:

   - the system testing group
   - the computer applications help desk
   - VDU batch input.

   How could these jobs be redesigned to give more job satisfaction?

2. In Exercise 10.1, a job specification was requested.
   (a) Write a job holder profile of the sort of person who would be able to fulfil the specification in terms of qualities, qualifications, previous education and experience.
   (b) For each element in the job holder profile that you have produced in (a) above describe ways of finding out whether an applicant has met the requirement.

3. To what extent is the Belbin approach to balanced teams compatible with having chief programmer teams?

4. Four different mental obstacles to good decision making were identified in the text: framing, faulty heuristics, escalation of commitment and information overload. What steps do you think can be taken to reduce the danger of each of these?

5. In exercise 10.8, the management style most appropriate for each of three different situations was asked for. Go back and consider how you as a manager would respond to each of these three situations in terms of practical things to do or avoid.

Chapter 11

Software quality

OBJECTIVES

When you have completed this chapter you will be able to:

☐ explain the importance of software quality to software users and developers

☐ define the qualities of good software

☐ design methods of measuring the required qualities of software

☐ monitor the quality of the processes in a software project

☐ use external quality standards to ensure the quality of software acquired from an outside supplier

☐ develop systems using procedures that will increase their quality.

Introduction

In this chapter, we will start by giving some of the reasons why the quality of software is increasingly being seen as important. While quality is seen as a good thing, a problem is that if we are not careful the 'quality' of a system may remain a rather a vague concept. We therefore need to define precisely what we mean by quality in a particular set of circumstances. Defining quality by itself, however, is not enough – we need to be able to judge whether a system meets our quality requirements and this leads to the need for the measurement. This would be of particular concern to someone like Brigette at Brightmouth HE College when she is in the process of selecting a payroll package.

For someone like Amanda at IOE who is developing software, waiting until the system finally exists before measuring it would be leaving things rather late. She would want to be able to forecast the likely quality of the final system while it was still under development, and also to make sure that the methods which were used will produce that quality. This leads to a slightly different emphasis – rather than concentrating on the quality of the final system, a potential customer for software might try to check that the developers are using the best methods. The last part of this chapter describes some of the methods that are likely to be of help here.

The place of software quality in project planning

Quality will be of concern at all stages of project planning and execution, but will be of particular interest at the following points in the Step Wise framework (Figure 11.1).

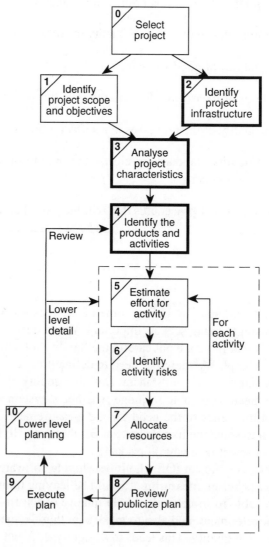

Figure 11.1 *The place of software quality in Step Wise.*

- **Step 2: Identify project infrastructure** – activity 2.2 within this step identifies installation standards and procedures. Some of these will almost certainly be about quality.
- **Step 3: Analyse project characteristics** – in activity 3.2 ('Analyse other project characteristics – including quality based ones') the system to be implemented will be examined to see if it has any special quality requirements. If, for example, it is extremely safety-critical then a whole range of additional activities may be added such as *n*-version development where a number of teams develop versions of the same software which are then run in parallel with the outputs being cross-checked for discrepancies.
- **Step 4: Identify the products and activities of the project** – it is at this point that the entry, exit and process requirements are identified for each activity. The nature of these requirements is described later in this chapter.
- **Step 8: Review and publicize plan** – at this stage the overall quality aspects of the project plan are reviewed.

The importance of software quality

We would expect quality to be a concern of all producers of goods and services. However, the special characteristics of software, and in particular its intangibility and complexity, make special demands.

- **Increasing criticality of software** – the final customer or user is naturally anxious about the general quality of software, especially its reliability. This is increasingly the case as organizations become more dependent on their computer systems and software is used more and more in areas which are safety critical, for example to control aircraft. This anxiety is bound to be increased by the intangible nature of the software.
- **The intangibility of software** – this makes it difficult to know that a particular task in a project has been completed satisfactorily. The products of these tasks can be made visible by demanding that the developer produce 'deliverables' that can be examined. However, visibility, by itself, is not enough as a 'deliverable' could be still be of inadequate quality.

  The intangibility of software presents particular problems - see Frederick P Brooks. 'No Silver Bullet: Essence and Accidents of Software Engineering'. *IEEE Computer* April 1987.

- **Accumulating errors during software development** – as computer system development is made up of a number of steps where the output from one step is the input to the next, the errors in the deliverables that are produced in the earlier steps will be added to those in the later steps to have an accumulating detrimental effect. In general, the later in a project that an error is found the more expensive it will be to fix. Yet it is not only the costs of correcting errors that must concern us. Because the number of errors in the system is unknown the debugging phases of a project are particularly difficult to control by management.

For these reasons quality management is an essential part of effective overall project management.

Defining software quality

Quality is a rather vague term and we need to define carefully what we mean by it. For any software system, there should be three specifications:

- a **functional specification** describing what the system is to do
- a **quality (or attribute) specification** concerned with how well the functions are to operate
- a **resource specification** concerned with how much is to be spent on the system.

Methodologies such as SSADM produce primarily functional requirements – so how are the required qualities of the proposed system, such its flexibility when change is needed, to be defined?

Exercise 11.1

At Brightmouth HE College, Brigette has to select the best off-the-shelf payroll package for the college. How should she go about this in a methodical manner?

One element of the approach could well be the identification of criteria against which payroll packages are to be judged. What might these criteria be and how could you check the extent to which candidate packages measure up against these criteria?

James A. McCall, 'An Introduction to Software Quality Metrics' In: J. D. Cooper & M. J. Fisher (eds.) *Software Quality Management* New York, Petrocelli, 1978.

There have been several attempts to identify specific product qualities that are appropriate to software. James A. McCall, for instance, grouped software quality into three sets of quality factors:

- product operation qualities
- product revision qualities
- product transition qualities.

The ISO 9126 standard presents an alternative set.

Note that the definitions below are those given by McCall, but the reader will come across others. In particular circumstances, additional qualities may be of interest.

Product operation quality factors

- **Correctness** – extent to which a program satisfies its specifications and fulfils the user's objectives.
- **Reliability** – extent to which a program can be expected to perform its intended function with required precision.
- **Efficiency** – the amounts of computer resources required by the software.
- **Integrity** – extent to which access to software or data by unauthorized persons can be controlled.

- **Usability** – effort required to learn, operate, prepare input and interpret output.

Product revision quality factors

- **Maintainability** – effort required to locate and fix an error in an operational program.
- **Testability** – effort required to test a program to ensure it performs its intended function.
- **Flexibility** – effort required to modify an operational program.

Product transition quality factors

- **Portability** – effort required to transfer a program from one hardware configuration and/or software system environment to another.
- **Reusability** – extent to which a program can be used in other applications.
- **Interoperability** – effort required to couple one system to another.

The relationship between any two quality factors may be:

- **indifferent** – the presence of one quality has no effect on the other
- **complementary** – the presence of one quality would suggest the presence of the other
- **conflicting** – the presence of one quality is likely to reduce the presence of the other.

Look at McCall's list of quality factors. Identify examples of pairs that are (a) indifferent, (b) complementary, and (c) conflicting.

Exercise 11.2

McCall's software quality factors reflect the external view of software that users would have. For instance, usability would be a key concern of users. These quality factors have to be translated into internal factors of which the developers would be aware – **software quality criteria** (Table 11.1).

The same software quality criteria often appear for more than one software quality factor. What is the significance of this?

Exercise 11.3

Defining quality is not enough. If we are to judge whether a system meets our requirements we need to be able to measure its qualities. For each criterion, one or more measures have to be invented which assess the degree to which the quality is present.

Table 11.1 *Software quality criteria*

The same software quality criterion may apply to more than one of the software quality factors.

Quality factor	Software quality criteria
Correctness	traceability, consistency, completeness
Reliability	error tolerance, consistency, accuracy, simplicity
Efficiency	execution efficiency, storage efficiency
Integrity	access control, access audit
Usability	operability, training, communicativeness, input/output volume, input/output rate
Maintainability	consistency, simplicity, conciseness, modularity, self-descriptiveness
Testability	simplicity, modularity, instrumentation, self-descriptiveness
Flexibility	modularity, generality, expandability, self-descriptiveness
Portability	modularity, self-descriptiveness, machine independence, software system independence
Reusability	generality, modularity, software system independence, machine independence, self-descriptiveness
Interoperability	modularity, communications commonality, data commonality

Measures may be:
- **relative quantity measures** where an attempt is made to quantify the presence of the quality, or
- **binary measures** where the quality is deemed either to be present or not present.

Some writers use the term metric interchangeably with measure. Software measurement specialists would, however, maintain that there is a technical difference between the two terms.

Any good relative measure must be able to relate the number of units to the maximum possible in the circumstances. The maximum number of faults in a program, for example, is going to be related to the size of the program so a measure of 'faults per thousand lines of code' is more helpful than 'total faults in a program' as a means of judging the quality of a program.

Trying to find measures for a particular quality helps to clarify ideas about what that quality really is. What is being asked is, in effect, 'how do we know when we have been successful?' An answer to this is essential if the quality objectives are to be communicated to a large number of people.

The measures may be **direct** where we can measure the quality directly or they can be **indirect** where the thing being measured is not the quality itself but an indicator of the degree to which the quality is present. By identifying measures the management are setting targets for project team members so care has to be taken that an improvement in the measured quality is always going to be valid. For example, the number of errors found in program inspections could be counted. This count could, of course, be improved by allowing more errors to go through to the inspection stage rather than eradicating them earlier – which is not quite the point!

In general, the user of software would be concerned with measuring what McCall called **quality factors** while the developers would be concerned with **quality criteria**.

The following should be laid down for each quality:

- **scale** – the unit of measurement
- **test** – the practical test of the extent to which the attribute quality exists
- **worst** – the worst acceptable value
- **plan** – the value that it is planned to achieve
- **best** – the best value that appears to be feasible (the 'state of the art' limit); this would be a level that is known to have been achieved elsewhere
- **now** – the value that applies currently.

In order to derive these **quality specifications** it may be necessary to break down a quality criterion into further subcriteria. Take the quality criterion 'communicativeness' which contributes to the quality factor 'usability'. One aspect of this might be the ease of understanding of the menu structure, i.e. how easy it is to find the command to carry out some function. Another aspect of communicativeness would be how informative the error messages were, while yet another would be the clarity of the 'help' pages.

Suggest quality specifications for a word processing package. Give particular attention to the way that practical tests of these attributes could be conducted.   **Exercise 11.4**

Practical software quality measures

Below are some ways that might be used to measure particular qualities. It is emphasized that the measures are illustrations only and should certainly not be treated as definitive! Each project will need to devise its own measures to meet its own specific needs. The measures described relate to the final software products of a project.

Reliability

This might be measured in terms of:

- **availability** – the percentage of a particular time interval that a system is usable
- **mean time between failures** – the total service time divided by the number of failures
- **failure on demand** – the probability that a system will not be available at the time required or the probability that a transaction will fail
- **support activity** – the number of fault reports that are generated.

Exercise 11.5

IOE Maintenance Group Accounts system has been installed, and is normally available to users from 8.00 am until 6.00 pm from Monday to Friday. Over a four-week period the system was unavailable for one whole day because of problems with a disc drive and was not available on two other days until 10.00 in the morning because of problems with overnight batch processing runs.

What were the availability and the mean time between failures of the service?

Maintainability can be seen from two different perspectives. The user will be concerned with the elapsed time between a fault being detected and it being corrected, while the programming management will be concerned about the effort involved.

Maintainability

This is closely related to flexibility, the ease with which the software can be modified. The main difference is that before an amendment can be made, the fault has to be diagnosed first. Maintainability can therefore be seen as flexibility plus a new quality **diagnosability** which might be defined as the average amount of time needed to diagnose a fault.

Extendibility

This is a component of the more general quality of flexibility. It can be defined as the productivity needed to incorporate a new feature into an existing system expressed as a percentage of the normal productivity when developing the software from scratch.

Worked example

The original IOE maintenance billing system comprised 5000 SLOC and took 400 work-days to implement. An amendment to the core system caused by the introduction of group accounts has lead to 100 SLOC being added which took 20 work-days to implement, thus:

> productivity for the original system
> > $= 5000/400$
> > $= 12·5$ SLOC/staff day

> productivity for the amendment
> > $= 100/20$
> > $= 5$ SLOC/staff day

> extendibility
> > $= 5/12·5 \times 100$
> > $= 40\%$

Product versus process quality management

To someone like Amanda at IOE, who is developing software, being able to measure the quality of the system only when it is completed would not be very satisfactory. They would want to be able to judge, while they were developing it, what the quality of the final system was likely to be.

The measurements described above can only be taken once the system is operational. It may then be too late to do anything to remedy problems. What would be more helpful would be measurements and other checks taken during development that could help control what the final system will be like – hence the attention given to the quality of the processes that create products.

The system development process is made up of a number of activities that are linked together so that the output from one activity is the input to the next (Figure 11.2). Thus program testing will depend on there being a program to test which will be the deliverable from the program coding stage. Errors can enter the process at any stage. They can either be introduced because of a defect in the way a process is carried out, as when a programmer makes a mistake in the logic of their program, or because information has not been passed clearly and unambiguously between stages.

This model should already be very familiar from the discussion of precedence networks where the dependence of one or more activities on the completion of one or more preceding activities is taken into account.

Errors that creep in at the early stages are more expensive to correct at later stages for the following reasons.

- The later the error is found the more rework at more stages of development will be needed. If an error in the specification is found at the testing stage, then this will mean rework at all the stages between specification and testing.
- The general tendency is for each successive stage of development to be more detailed and less able to absorb change.

Errors should therefore be eradicated by careful examination of the deliverables of each stage before they are passed on to the next. To do this, the following **process requirements** should be specified for each activity.

- **Entry requirements** which have to be in place before an activity can start. An example would be that a comprehensive set of test data and expected results be prepared and approved before program testing can commence.
- **Implementation requirements** which define how the process is to be conducted. In the testing phase, for example, it may be laid down that whenever an error is found and corrected, all test runs must be repeated, even those that have previously been found to run correctly.
- **Exit requirements** which have to be fulfilled before an activity is deemed to have been completed. For example, for the testing phase to be recognized as being completed, all tests will have to have been run successfully with no outstanding errors.

These requirements may be laid out in installation standards, or a *Software Quality Plan* may be drawn up for the specific project if it is a major one.

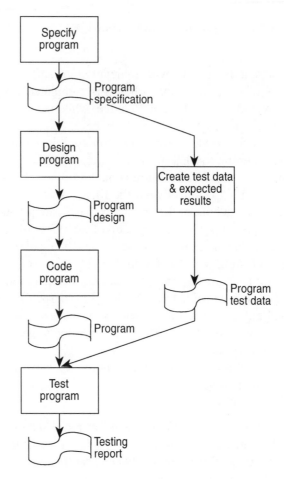

Figure 11.2 *An example of the sequence of processes and deliverables.*

Exercise 11.6

In what cases might the entry conditions for one activity be different from the exit conditions for another activity that immediately precedes it?

Exercise 11.7

Amanda at IOE already has a quality manual that she can consult. Brigette at Brightmouth HE College has to specify her own entry and exit requirements. What might she specify as the entry and exit requirements for the process **code program** shown in Figure 11.2?

External standards

BS EN ISO 9001

At IOE, a decision might have been made to use an outside contractor to produce the maintenance group accounts subsystem rather than develop the software in-house. As a client using the services of an outside contractor they would be concerned that the contractor is following the best quality practices. It is now common to include in contracts terms covering the types of technique that a contractor will use. Various national and international standards bodies, including the British Standards Institution (BSI), have inevitably got involved in the creation of standards for quality management systems. The British standard is now called BS EN ISO 9001:1994, which is identical to the international standard, ISO 9001:1994. The British standard until recently was called BS 5750.

The Civil Service practice is, for instance, to demand that contractors use SSADM, the standard systems analysis and design method, and PRINCE, the project control standard when information systems are being developed.

Standards such as ISO 9000 series try to ensure that a monitoring and control system to check quality is in place. They are concerned with the certification of the development process, not of the end-product as in the case of crash helmets and electrical appliances with their familiar kite-marks. The ISO 9000 series govern quality systems in general terms and not just those in the software development environment.

There has been some controversy over the value of these standards. Stephen Halliday, writing in *The Observer,* had misgivings that these standards are taken by many customers to imply that the final product is of a certified standard although as Halliday says 'It has nothing to do with the quality of the product going out of the gate. You set down your own specifications and just have to maintain them, however low they may be'. In the past, misgivings have also related to the lack of control over who can set themselves up as a BS 5750 auditor, but in the case of IT, this has been resolved. Finally there has been a concern that a preoccupation with certification might distract attention from the real problems of producing quality products.

Putting aside these reservations, let us examine how the standard works. A primary task is to identify those things which are to be the subject of quality requirements. Having defined the requirements, a system must be put in place which checks that the requirements are being fulfilled and that corrective action is being taken where necessary.

An overview of BS EN ISO 9001 QMS requirements

In order for a quality management system (QMS) to meet the standard it has to conform to certain requirements which are summarized below.

(a) The management must define and document the policy concerning quality and must ensure that this policy is communicated to all levels of the organization.

(b) All quality control procedures must be documented.

Remember that these standards were originally designed for all kinds of production – not just software development.

(c) All contracts to supply goods or services should contain mutually agreed requirements that the developer is capable of delivering.

(d) There should be procedures to control and verify the design of the system to be supplied so that it meets the requirements agreed with the customer.

(e) There should be procedures to approve design and other documentation.

(f) Where components of the system to be supplied to the client are obtained from third parties there must be procedures to ensure, check and maintain the quality of these components.

(g) Individual products should be identifiable as should their components.

(h) The process by which the final product is created should be planned and monitored.

(i) Inspection and testing should take place during the development phase, at its completion and before delivery. Tests and inspections should also be carried out on components obtained from third parties.

(j) The equipment used in the production process itself should be properly controlled with respect to quality.

(k) The testing status of all components and systems should be clearly recorded at all times.

(l) Care must be taken to ensure that items which are known to be defective are not inadvertently used.

(m) When a defect is detected, measures must be undertaken to remove the defective part and to ensure that the defect does not occur again.

(n) Satisfactory procedures must be in place to deal with correct handling, storage, packaging and delivery of the product.

(o) Sufficient records must be maintained to demonstrate that the quality system is working satisfactorily.

(p) The software quality management system should be audited on a regular basis.

(q) Servicing and support activities must be subject to the quality management system.

(r) The developer must establish appropriate statistical techniques to verify the acceptability of the final product.

Exercise 11.8   Identify specific instances in a software development environment where the requirements about the control of equipment (j), the recording of the testing status of all components (k), and the correct handling, storage, packaging and delivery of the product (m) would be relevant. What procedures would apply in a software environment in relation to these requirements?

Bearing in mind the criticisms of BS EN ISO 9001 that have been mentioned, what precautionary steps could a project manger take where some work of which the quality is important is to be contracted out?

Exercise 11.9

TickIT

The ISO 9000 standards refer to quality management systems in general but the DTI have formulated the TickIT standards which give an interpretation of these standards which applies specifically to software development. This includes such requirements as:

However, some parts do refer to software, e.g. ISO 9000-3.

- a detailed development plan is required before development is embarked upon
- change control procedures should be used at all stages of development
- design reviews should take place
- the suitability of the design methodology should be reviewed
- progress should be reviewed on a systematic basis
- it should be possible to trace back the features of software design to specifications and requirements
- designs should be properly documented
- suitable test plans, specifications and records should be produced
- a code of practice should be in place which governs the way the software is developed.

The code of practice should include the requirements that:

- the design should be broken down into levels, each with identifiable inputs and outputs
- software should be organized into modules
- a module should normally perform a single function or a set of related functions
- a plain language description should exist for each module.

A TickIT auditor can certify that a particular organization conforms to these standards. This is called **certification** . The bodies doing this certification have to be **accredited** by the National Council for Certification Bodies (NACCB) on behalf of the DTI. The scheme is now administered by DISC, a part of the British Standards Institution.

Capability process models

Rather than just checking that a system is in place to detect faults, a customer may wish to check that a supplier is using software development methods and tools which are likely to produce good quality software. Even the TickIT

See H. S. Watts, Managing the Software Process, Addison-Wesley, New York, 1989

recommendations may be regarded as fairly minimal. A customer may feel more confident, for instance, if they know that their software supplier is using structured methods. In the United States, an influential **capability process model** has been developed at the Software Engineering Institute. This attempts to place organizations producing software at one of five levels of process maturity which indicate the sophistication and quality of their software production practices. These levels are defined as follows.

One survey showed that of the organizations that have been assessed in the USA, 81% were placed at level 1, 12% at level 2 and 7% at level 3. No organizations were placed at level 4 or 5. It has been suggested that some individual project teams within some organizations may be at a higher level, e.g. the IBM team dealing with the on-board space shuttle software.

- **Level 1: Initial** – the procedures followed tend to be haphazard. Some projects may be successful, but this tends to be because of the skills of particular individuals including project managers. The is no level 0 and so any organization would be at this level by default.
- **Level 2: Repeatable** – organizations at this level will have basic project management procedures in place. However, the way individual tasks are carried out will depend largely on the person doing it.
- **Level 3: Defined** – the organization has defined the way that each task in the software development life cycle should be done.
- **Level 4: Managed** – the products and processes involved in software development are subject to measurement and control.
- **Level 5: Optimizing** – improvement in procedures can be designed and implemented using the data gathered from the measurement process.

The assessment is done by a team of assessors coming into the organization and interviewing key staff about their practices using a standard questionnaire to capture the information. A key objective is not just to assess, but to recommend specific actions to bring the organization up to a higher level.

Assessing software products

The concern in the last two sections has been with the assessment of organizations and the processes that they use to produce software, but many purchasers of software, including project managers contemplating the purchase of software tools may be more directly worried about the quality of the software product itself. Compilers for some programming languages, for example, are subject to certification. In addition, a recent standard, ISO 9126, attempts to address product quality. Much progress, however, has still to be made in this area.

Techniques to help enhance software quality

So far in this chapter we have looked at the steps a customer might take to ensure the quality of software produced by an outside supplier. We now need to look at what techniques a project team might wish to employ to help them improve their own software development processes. Three main themes emerge.

- **Increasing visibility** – a landmark in this movement towards making the software development process more visible was the advocacy by the American software guru, Gerald Weinberg, of 'egoless programming'. Weinberg encouraged the simple practice of programmers looking at each other's code.

  Gerald Weinberg, *The Psychology of Computer Programming* Van Nostrand Reinhold, 1971.

- **Procedural structure** – at first programmers were more or less left to get on with writing the programs although there might be some general guidelines. Over the years there has been the growth of methodologies where every process in the software development cycle has carefully laid down steps.
- **Checking intermediate stages** – it seems inherent in human nature to push forward quickly with the development of any engineered object until a 'working' model, however imperfect, has been produced which can then be 'debugged'. One of the elements of the move towards quality practices has been to put emphasis on checking the correctness of work at its earlier, conceptual, stages.

  The creation of an early working model of a system may still be useful as the creation of prototypes shows.

We are now going to look at some specific techniques in more detail. The push towards more visibility has been dominated by the increasing use of walkthroughs, inspections and reviews. The movement towards more procedural structure inevitably leads to discussion of structured programming techniques and to its later manifestation in the ideas of 'clean-room' software development.

The interest in the dramatic improvements made by the Japanese in product quality has led to much discussion of the quality techniques they have adopted such as the use of quality circles and these will be looked at briefly. Some of these ideas are variations on the theme of inspection and clean-room development, but they are seen from a slightly different angle.

Inspections

The principle of inspection can be extended to any document that is produced at any stage of the development process. For instance, test data needs to be reviewed – its production is usually not a high profile task even though errors can get through to operational running because of its poor quality.

The underlying procedure with inspections is that when a piece of work is completed, copies of the work are distributed to co-workers who then spend some time going through the work noting any defects. A meeting is then held where the work is discussed and a list of defects requiring rework is produced. The work to be examined could be, for instance, a program listing that is free of compilation errors.

The main problem is maintaining the commitment of participants to a thorough examination of the work they have been distributed with after the novelty value of reviews has worn off a little.

Our own experience of using this technique has been that:

- it is a very effective way of removing superficial errors from a piece of work
- it motivates the programmer to produce a better structured and self-explanatory program because they know that other people will be criticizing it

- it helps spread good programming practices as the participants discuss the advantages and disadvantages of specific pieces of code
- it can enhance team spirit.

The item will usually be reviewed by colleagues who are involved in the same area of work, so that a programmer, for example, will have their work reviewed by fellow programmers. However, to reduce the problems of incorrect communication between different stages there may be representatives from the stages that precede and follow the one which produced the work under review.

IBM have put the review process on a much more structured and formal basis, and have produced statistics to show its effectiveness. A Fagan inspection (named after the IBM employee who pioneered the technique) is a much more formalized procedure which is led, not by the author of the work, but by a specially trained 'moderator'.

See M. E. Fagan's article 'Design and code inspections to reduce errors in program development' in *IBM Systems Journal* 15(3).

The general principles behind the Fagan method

- Inspections are carried out on all major deliverables.
- All types of defect are noted – not just logic or function errors.
- Inspections can be carried out by colleagues at all levels except the very top.
- Inspections are carried out using a predefined set of steps.
- Inspection meetings do not last for more than two hours.
- The inspection is lead by a **moderator** who has had specific training in the technique.
- The other participants have defined roles. For example, one person will act as a **recorder** and note all defects found and another will act as **reader** and take the other participants through the document under inspection.
- Checklists are used to assist the fault-finding process.
- Material is inspected at an optimal rate of about 100 lines an hour.
- Statistics are maintained so that the effectiveness of the inspection process can be monitored.

Exercise 11.10

This exercise needs to be done in groups. Select for review a small program that has been written by one of your colleagues.

Choose a moderator, a reader and a recorder for the group. Spend about 20 minutes examining listings of the program individually and then come together to review the code jointly.

Structured programming and clean-room software development

One of the people most closely associated with the origins of structured programming is Dijkstra. In the late 1960s, software was seen to be getting more complex while the capacity of the human mind to hold detail remained limited. It was also realized that it was impossible to test any substantial piece of software completely – there were just too many possible combinations of inputs. The most that testing could do was prove the presence of errors, not their absence. It was suggested by Dijkstra and others that, because of this, the only way that we could reassure ourselves about the correctness of software was by actually looking at the code.

The way to deal with complex systems, it was contended, was to break them down into components which were of a size for the human mind to comprehend. For a large system there would be a hierarchy of components and sub-components. For this decomposition to work properly, each component would have to be self-contained with only one entry and exit point.

The ideas of structured programming have been further developed into the ideas of clean-room software development by people such as Harlan Mills of IBM. With this type of development there are three separate teams:

- **a specification team** which obtains the user requirements and also a **usage profile** estimating the volume of use for each feature in the system
- **a development team** which develops the code but which does no machine testing of the program code produced
- **a certification team** which carries out testing.

Any system is produced in increments each of which should be capable of actual operation by the end user. The development team does no debugging; instead, all software has to be verified by them using mathematical techniques. The argument is that software which is constructed by throwing up a crude program which then has test data thrown at it and a series of hit-and-miss amendments made to it until it works is bound to be unreliable.

The certification team carry out the testing which is continued until a statistical model shows that the failure intensity has been reduced to an acceptable level.

Formal methods

In the section above on clean-room development, the use of mathematical verification techniques was mentioned. These techniques use unambiguous, mathematically-based, specification languages of which Z and VDM are examples. They are used to define **pre-conditions** and **post-conditions** for each procedure. Pre-conditions define the allowable states, before processing, of the various items of data that a procedure is to work upon. The post-conditions define the state of those data items after the procedure has been executed. Because the mathematical notation is precise, a specification expressed in this way should be unambiguous. It should also be possible to prove mathematically

E. W. Dijkstra in 1968 wrote a letter to a learned computing journal which was entitled 'Go To Statement Considered Harmful'. This unfortunately led to the common idea that structured programming was simply about not using GO TOs.

David Rann, John Turner and Jenny Whitworth, *Z: A Beginner's Guide* in this series describes one of these languages.

(in much the same way that at school you learnt to prove Pythagoras' theorem) that a particular algorithm will work on the data defined by the pre-conditions in such a way as to produce the post-conditions. It needs hardly be said that in many cases this will be more easily said than done. In fact structured programming can be seen as an attempt to analyse a program structure into small, self-contained, procedures that will be amenable to this formal verification approach.

Software quality circles

Much interest has been shown in Japanese software quality practices. The aim of the 'Japanese' approach is to examine and modify the activities in the development process in order to reduce the number of errors that they have in their end-products. Testing and even techniques such as Fagan inspections can assist the removal of errors – but the same types of error may occur again and again in successive products created by a specific type of process. By uncovering the source of errors, this repetition can be eliminated. To do this needs the involvement of all the staff in identifying the causes of errors.

Staff are involved in the identification of sources of errors through the formation of **quality circles**. These can be set up in all departments of an organization including those producing software where they are known as software quality circles (SWQC).

A quality circle is a group of four to ten volunteers working in the same area who meet for, say, an hour a week to identify, analyse and solve their work-related problems. One of their number is the group leader and there is likely to be an outsider, a **facilitator**, who can advise on procedural matters. In order to make the quality circle work effectively training needs to be given.

Problem solving by quality circles

The steps that the circle go through in solving problems are:

(a) identify a list of problems
(b) select one problem to solve
(c) clarify the problem
(d) identify and evaluate the causes
(e) identify and evaluate the solutions
(f) decide on a solution
(g) develop an implementation plan
(h) present the plan to management
(i) implement the plan
(j) monitor the plan
(k) consider wider applicability of solution
(l) restart from (b).

Exercise 11.11.

What are the important differences between a quality circle and a review group?

A number of specific techniques characterize quality circles, the most prominent of which is **brainstorming.** A subject or problem for which ideas are needed is nominated and the group then suggest as many ideas as possible. As ideas are suggested they are written down on a flip-chart. Other members of the group do not, at this stage, make any comments or criticisms of any suggestions made. At the end of the session the group go through the ideas listed and put similar ideas together and combine overlapping ideas. Typically this technique would be used to generate the initial list of problems or a list of possible solutions to a particular problem.

People may feel inhibited from contributing ideas to a group and brainstorming can help to reduce this inhibition.

Also associated with quality circles is the compilation of **most probable error lists.** For example, at IOE, Amanda may find that the maintenance group accounts project is being delayed because of errors in the requirements specifications. The project team could be assembled and spend some time producing a list of the most common types of error that occur in requirements specifications. This is then used to identify measures which can reduce the occurrence of each type of error. They might suggest, for instance, that test cases should be produced at the same time as the requirements specification and that these test cases should be dry run at an inspection. Another result might be a checklist for use when conducting inspections of requirement specifications.

Exercise 11.12

This exercise has to be carried out as a group. Select a particular area of common experience where problems have arisen in the past. For example if you are a group of students you could use the course or module you are undertaking, or a recent assignment that you have just completed. By means of a brainstorming session, identify all the problems that the participants have had. At the end of the brainstorming session, group together similar problems and combine overlapping ones.

The effectiveness of quality circles

For quality circles to work there must be full support for them at all levels of management. First-line management may feel threatened by them as they may appear to undermine their authority. After all, problem solving is one of their main tasks. The proponents of quality circles see them as a way of giving management more time for planning and development. Any manager will have to devote time to 'fire-fighting' dealing with ad hoc crises, and this can detract from longer term activities which will be able to improve the effectiveness of the organization.

The problems needing crisis management are often technical in nature. Quality circles can take pressure off management by encouraging problem solving activity at lower levels of the organization and by preventing crises occurring as their roots are tackled on a systematic basis.

Conclusions

Important points to remember about software quality include the following.

- Quality by itself is a vague concept and practical quality requirements have to be carefully defined.
- There have to be practical ways of testing for the relative presence or absence of a quality.
- Most of the qualities that are apparent to the users of software can only be tested for when the system is completed.
- Ways of checking during development what the quality of the final system is likely to be are therefore needed.
- Some quality enhancing techniques concentrate on testing the products of the development process while others try and evaluate the quality of the development processes used.

Further exercises

1. McCall suggests that simplicity, modularity, instrumentation and self-descriptiveness are software quality criteria, i.e. internal characteristics that promote the external quality of testability.

    (a) Explain what is meant by each of the four criteria above.
    (b) Describe possible measures for each of the criteria.
    (c) Describe practical ways in which the measures could be assessed.

2. Discuss how meaningful the following measurements are.

    (a) The number of error messages produced on the first compilation of a program.
    (b) The average effort to implement changes requested by users to a system.
    (c) The percentage of lines in program listings that are comments.
    (d) The number of pages in a requirements document.

3. What might the entry, implementation and exit requirements be for the process *design program structure*?

4. What ISO 9000/BS 5750 requirements have a bearing on the need for an effective configuration management system?

Chapter 12

Planning for small projects

OBJECTIVES

When you have completed this chapter you will be able to:

- [ ] avoid some of the pitfalls that occur with students projects

- [ ] produce an initial planning document for a small, IT-related project

- [ ] plan further reading on software planning and control.

Introduction

Many of the readers of this book are students who will have to plan their own projects that they will have to carry out as part of their course of studies. In some cases, these will be undertaken for an external client. In other cases, a piece of software, perhaps of an experimental nature, may be produced where there is no identifiable client, apart from a project tutor. Although the projects that are carried out for 'real' clients are more convincing tests of the student, they are in many ways more risky than the purely academic ones.

One of the problems that students face when planning projects is applying techniques that they may have learnt on software project planning courses and which were designed for much larger-scale projects than their own. In this chapter we present an outline of how students should set out their plans. It is based on a structure that we have recommended to our own students over the years. It contrasts with the material in Appendix A on PRINCE which is designed to support the management of large projects. The overall Step Wise approach is still applicable to the planning of your project – but the techniques used at the different steps of the planning process will need to be carefully chosen as appropriate to the scaled-down application

Some problems with student projects

Note that here we are
discussing a practical
application of the risk
identification and
avoidance policies
described in Chapter 8.

There are some problems or risks that seem particularly to affect student projects.

Use of unfamiliar tools

Very often a student will be using a new software tool (for example, an application builder in a Windows environment) that they have not used before. Clearly, time will need to be allocated in the project plan to learning the package. When trying to formulate plans, because of their ignorance of the software tool, the student may have difficulties estimating how long tasks will take. There will also be risks that unexpected technical problems may halt or delay the project's progress. A student may have other things on their mind, such as examinations, in the period leading up to the start of the project, but the risks of technical problems will be reduced if they are able to try out the software tools at this point.

Uncertain design requirements

Many project assignments require the student to demonstrate a careful analysis and design process and then to build at least part of the application. Until the analysis has been done, it may be difficult to plan exactly how design and software building is to be executed.

Two points may be worth making here. The first is that the structure of the project is going to be dictated to a large extent by the amount of time that is available.

Say that you have 10 weeks in which to carry out a project that involves analysing user requirements, designing a new system and building it. It is not a bad idea to start planning on the basis of doing the project in 9 weeks in order to allow for slippage. Working backwards from the end, of those 9 weeks, it might be decided that the last 2 should be reserved for testing and evaluation. This may seem an excessive amount of time to some students, but with most assessment schemes your project is likely to gain really good marks if you can demonstrate that it is of good quality and that you have evaluated it carefully. You might decide to allocate proportions of the remaining first 7 weeks to analysis, design and system building so that you get the following skeleton schedule:

- **weeks 1–2** – analysis
- **week 3** – design
- **weeks 4–7** – system building
- **weeks 8–9** – testing and evaluation
- **week 10** – contingency.

The actual breakdown will vary depending on the circumstances of your particular project. A very well structured problem area may mean that you can spend less time on analysis, while, on the other hand, if you know the software building tools that you are going to use, you may decide to reduce the time for analysis in favour of devoting more effort to a more sophisticated operator interface.

The second point, and one that we have already emphasized, is that you should be prepared to delay planning a particular phase of a project in detail until more information becomes available. When you have completed your analysis phase at the end of the second week in the above plan, you should be in a much better position to plan the design and system building phases in more detail – you will know, for example, what the main transactions are going to be in an information systems application. You should also be in a position to cut down the scope of the application to fit the time available to build it!

In Chapter 6 we discussed the practice of design to cost, i.e. designing the system to fit the resources available to build it.

Incomplete systems

Sometimes students simply run out of time and so do not have a working system to demonstrate. In the case of student projects, it is a good idea to try and arrange things so that you have something, even if it is not much, to demonstrate from a relatively early stage of the project. In the skeleton plan described above it would not be a bad idea to have certain features of the application up and running after the first week or so of system building. Having got these 'in the bag' so to speak, you can go on and add new functions or features, secure in the knowledge that at any point you will have at least something to demonstrate. You may find that you can even break the work down into increments to give you something similar to the following:

In Chapter 4 we discussed the incremental approach which is relevant here.

- **weeks 1–2** – analysis
- **week 3** – design increment 1
- **week 4** – build/test increment 1
- **week 5** – design increment 2
- **week 6** – build/test increment 2
- **week 7** – design increment 3
- **week 8** – build/test increment 3
- **week 9** – evaluate complete system
- **week 10** – writing up/contingency.

If something went wrong so that increment 3 could not be completed on time, you would still have increments 1 and 2 to demonstrate and in your project evaluation report you could describe your proposed design for increment 3.

In the skeleton plan above we have allocated week 10 for writing up. As a general rule, it is best to try and write up as much of your project as you can as you go along. It will not save you any time if you leave it and you will be able to write more clearly and fully about your analysis process, for example, while it is still clear in your mind. Pausing to do this writing should also help you to reflect on what you are doing and help you consider coolly what needs to be done next.

Lack of commitment from clients

In most cases, where a project is for an external client, the student will not be being paid. The advantage of this is that the outside organization may be attracted to the chance of having a free resource and take on a project for a student about whose capabilities they know little or nothing. The danger is that because the resource is free, there may be little commitment from the client to the project. If they had to pay for the work, they would think more carefully about whether they really needed the work before agreeing to the project and they would pay attention to getting value for money.

There is no such thing as a completely free project, even when the student's efforts are free. The student may need access to hardware and software facilities to be provided by the client and where even this is not the case the client needs to be prepared to give up some spare time to discuss requirements and to evaluate intermediate results. It has to be said that sometimes clients can let students down as far as this is concerned. Our advice to students would be to try and get to know your client thoroughly before the project starts. Try, for instance, to meet all the people in the organization who will be affected by your work before you actually get going on the project. Show a copy of your initial project plan to the client and get them to comment on it. Arrange beforehand to have regular meetings with them to discuss progress.

Content of a project plan

We discuss below what should be in your project planning document. It is suggested that the plans for small projects being done for outside clients should follow this format. Specific course requirements (e.g. learning objectives) are not covered.

1 Introduction

1.1 **Identity of client** – i.e. the organization or department for whom the work is to be done.
1.2 **Short description of project** – not more than two or three brief lines.
1.3 **Identity of the project authority** – the person or persons within the client organization who will have authority over the project's direction. It is essential that such an authority is identified.

2 Background

This may include:

- relevant information about the client's business
- descriptions of the existing software/hardware environment
- circumstances or problems leading to the current project
- work already carried out in the area of the project

- stakeholders in the projects, i.e. all those who will be affected by the project or who have some other interest in it.

3 Objectives of the project

These may already have been defined in a terms of reference (TOR) document. If so, then it may be attached as an appendix to the plan.

The objectives must define what is to be achieved and the method of measuring the extent of that achievement. One problem with small projects conducted by students is that the project's success is evaluated in course terms soon after its completion, whereas the project's true value to the users may take much longer to emerge (if ever!). As this document is in part for the benefit of the client the objectives from the client's viewpoint should have the emphasis here.

Where there are several objectives, an order of priority should be given to them if this is possible.

4 Constraints

It may be convenient to merge this into the project objectives, above. Constraints might include:

- externally imposed time scales
- legal requirements
- specific standards
- limitations on the people who can be approached for information.

5 Methods/technology to be used

These may have already have been laid down for you, or it may be that part of the project will involve the selection of the most appropriate technologies etc. In other cases you need to specify the general approach you will take – for instance that you are going to use SSADM or a soft system methodology (SSM) approach. In a small project it is unlikely that you will have time for a full SSADM approach and you may decide to use a subset of the techniques – this should be specified.

The methods selected will, of course, govern much of what will go into section 6 below on project products and section 7 on activities. When discussing prototypes, we emphasized that a prototype should always be a tool for learning or clarifying something (e.g. the best interface for the user). If you claim you are producing a prototype, then you must be prepared to define learning objectives for the prototype, a method of evaluation and an analysis of what has been learnt.

If you are developing software then the choice of software tools should be stated in this section.

Some justification of the decisions made here should be given as they can be crucial to the success of the project.

The training and other resource requirements (e.g. the need to purchase a particular package) that result from the decisions should be noted.

6 Project products

This is a list of *all* the products or deliverables that the project will produce, e.g. software modules, documentation, user guides and reports.

Intermediate products, e.g. design documents, should be included.

7 Activities

This is a list of the main activities that the project will involve. There must be activities to produce all the products listed in 6. Also, in general, each activity should result in some deliverable: avoid tasks like 'familiarization with departmental procedures' in favour of 'documentation of departmental procedures'. In identifying activities, new interim products may be discovered.

For each activity, define:

- **pre-requisites** – what has to be done before this activity can start
- **dependent activities** – activities that need this one to be completed first
- **estimated time/effort** – this may be a range of values
- **quality checks** – details of how you are going to verify and validate the product of the activity.

PERT or Gantt charts may be used but are often not needed.

8 Resources

This includes staff time, accommodation and hardware/software requirements.

9 Risk analysis

Identify the main things that can be seen as possibly going wrong. Typically this might include:

- unavailability of resources (e.g. delay in getting a software package)
- unavailability of key client personnel
- technical problems (e.g. software bugs).

A priority can be given to each risk by allocating a **probability rating** (1–10) and a **seriousness of impact rating** (1–10). Multiplying the two together gives an overall score for priority purposes.

For the most serious risks (i.e. those with the highest scores), **preventive** measures to reduce or remove the risk should be specified. For example, in order to prevent problems with the unavailability of key client personnel, meetings may be arranged with them at the planning stage and holiday plans may be ascertained. In some cases **contingency** measures which can be undertaken once the risk has actually materialized may be more appropriate.

Conclusions and further reading

In this chapter we have tried to show how some of the broader issues of software planning that have been covered elsewhere in the book can be related to the kind of task a student might be asked to undertake as a project. On the other hand, a student undertaking a substantial industrial placement might be involved in a project team undertaking a large project and using a method such as PRINCE, described in Appendix A, to control the project.

Readers may wish to follow up some of the topics touched upon in this book in more detail and to assist this we would like to suggest the following books for further reading.

Ken Bradley *PRINCE A Practical Handbook* Butterworth-Heinemann, 1993

Barry Boehm *Software Engineering Economics* Prentice-Hall, 1981. Along with the Brooks' book one of the most frequently cited books on software project management. Written by the inventor of COCOMO, Chapters 5 and 6 are the most important.

Frederick Brooks *The Mythical Man-Month: Essays on Software Engineering* Addison Wesley, 1982. A slightly dated but classic exposition of the central issues of software project management from the man who was in charge of the IBM 360 Operating System development project. You should try and look at it at some time.

Tom Gilb *Principles of Software Engineering Management* Addison-Wesley, 1988, Chapter 7 'Incremental delivery'.

Charles B. Handy *Understanding Organizations* Penguin, 1993 (4th edition)

F. L. Harrison *Advanced Project Management* Gower, 1981. A general project management book – not just software projects.

Charles R. Symons *Software Sizing and Estimating Mk II FPA* John Wiley & Sons, 1991. A book by the inventor of Mark II function points.

Tom DeMarco and Lister *Peopleware* Dorset House, 1987

Martyn A. Ould *Strategies for Software Engineering: The Management of Risk and Quality.* John Wiley & Sons, 1990. Technical plans and process model selection – Chapters 2 and 3.

Roland Vonk *Prototyping: the effective use of CASE technology* Prentice-Hall, 1990, Chapter 3.

Neal Whitten *Managing Software Development Projects* John Wiley & Sons 1989. This gives a flavour of the IBM approach.

Appendix A

PRINCE project management standards

Introduction to PRINCE

It is claimed that PRINCE stands for 'PRoject control IN Computer Environments'!

In a large organization there may be many large software development projects going on at the same time. It would be helpful if the rules and procedures by which each project is run were standardized rather than being re-invented for each new project. With large projects much of the work may be contracted out to external organizations. Here the need for agreed project management standards is even greater. The UK government recommends such a set of standards known as PRINCE.

PRINCE standards can be applied to any IT-related project. It can be used equally well for non-IT projects.

Although the standard fits in well with SSADM, it can be used to control projects using other analysis and design methods. The projects controlled by PRINCE do not need to include the development of software at all – PRINCE has been used for procurement and system reconfiguration projects. Because the methodology implies the making of an investment in order to overcome the problems of communication and coordination in a large project, it may not be cost-effective to use the full set of PRINCE measures on a small project (e.g. where only one or two people are involved and where the duration is less than three months).

PROMS-G is the project management specialist group of the British Computer Society.

Some idea of the extent of the use of PRINCE is given by a recent (1994) survey of members of PROMS-G found that 40% of respondents used PRINCE, although one in three of those using it had extended or modified it to meet their own needs – a practice that is allowed and encouraged by PRINCE.

PRINCE is constantly under review and version 2 of the method is currently (1995) under development.

Project organization

PRINCE roles

See Chapter 1.

The importance of identifying project stakeholders has already been discussed. PRINCE identifies three main groups of interests in the development of an information system:

- the organization management
- the end user
- the developers.

Each of these interest groups are likely to be made up of various subgroups. For example, the users of a system may come from a number of different departments and there may be several different groups representing different specialisms among the developers.

PRINCE specifies certain **roles** rather than jobs. Depending on the circumstances, a role may in fact be carried out by more than one person, or more than one role may be assumed by one member of staff.

PRINCE defines project management roles.

The Project Board

The need to identify a project authority has been stressed. With PRINCE, the overall authority for a project is vested in a **Project Board**. This will have people with responsibility for the following roles:

- **the Executive role** – which should provide overall guidance and ensure the project is meeting its business objectives
- **the Senior User role** – which should represent the users of the final product of the project
- **the Senior Technical role** – which should represent those responsible for the technical implementation and for operations.

We use capitalized initial letters to indicate a term that has a precise meaning in the PRINCE standards, e.g. Project Board.

The Project and Stage Managers

Although the Project Board has overall authority, the day to day running of the project is carried out by the **Project Manager** role. A project may have distinct stages where different types of expertise are required. For instance a systems analysis and design phase may be followed by the actual development of the software. PRINCE allows for a **Stage Manager** role where a specialist may take responsibility for the management of an individual stage. PRINCE also allows for different Stage Managers to assume the Project Manager role for different stages, although this would seem to raise problems with continuity.

The Project Assurance Team

Nearly all projects come under pressure at some time and a great temptation is to cut corners in order to get the job done. This often means that good project or quality management practices are neglected. PRINCE partly addresses this problem by having a **Project Assurance Team (PAT)** which reports in the first instance to the Project Manager. The PAT comprises the three following roles.

The **Business Assurance Coordinator (BAC)** has responsibilities which include monitoring the progress of the project against its financial and resource plans, setting up and documenting project meetings and maintaining project files.

The User Assurance Coordinator (UAC) coordinates matters from the users' point of view and acts as a channel of communication with the users. This includes taking the responsibility for obtaining approval for implementation plans (e.g. concerning data take-on), the assessment by users of alternative proposals, and the definition of the criteria which will form the basis for acceptance of the system by its users. The UAC is there not just to ensure the project team fulfils its obligations to the users but also to ensure that the users fulfil theirs, e.g. by approving documents on time.

The Technical Assurance Coordinator (TAC) coordinates technical matters such as the application of technical standards, oversees the formulation and implementation of technical plans and assesses the impact of modifications from a technical point of view.

The Project Support Office

The Project Support Office helps to ensure continuity between successive projects.

Project teams often exist as an entity only for the duration of the project and are then dispersed. There is thus a potential problem of the lack of continuity which can lead to useful information about productivity rates, for example, being lost. PRINCE recommends the establishment of a **Project Support Office (PSO)**, a central group which provides support for the all the projects being undertaken in an organization. The PSO may provide personnel who undertake the BAC and TAC roles for a project. The UAC, however, should always come from the user environment.

The Configuration Librarian

The Configuration Librarian controls the versions of documents and software produced by the project.

A large project will produce a mass of documentation which will go through a process of constant modification. Project team members need to be assured that they are dealing with the latest version of any document – yet it is very easy for documents not to be updated, for them to get lost or for linked documents to become incompatible. These considerations, of course, also apply to the software components of a project. Hence there is a recommendation for a **Configuration Librarian** who controls the project's library of documentation and software.

Project initiation

In the case of information systems, it is very unlikely that any system will be completely self-contained. It is more likely that it will be just one component in the set of interlinked systems in use by the organization in question. The organization should therefore have an overall IS Strategy which contains a shopping list of desirable projects. There is also likely to be some kind of technical plan which lays down standards to ensure compatibility between systems.

In a PRINCE environment, the responsibility of ensuring that an IS strategy is in place which supports the business objectives of the organization should be vested in an IS Steering Committee. There is also a need to deal with the allocation of resources between projects and the general co-ordination of IS development. The IS Steering Committee would not be the best vehicle for this as it will be composed of representatives of the business management who will not be interested in the details of IS implementation. This will be devolved to an IT Executive Committee (ITEC) and it is this that will appoint the Project Board for a particular project. The Executive member of the Project Board should be a member of the ITEC and report back to it.

The responsibilities of the ISSC and ITEC may be taken up by one or several authorities in real organizations.

The Project Initiation Meeting

The PRINCE approach makes the focus of project initiation the **Project Initiation Meeting.** This should do the following:

- authorize the project to go ahead
- allocate responsibilities for the project, including appointing the Project Manager
- agree the **project brief** based on the terms of reference set down by the ITEC
- agree the boundaries of the project
- approve the project plan and first stage plan
- approve the formal **Project Initiation Document** (PID) which documents:
  the business case for the project
  the project brief
  the project boundary
  the project organization
  the project plan.

The PID in effect constitute the terms of reference for the project as agreed by the Project Board.

Practical considerations

There are some obvious problems with the approach described in the PRINCE documentation. If, for example, the Project Manager is to be appointed only at this meeting, who is to prepare the plans that the meeting is to approve? In reality the tasks that are to be carried out by the Project Initiation Meeting are likely to be done at more than one meeting.

What might happen is this. The main project is almost certainly to be preceded by a feasibility study. This may not itself be subject to full PRINCE controls as it will only use one or two people for a number of weeks. A Project Board will be set up at the same time and their first task will be to consider and make recommendations on the basis of the feasibility report. If the decision is to go ahead then planning will be undertaken which will be formally approved by the Project Initiation Meeting.

Knowing when a project starts can be a real difficulty for people using PRINCE for the first time.

The possibility of tailoring PRINCE for individual projects is seen by practitioners as a great advantage over the prescriptiveness of PROMPT, the precursor of PRINCE.

The Project Initiation Document and Project Plan are important for many reasons including the fact that they will specify the quality requirements for the projects, the tolerances that will be allowed on activities before exception planning takes place, the stages of the project and the frequency of mid-stage assessments. The detailed methods of project control can therefore be specified taking into account the particular circumstances of the project.

Project structure

The PRINCE project structure is illustrated by Figure A.1. The focal point of the Project Initiation process is the Project Board's Project Initiation Meeting which approves the Project Initiation Document (PID). As we have seen, the PID comprises the Terms of Reference for the project, the Project Plan and the Stage Plan for the first stage.

It should be well established that it is dangerous to plan in too much detail too far ahead because circumstances are bound to change and more information is likely to come to light as time goes on. The PRINCE standards recognize this by requiring only an outline plan at the beginning of the project and a detailed Stage Plan just before the relevant Stage is embarked upon.

An End-Stage Assessment approves the completion of work on one Stage and authorizes the start of the next.

An **End-Stage Assessment (ESA)** is a formal meeting of the Project Board, the Project Assurance Team, and the Project Manager. It has to be convinced that the products of the current stage have been completely and correctly produced within budget. It then reviews the plans for the next stage and approves the beginning of work on that stage.

Mid-Stage Assessments are not mandatory in PRINCE.

Mid-Stage Assessments (MSA) are meetings that are called part-way through a stage and which have the same attendees as the ESA. They will usually be called at set time intervals, e.g. every 2 months. Their objective is to ensure that satisfactory progress is being made.

The general philosophy of PRINCE is that all the deliverables of one stage need to be completed before the next stage can be commenced. Sometimes, however, it is convenient to authorize limited work on the next stage before all the products of the preceding stage have been completed. An MSA would have to be called to do this.

A third reason why an MSA might be called is to deal with unforeseen circumstances which require the approval of an Exception Plan.

MSAs provide external monitoring of the project. At more frequent intervals there would be internal project progress meetings or **Checkpoints.**

Arranging the PIR can be a problem as it is outside the current project.

Project Closure is approved by a special meeting of the Project Board. The satisfactory completion of the project is recorded in a number of **Acceptance Letters** by the various parties to the project. The meeting would also ensure that a **Project Evaluation Report** has been produced by the Project Manager as the result of a Project Review. The meeting would also ensure that arrangements have been made for a **Post Implementation Review** (PIR) after a suitable period of operational running, say 6 months.

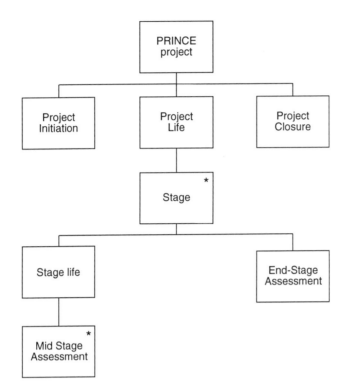

PRINCE divides a project into stages.

Figure A.1 *PRINCE project structure (* indicates iteration).*

PRINCE plans

The PRINCE approach assumes that a project can be seen as a hierarchy of levels of products and activities, each lower level breaking the components of the one above into more detail. To match this, PRINCE suggests a hierarchy of plans. At each level the plans are derived from the outline supplied by the plan for the level above.

At each level the plans are subdivided into:

- the **Technical Plan** which gives details of the activities that will have to be carried out, and
- the **Resource Plan** which gives estimates of the amount and cost of each type of resource needed to carry out the activities described in the Technical Plan.

This division into the Technical and Resource Plans is a way of addressing the problem that not all managers (especially those from the user side) will be able to comprehend all the technical aspects of a project. They will still, however, be concerned with the resources being consumed and completion dates.

The levels of planning comprise the following.

PRINCE only requires
plans to a level of detail
that is useful and
sensible.

- **Project Plan** – this is produced for the whole project at the beginning and is approved by the Project Initiation Meeting.
- **Stage Plans** – these are prepared for each stage before work commences on it to show in greater detail the activities and requirements for that stage.
- **Detailed Plans** – these cover specific activities within the stage.
- **Individual Work Plans** – these lay down the work to be carried out by an individual.
- **Exception Plans** – drawn up where unforeseen circumstances mean that plans have to be altered.

Contents of plans

Project, Stage and Detailed Plans (both Technical and Resource) have the same basic contents.

Graphical summary

Either a graph of costs against time for Resource Plans or an activity bar chart for Technical Plans.

Plan description

This provides a narrative description of the plan. It allocates responsibilities, specifies **control tolerances**, and lays down monitoring and reporting procedures. A tolerance is the variation to a plan that is to be allowed without special action having to be taken. For example it could be the number of days that an activity can be later than its planned completion. The ramifications of this are explored further in the section on 'Project control'.

Plan assumptions

The assumptions upon which the plan is based are written down so that changes in circumstances which alter the validity of the plan can be watched.

External dependencies

Activities or resources outside the control of the project upon which the project depends are mentioned as are other projects which depend on the successful completion of the current one.

Plan business risks

Other potential threats to the plan are identified here.

Planning: stages and techniques

Those familiar with SSADM will know that it lays down a set of **procedural standards** which dictate on a step-by-step basis what will be done. It also contains a set of **techniques** which will be used to carry some of those steps. In some cases, the same technique (e.g. data flow diagrams) can be employed at more than one point. With PRINCE, the emphasis is on the procedural standards. Some techniques are described in outline, but much is left to the discretion of the practitioner. This can be of advantage because it means that existing techniques and software tools can fit into the PRINCE framework – another example of the flexibility of PRINCE.

PRINCE regards the processes of producing Product Breakdown Structures, Product Flow Diagrams and preliminary activity networks as essentially technical in nature. This has to be followed by a management process which is described in the section below headed 'The management planning process'.

Identification of the project products

The project brief passed to the Project Board at the initiation of the project will identify the major products the project must create in order to meet its business justification. This list will need to be expanded. There will be a large number of **technical** products including training material and operating instructions and also products to do with the **management** and the **quality** of the project.

The products will form a hierarchy. The main products will have sets of component products which in turn may be made up of subcomponent products and so on. These relationships can be documented in a **Product Breakdown Structure (PBS)**, illustrated in Figure A.2.

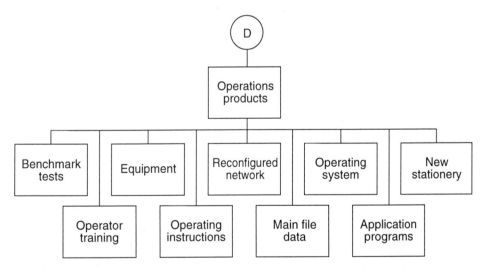

Figure A.2 *Example of part of a Product Breakdown Structure.*

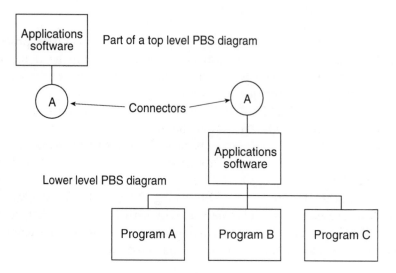

Figure A.3 *Use of connectors to expand a product at a lower level.*

Note that where a product needs to be further analysed into components connector symbols may be used (see Figure A.3). Some products may not be one-off items but may represent collections of items that are accumulated throughout the course of the project, e.g. progress reports. The repetitive accumulating nature of the item can be indicated by an asterisk in the top right hand corner of the box. Those used to entity life histories in SSADM or Jackson Structured Programming may be reassured that it is acceptable to mix boxes with asterisks with boxes which do not have them on the same level in this type of diagram.

Each product at the bottom of the PBS that is not further subdivided should be documented by a **Product Description** which contains:

- **name/identity** of the product
- **purpose** of the product
- **derivation** of the product (i.e. from what other products is it derived)
- **composition** of the product
- **form** of the product
- relevant **standards**
- **quality criteria** that apply.

As a guideline to how far products should be broken down, a principle suggested by the PRINCE documentation is that separate products should not be identified if they are the result of the same process. This is only a guideline, however, and exceptions can be imagined. The PRINCE documentation supplies a standard skeleton PBS which can be used as a starting point.

Analysis of product flows

Some products will be derived from others. For example, a program module may be derived from a program design which in turn is derived from a program specification. Each of the processes of creating a new product from an old one is known as a **transformation.** The thinking through of these transformations by the planner will help to identify intermediate products that may have previously been overlooked. SSADM with its detailed step-by-step approach supplies a ready-made set of transformations and intermediate products.

Figure A.4 shows part of a Product Flow Diagram (PFD). The use of an oval around a product name indicates a product that originates outside the project. The lines represent dependencies between products. The flow of dependencies is from top to bottom or from left to right depending on convenience, but not both in the same diagram.

Production of an activity network

Transformations take a set of products, perform activities and a quality process and produce another set of products (Figure A.5).

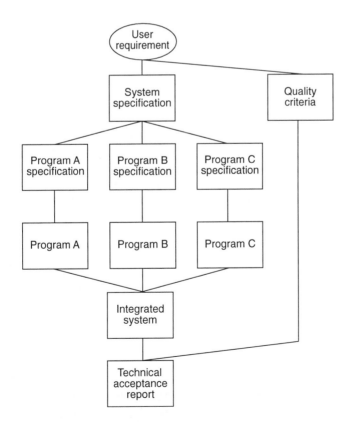

Figure A.4 *Example of part of a Product Flow Diagram.*

Figure A.5 *A transformation.*

For each transformation the activities involved and the logical dependencies between them must be identified. As a general guideline activities should be between 1 day and 2 weeks in duration.

In order to produce a valid activity network, constraints on activities need to be identified – these can be internal to the project or external. Where the constraint is external then it should, if possible, be indicated as an external product upon which the activity in question is dependent. For example a compiler may need to be delivered and installed by an external supplier before module coding can start. These constraints should be of a technical nature – staffing resource constraints (for example, having to hold up system testing until testing staff are available) depend upon management decisions about which staff are to be made available, and these questions are addressed at a later stage.

The activities and their dependencies are documented using a standard activity network diagram. PRINCE recommends the use of **precedence networks** where the activities are shown as boxes as opposed to arrow networks where events are represented as circles and activities as lines between the circles.

Estimates of resources and activity durations

PRINCE does not lay down a specific estimating method. It does recommend that two sets of estimates be produced independently. Before estimating is started, the types of resource that are available in terms of specific expertise and experience should be defined.

Selection of control points and baselines

A control point is a point in the project where the Project Board reviews the progress of the project and confirms or revises its direction. They are the ESAs (End-Stage Assessments) and MSAs (Mid-Stage Assessments) previously mentioned. They will require the creation of special products in the form of reports and plans and these need to be included in the Product Breakdown Structure.

Chapter 9 on monitoring and control discusses control points in some detail.

A **baseline** is a snapshot of the state of all the products at one time – this would normally coincide with a control point and is the agreed set of products upon which the project can proceed.

The management planning process

The technical planning will have come up with a logical sequence of activities presented in the form of an activity network. The calculation of the completion date of the project is a management task rather than a technical one as it will depend upon the willingness of management to allocate staff and other resources.

The date when the users must have the system and the availability of staff to develop and implement the system are checked and the activity network is amended to accordingly. For example there may be three programs which could be coded in parallel, but as there is only one programmer available they will have to be done one after the other and so the start of work on the second program becomes dependent on the completion of the first and the start of the third program on the completion of the second one.

The next management activity is to allocate individual staff to the activities that have been identified.

The technical planning phase should have come up with overall estimated demand for each type of staff. The job now is to decide when and for how long staff and other resources will be needed, and to convert the figures in the resource estimates, which will be in staff-hours, say, into real financial costs.

Project control

How progress is recorded

The Project Board checks on the progress of the project through formal End-Stage and Mid-Stage Assessment meetings (ESAs and MSAs).

Control also has to take place at a lower level than this. Each group within the project team which has a team leader will have regular **checkpoint meetings**, for example, each week. The progress made by each member of the group will be recorded and any local difficulties will be resolved. Information about progress will be used to add details of current progress to the stage plan with and may also be used by the team leader to produce a **checkpoint report** that goes to the Project Manager. The team leader may then prepare **work-to lists** for each group member covering the tasks to be undertaken in the period up to the next checkpoint.

Each month (or at some other agreed interval) the Project Manager will produce a **highlight report** that will summarize the information on the checkpoint reports and draw attention to areas of concern. This report will be circulated to members of the Project Board.

What happens when things go wrong

The problem may be a **technical exception** – for example there may be a major flaw in the user requirements or in the overall design of the system which is only discovered during development. It may also be that something in the system requirement cannot be delivered because of unforeseen technical difficulties. The first stage is to produce a **Project Issue Report (PIR** but note that PIR can also stand for Post Implementation Review!) which describes the problem. The Project Manager will analyse all Project Issue Reports and may decide that the problem is such that a change is needed to the System Requirements. This would be initiated through a **Request For Change (RFC).** Alternatively the Project Manager may decide that the best course of action is to not implement that part of the system where the problem has occurred and an **Off-Specification Report (O-SR)** is raised.

Each stage plan will identify tolerances, the degree to which the plan can be deviated from without the project's objectives being threatened. The tolerance may be expressed in terms of cost or the duration of particular activities. When the project is executed, a deviation from the plan may be forced that is so great that the plan is invalidated and in this case an **Exception Plan** has to be drawn up.

The Exception Plan must give the following information:

- an explanation as to how the exceptional circumstances have occurred
- the outcome if no action is taken
- recommended action
- impact of the recommended action on the Stage and Project Plans
- new assumptions – pre-requisites and risks
- impact on the business plan.

The Project Manager would formulate the Exception Plan which would require the approval of the Project Board.

Quality assurance

Quality criteria

Chapter 11 deals with quality in a wider sense.

PRINCE lays down that as part of the planning process the quality criteria which apply to each product must be identified and agreed. These would include:

- **performance**, e.g. response time, throughput, and constraints
- **usability**
- **external interfaces to other systems**
- **compatibility**, e.g. with existing systems
- **reliability** and **maintainability**.

In some cases there may be conflicts between different quality requirements – for example a system may be able to have a fast response time only by using the characteristics of the host hardware in such a way that it makes portability (a component of compatibility) very difficult. In this case the quality requirements will have to be put into some kind of order of priority.

Typically a product will be the result of a series of transformations which will each have some intermediate product. These intermediate products will be identified in the Product Flow Diagram. Quality checks on the intermediate products will help to eradicate errors at an early stage.

For each of the quality criteria a way of checking that the standard has been met must be specified, for example, a set of tests or a review or both. The resources required to carry out the quality checking must be identified.

Quality planning

The activity network will have to contain details of tasks needed to carry out the quality checking activities and this in turn will lead to the allocation of specific resources for these tasks.

Quality reviews

These form the mainstay of the PRINCE quality process. The reviews vary in formality and scale. At the lowest level they could be **a group of two** where two people work together and check each other's work. **A group of three** is similar – here there might be two trainees assigned to a more experienced member of staff.

A **formal review** requires the presence of three roles:

- **the chair** who runs the review meeting, and records the actions of the meeting
- **the presenter** who is normally the author of the work that is under review
- **the reviewers** who examine the work and note errors.

The review process is monitored by the Business Assurance Coordinator who checks that reviews specified in the PRINCE plans are in fact carried out. Before the meeting, copies of the item under review are distributed to the reviewers. Each item is the result of some process and copies of the documents that were input to that process must be given to the reviewers so that they can check the consistency of the product. There may also be specific check-lists of things to be scrutinized in that particular type of product.

> The PRINCE quality review process is structured around documents – there are other ways to do quality reviews and these should be used if appropriate.

The reviewers examine the product and produce a **Quality Review Error List** which should be passed to the presenter before the Quality Review if possible. Where appropriate they may annotate their copy of the product with their queries.

The meeting is convened by the chair. The presenter introduces the product and the reviewers make general comments about their concerns. The presenter will then 'walk-through' the detail of the product. The reviewers will make their comments and the chairman will make notes of the remedial action that needs to be taken on a **Quality Review Follow-Up Action List.**

The review may decide that the work is of such poor quality that it needs to be taken away and be redone and re-reviewed. Less drastically and more frequently there will be a need for the correction of some defects. This will normally be carried out by the presenter. The review will decide who will sign off the rework – normally it would be the chair.

A **Result Notification** is sent to the Business Assurance Coordinator to signify that the review has taken place. If the review does not take place as scheduled for some reason then an **Exception Memo** is sent to the BAC.

Configuration management

Configuration management has already been touched upon in Chapter 9.

A **configuration** is a set of related products which would include hardware, software, data and documentation. There is a need to control the configuration to ensure, for example, that the different versions of interlinked components that will be developed during the course of the project are in step. Hence there is an essential need for **configuration management.** The individual products in the configuration are known as **Configuration Items (CIs).** Configuration management is concerned with such matters as the identification of these items, their secure filing, the control of changes to them and the distribution of copies to project team members and others who have need of them.

PRINCE provides a base standard for configuration management which may be replaced or augmented by appropriate local standards.

PRINCE lays down a specific role of **Configuration Librarian**. It also states that a Configuration Plan needs to be formulated as part of the overall Project Plan. Among other things the Configuration Plan will specify the coding system to be used to identify Configuration Items. In a well-organized development environment much of this plan will simply be referring to standard procedures, but an individual project may have special problems that need to be addressed. For example, it may be that a 'core' system is to be produced by an organization with variations for each of its European subsidiaries.

Each identified configuration items will be subject to a number of transformations during the life-time of the project and the Configuration Librarian must be aware of these and document them. These details will be held in a set of **Configuration Item Description Records** which will contain the following information:

- **CI name**
- **CI description**
- **CI life-cycle** – a description of the life-cycle that this item goes through

- **parent CI(s)** – the CIs that were used to create the current CI
- **child CI(s)** – the CIs that the current CI will be used to create
- **officer responsible**
- **date of responsibility**
- **CI source** – who produced the CI
- **current life-cycle phase**
- **current life-cycle step**
- **latest baseline identity**
- **product list** – list of all the products required for this stage/step of the CIs life-cycle
- **change history.**

The Configuration Librarian will need to set up a separate folder for each item which will hold the record described above and the latest version of the item along with previous versions. Where the item is in machine-readable format then the appropriate computer directory system needs to be established.

As work is carried out on a product it will be in a state of continual change. If for example a program module needs to be amended, it is possible that the programmer may implement those changes in increments. They may also have to make further alterations to clear errors that are found during 'debugging'. At some stage, however, the programmer will feel that the module is in a fit state to be released to a wider world. This version of the module, which under a PRINCE regime will have been subject to a quality review, will be a **baseline**. It is important that once an item becomes a baseline, any changes to it which will in effect create a new baseline, are carefully controlled.

Copies of products, e.g. data base record specifications, may need to distributed to a large number of staff in order that they can use the information in their own work. The Configuration Librarian needs to keep careful record of these **releases** in order to know who needs to be notified of any changes to the product.

Appendix B

Answer pointers

Chapter 1

The order you put these projects is, of course, to a large degree subjective. Here is one example of a possible ordering.

1. **Building the Channel Tunnel.** Almost everybody puts this one first. The huge scale of the task, the relative novelty of the project, all the different specialisms involved and the international nature of the project make it special.

2. **Writing an operating system.** This is a prime example of a software development project.

3. **Amending a financial system to start the financial year on 1st January rather than 1st April.** This project is modifying an existing system rather than creating a new one from scratch. Many software projects have this characteristic and it does not make them any less a software project.

4. **Installing a new version of a word processing package in an organization.** Although no software is being produced or modified, many of the stages that are associated with software projects will be involved and the techniques of software project management would be appropriate.

5. **Investigation into the reasons why a user has a problem with a computer system.** This will have many of the stages common to software projects, although the precise nature of the end result is uncertain at the outset. It could be that the user needs some simple remedial training. On the other hand, it could turn out to be quite a considerable software modification task.

6. **Getting married.** There should be lots of arguments about this one! Some will be reluctant to give a high rating to this because of its personal nature. The degree to which this is 'project-like' may depend very much upon the cultural milieu in which it takes place. Very often it requires a high degree of planning, involves lots of different people and, for most people, is a non-routine operation.

7. **A research project into what makes a good human–computer interface.** Compared to some of the projects above, the objectives of the research project are more open-ended and the idea of a specific client for the end

product may be less well-defined. Research projects are in some ways special cases and the approach to their planning needs a rather different approach which is outside the scope of this book.

8. **Producing an edition of a newspaper.** In some ways this has all the characteristics of a project. There are lots of different people with lots of different specialisms whose work needs to be coordinated in order to produce an end product under very tight time constraints. What argues against this as a typical project is that it is repeated. After a while everyone knows what they need to do and most of the problems that may arise are familiar and the procedures to deal with them are well-defined.

9. **A second year programming assignment for a computing student.** This is not being done for a customer, although it could be argued that the tutor responsible for setting and assessing the assignment is, in effect, a surrogate client. Not all the stages of a normal project will be gone through.

1.2 Brightmouth HE College payroll: Stages of a project

1. **Project evaluation.** All the costs that would be incurred by the college if it were to carry out its own payroll processing would need to be carefully examined to ensure it would be more cost effective than letting the local authority carry on providing the service.

2. **Planning.** The way that the transfer to local processing is to be carried out needs to be carefully planned with the participation of all those concerned. Some detailed planning would need to be deferred until more information was available, e.g. which payroll package was to be used.

3. **Requirements analysis.** This is finding out what the users need from the system. To a large extent it may consist of finding out what the current system does as it may be assumed that in general the new system is to provide the same functions as the old. The users may have additional requirements, however, or there may even be facilities that are no longer needed.

4. **Specification.** This involves documenting what the new system is to be able to do.

5. **Design/coding.** As an 'off-the -shelf' package is envisaged, these stages will be replaced by a package evaluation and selection activity.

6. **Verification and validation.** Tests will need to be carried out to ensure that the selected package will actually do what is required. This task may well involve parallel running of the old and new systems and a comparison of the output from them both to check for any inconsistencies.

7. **Implementation.** This would involve such things as installing the software, setting system parameters such as the salary scales, and setting up details of employees.

8. **Maintenance/support.** This will include dealing with users' queries, liaising with the software house and taking account of new payroll requirements.

1.3 The nature of an operating system

Many large organizations which are committed to computer-based information systems may have specialists responsible for the maintenance of operating systems. However, as an operating system is primarily concerned with driving the hardware it is argued that it has more in common with what we have described as industrial systems.

1.4 Brightmouth HE College payroll: Objectives-driven vs. product-driven

This project is really driven by objectives. If in-house payroll processing turns out not to be cost effective then the project should not try and implement such a solution. Other ways of meeting the objectives set could be considered: for example, it may be possible to contract out the processing to some organization other than the local authority at a lower cost.

1.5 Brightmouth HE College payroll: Sub-systems

The danger here is to think only in terms of software modules. The payroll system will contain both technical and human elements. A breakdown into sub-systems will vary tremendously according to your particular viewpoint. Figure B.1 is a diagrammatic representation of just one possible answer.

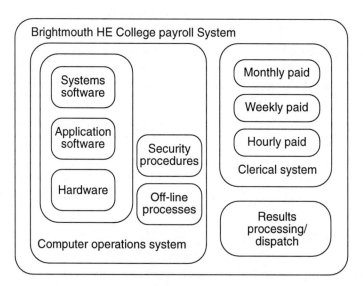

Figure B.1 *A systems map of Brightmouth HE College payroll.*

The environment of the system would contain:

- Inland Revenue
- Pension funds
- Department of Social Security (for National Insurance)
- Bankers Automated Clearing Scheme (BACS)
- Trades unions (staff may have subscriptions deducted at source)
- Software suppliers

- Hardware suppliers
- Other office equipment suppliers
- A security firm if some staff are paid in cash
- District audit
- College management
- Site management (who are responsible for physical accommodation)
- Staff

Planning:

- staffing requirements for the next year.

Representing the section:

- at the group meeting
- when communicating with the personnel manager about replacement staff
- when explaining about the delay to users.

Controlling, innovating, directing:

- deciding what needs to be done to make good the progress that will be lost
  through temporarily losing a member of staff.

Staffing:

- deciding which member of staff is to do what
- discussion with personnel about the requirement for temporary staff
- planning staffing for the next year.

Note: the same activity may involve many different roles.

The original objective might have been formulated as: 'To carry out payroll processing at less cost while maintaining the current scope and quality of services'.

In order to achieve this, subobjectives or goals may have been identified, e.g.

- to transfer payroll processing to the HE College by 1st April
- to implement in the new system those facilities that exist in the current system less those identified in the initial report as not being required
- to carry out the implementation of the payroll processing capability within the financial constraints identified in the initial report.

It should be noted that the objectives listed above do not explicitly mention things such as putting into place ongoing arrangements to deal with hardware and software maintenance, security arrangements and so on. By discussing and trying to agree objectives with the various people involved the true requirements of the project can be clarified.

Measures of effectiveness for the subobjectives listed above might include the following.

- **Date of implementation** – was the new system being used operationally by the agreed date?
- **Facilities** – in parallel runs were all the outputs produced by the old system and still required also produced by the new system?
- **Costs** – how did the actual costs incurred compare with the budgeted costs?

1.8 Brightmouth HE College payroll: stakeholders

Most of the external entities identified in Exercise 1.5 would also be stakeholders in the project.

Major stakeholders would include:

- the finance department
- the personnel department – they would need to supply most of the employee details needed
- heads of departments – they would need to submit details of hours worked for part-time staff
- staff – who would naturally be concerned that they are paid correctly
- site management – the new arrangements may mean that the office layout has to be rearranged physically
- software and hardware vendors.

One group of stakeholders that may not be readily identified at first is the local authority and its staff. It may seem strange to list the people who used to do the job, but who are no longer required. The project manager's job will be made a lot easier if their cooperation and help can be obtained. The project manager would do well to sound out tactfully how the local authority staff feel about losing this work. It may be that they are pleased to be shot of the workload and hassle involved! Arrangements may be possible which take into account existing local authority staff. For example, if the college need to recruit new staff to deal with payroll, it may smooth things to give the job to a member of the local authority staff who already deals with this area.

Chapter 2

2.1 External stakeholders in IOE accounts system

The main stakeholders who needs to be considered are the IOE customers. It may be worth consulting some representative customers about the layout of the new monthly statement for example.

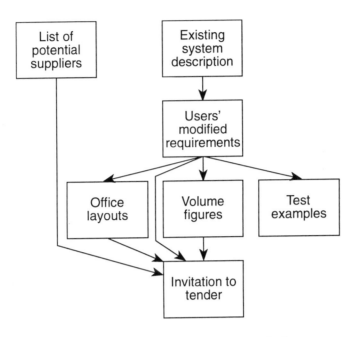

2.2 Figure B.2 is the product flow diagram for invitation to tender for Brightmouth HE College payroll

Figure B.2 *Product flow diagram for 'Invitation to tender'.*

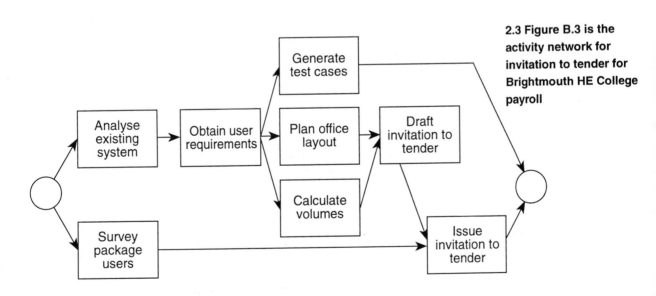

2.3 Figure B.3 is the activity network for invitation to tender for Brightmouth HE College payroll

Figure B.3 *Brightmouth HE College payroll project activity network fragment.*

2.4 Figure B.4 shows an activity network including a checkpoint

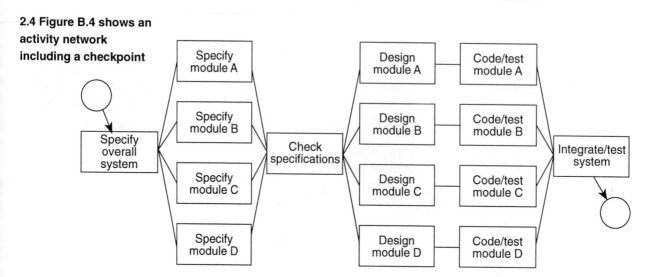

Figure B.4 *Fragment of the IOE maintenance group accounts activity network.*

2.5 Quality checks on user requirements

The users will need at least to read and approve the system specification. This may be rather late to make major changes, so user approval of earlier documents such as interview notes would be helpful.

Chapter 3

3.1 Costs and benefits for the Brightmouth College payroll system

Table B.1 lists costs and benefits for the proposed Brightmouth HE College payroll system. It is not comprehensive but illustrates some of the types of items that you should have listed.

3.2 Ranking project cash flows

Obviously you will have your own views about which have the best and worst cash flows. You should, however, have considered the following points: project 2 requires a very large investment compared to its gain – in fact we could obtain £100,000 by undertaking both projects 1 and 3 for a lesser cost than project 2. Both projects 1 and 2 produce the bulk of their incomes relatively late in their lives compared with project 3 which produces a steady income over its life.

3.3 Calculating payback periods

The payback periods for each of the projects will occur during the year indicated: project 1 year 5, project 2 year 5, project 3 year 4 and project 4 year 4 (end).

We would therefore favour project 3 or 4 over the other two. Note that, in reality, with relatively short-term projects such as these we would produce a monthly (or at least quarterly) cash flow forecast and it is therefore likely that project 3 would be seen more clearly to have a shorter payback period than project 4.

Table B.1 *Costs and benefits for the Brightmouth College payroll system*

Category	Cost/benefit
Development costs	software purchase – software cost plus selection & purchasing cost project team employment costs
Setup costs	training include costs of trainers and operational staff time lost while training staff recruitment computer hardware & other equipment which may have a residual value at end of projected life accommodation – any new/refurbished accommodation and furniture required to house new system. initial systems supplies – purchase of stationary, disks and other consumables
Operational costs	operations staff – full employment costs stationary – purchase and storage* maintenance & standby – contract or estimation of occurrence costs accommodation including heating, power, insurance etc.*
Direct benefits	saving on local authority fees later payment – increase interest income through paying salaries later in the month
Indirect benefits	improved accuracy – assumes that direct costs of correcting current errors that should not occur with a computerized system is known (e.g. takes one person one day per week) Note: benefit should measure what can be done with that additional time
Intangible benefits	improved management information – this should lead to improved decision making but it is very difficult to quantify the potential benefits

* *These items, and some other elements, may show corresponding savings or costs through no longer being required. For example, although new office furniture may be required for the new system, the existing furniture might be redeployed or sold.*

The return on investments for each of the projects is: project 1 10%, project 2 2%, project 3 10% and project 4 12·5%. Project 4 therefore stands out as being the most beneficial as it earns the highest return.

3.4 Calculating the return on investment

3.5 Calculating the net present value

The net present value for each of the projects is calculated as in Table B.2.

Table B.2 *Calculating the net present value of projects 2, 3 and 4*

| | | Discounted cash flow (£) | | |
Year	Discount factor	Project 2	Project 3	Project 4
0	1·0000	−1,000,000	−100,000	−120,000
1	0·9091	181,820	27,273	27,273
2	0·8264	165,280	24,792	24,792
3	0·7513	150,260	22,539	22,539
4	0·6830	136,600	20,490	20,490
5	0·6209	186,270	18,627	46,568
NPV		−179,770	13,721	21,662

On the basis of net present value, project 4 clearly provides the greatest return and project 2 is clearly not worth considering.

3.6 Calculating the effect of discount rates on NPV (Table B.3)

Table B.3 *The effect on net present value of varying the discount rate*

| | Cash flow values (£) | | |
Year	Project A	Project B	Project C
0	−8,000	−8,000	−10,000
1	4,000	1,000	2,000
2	4,000	2,000	2,000
3	2,000	4,000	6,000
4	1,000	3,000	2,000
5	500	9,000	2,000
6	500	−6,000	2,000
Net Profit	£ 4,000	£ 5,000	£ 6,000
NPV @ 8%	£ 2,111	£ 2,365	**£ 2,421**
NPV @ 10%	£ 1,720	**£ 1,818**	£ 1,716
NPV @ 12%	**£ 1,356**	£ 1,308	£ 1,070

In each case the 'best' project is indicated in bold. In this somewhat artificial example, which project is best is very sensitive to the chosen discount rate. In such a case we must either have a very strong reason to use a particular discount rate or take other criteria into account when choosing between the projects.

3.7 Project evaluation using cost–benefit analysis

Expected sales of £500,000 per year over 4 years would generate an expected net income of £1·2m (after allowing for annual costs of £200,000) which, by almost any criteria, would provide a good return on an investment of £750,000.

However, if sales are low, and there is a 30% chance of this happening, the company will loose money – it is unlikely that any company would wish to knowingly take such a risk.

This example illustrates one of the basic objections to using this approach for one-off decisions. Were we to repeat the project a large number of times we would expect, **on average**, an income of £500,000 per annum. However, the company is only developing this package once – they can't keep trying in the hope of, on the average, generating a respectable income. Indeed, a severe loss on this project may mean it is the last project they are able to undertake.

Chapter 4

(a) A payroll system is a data-oriented or information system which is application specific.

4.1 Classification of systems

(b) The bottling plant system is a process control or industrial system.

(c) This looks like an information system that will make heavy use of computer graphics. The plant itself may use control software which may be safety critical but this is not the subject of the project under consideration.

(d) Project management software tools are often categorized as general packages. There would be a considerable information systems element to them.

(e) This could use an information retrieval package which is a general software package. It is also a strong candidate for a knowledge-based system.

The user staff could, arguably, be regarded as a project resource. The writers' view is that it is useful to add a fourth category of risks – those belonging to the **environment** in which the system is to be implemented.

4.2 Identification of risks

Among the risks that might be identified at Brightmouth HE College are:

* conflict of views between the finance and personnel departments
* lack of staff acceptance for the system, especially among personnel staff
* lack of cooperation by the local authority which used to carry out payroll work
* lack of experience with running payroll at the college
* lack of administrative computing expertise at the college
* possible inadequacy of the chosen hardware
* changes to the payroll requirements.

(a) This would appear to be a knowledge-based system which is also safety-critical.

4.3 Selection of project approaches

Techniques associated with knowledge based systems could be used for constructing the system.

Testing would need to be very carefully conducted. A lengthy parallel run where the system is used to shadow the human decisions made in real cases and the results compared could be considered. Another approach would be to develop two or more systems in parallel so that the advice offered could be cross-checked.

(b) This is an information system which will be on a relatively large scale. An SSADM approach would be justified. When student loans were first introduced there was no existing system and so there might have been some scope for a prototype.

(c) This is a process control system which is highly safety critical. Measures that might be adopted to ensure the reliability of the system include:

- use of mathematics-based specification languages to avoid ambiguity
- developing parallel versions of the same software so that they can be cross-checked
- statistical control of software testing to allow for the estimation of the reliability of the software.

4.4. Feedback between project review and feasibility study

The review may find that the benefits forecast in the original feasibility study report have not been achieved. 'Corrections' to the existing system may allow those benefits and other ones to be realized. This would lead to a proposal for a new project to modify the installed option

4.5. Stages of a project where a prototype may be appropriate

(a) A prototype could be useful as part of the feasibility study. A mock-up of an executive information system loaded with current management information could be set up manually and then be tried out by the managers to see how easy and useful they found it.

(b) A prototype could be used to assist in the design of the user dialogues. SSADM allows for prototypes for this purpose as part of its requirement specification module.

(c) A prototype of the most response critical transactions could be made at the physical design stage to see whether Ingres/Vision could produce software which gave a satisfactory performance.

Chapter 5

Table B.4 *Productivity rates*

5.1 Calculating productivity rates and using productivity rates to project effort (Tables B.4 and B.5)

Project	Work - months	LOC	Productivity (SLOC/month)
a	16·7	6050	362
b	22·6	8363	370
c	32·2	13334	414
d	3·9	5942	1524
e	17·3	3315	192
f	67·7	38988	576
g	10·1	38614	3823
h	19·3	12762	661
i	59·5	26500	445
Overall	249·3	153868	617

Table B.5 *Estimated effort*

Project	Estimated work-months	Actual	Difference
a	6050/617 = 9·80	16·7	6·90
d	5942/617 = 9·63	3·9	−5·73

There would be an under-estimate of 6·9 work-months for project a and an over-estimate of 5·7 for project d.

5.2 Course staff costs program – activities required

A list of activities might include:

- obtain user requirements
- analyse the structure of the data already held
- design report and write user proposal
- write test plan
- write technical specification
- design software
- write software
- test software
- write operating instruction
- carry out acceptance testing.

The most difficult tasks to estimate are often those which are most sensitive to the size and the complexity of the software to be produced, in this case the design, writing and testing of the software. Writing the technical specification may also be difficult because of this, but estimating problems tend to be concealed here as deadlines can be met by omitting detail which can be added latter when deficiencies are found.

The duration of activities that are to be carried out by users may also present problems as this may depend upon their sense of priorities.

5.3 Effort drivers for a student assignment

The most obvious effort driver would seem to be the number of words required. Difficulty factors might include:

- **availability of material**, e.g. in the library
- **familiarity** of the student with the topic
- **breadth/depth** required, i.e. is a broad survey of a wide field required or an in-depth study of a narrow area?
- **technical difficulty,** i.e. some topics are easier to explain than others.

It could be argued that time available is the constraint. The student just does what can be done in the time available (see 'design to cost').

5.4. COCOMO estimates

Table B.6 *Comparison of COCOMO estimates and actual effort*

LOC	Actual (work-months)	COCOMO estimates	Difference (work months)	Difference (%)
6050	16·7	15·9	−0·8	−4·9
8363	22·6	22·3	−0·3	−1·2
13334	32·2	36·4	4·2	13·1
5942	3·9	15·6	11·7	299·7
3315	17·3	8·4	−8·9	−51·2
38988	67·7	112·4	44·7	66·0
38614	10·1	111·2	101·1	1001·5
12762	19·3	34·8	15·5	80·2
26500	59·5	74·9	15·4	25·9

This illustrates the need for the calibration of COCOMO to suit local conditions.

5.5 Albrecht function points

- External input types – none
- External output types – the report, i.e. 1
- Logical internal file types – the accounting feeder file, i.e. 1
- External interface file types – payroll file, staff file – timetabling, courses file – timetabling, accounting feeder file, i.e. 4

Because the accounting feeder file is outgoing, it is counted once as a logical interface file type and once as an external interface file type.

- External enquiry types   none
- External output types $1 \times 7 = 7$
- Logical internal file types $1 \times 10 = 10$
- External interface types $4 \times 7 = 28$

Total   45

Estimated lines of Cobol $= 35 \times 105 = 3710$

5.6 Calculation of SLOC from Albrecht function points

- Input data types   6
- Entities accessed   1
- Output data types   1

5.7 Mark II function points

Unadjusted function points $= (0.58 \times 6) + (1.66 \times 1) + (0.26 \times 1) = 5.4$.

First, we estimate the number of bottom level DFD processes that are not further subdivided:

5.8 Estimate of time to do EPDs

- second level DFD processes are estimated as A1 $\times 2.5 = 15$
- third level DFD processes are estimated as A7 $\times 0.75 = 11.25$
- half the second level DFD processes are not further expanded $= 7.5$
- total number of bottom level DFD processes is $7.5 + 11.25 = 18.75$ or 19 when rounded.

Estimated time to do EPDs is $19 \times 0.25 = 4.75$ days.

Figure B.5 gives an outline program structure. The numbers in circles are our estimates of the lines of Cobol code needed to implement each subprocess in the program. They should add up to 95 SLOC. Note that these do not include data declarations.

5.9 SLOC estimate for customer insertion program

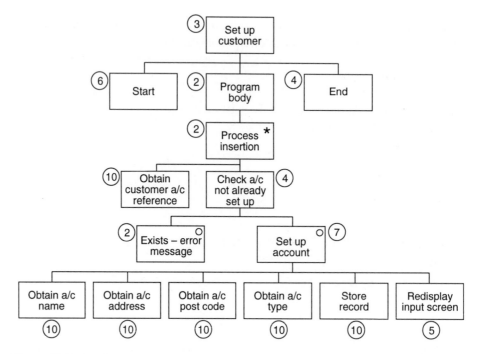

Figure B.5 *Outline program structure for 'set up customer' transaction.*

Chapter 6

6.1 Errors drawing activity networks

(a) Activity A dangles, giving the project two 'end events'. This network should be drawn as below. To aid comparison with the original the nodes have not been renumbered, although we would normally do so.

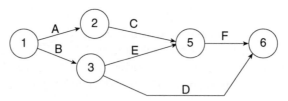

(b) Once again, this network has two end nodes, but in this case the solution is slightly different since we should introduce a dummy activity if we are to follow the standard CPM conventions.

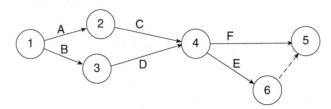

(c) Either this one has a dangle (although, because of the way it is drawn, it is less obvious) or activity E has its arrow pointing in the wrong direction. We need a bit more information before we can redraw this one correctly.

(d) Strictly speaking, there's nothing wrong with this one – it's just badly drawn and the nodes are not numbered according to the standard conventions. It should be redrawn as in the following example.

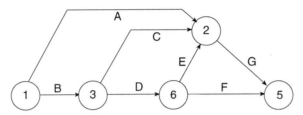

In this diagram the nodes have retained their original numbers (to aid identification) although they should of course be renumbered sequentially from left to right.

(e) This one contains a loop – F cannot start before G has finished, G cannot start before E has finished and E cannot start before G has finished. One of the arrows is wrong! It's probably activity F that's wrong but we can't be sure without further information.

Brigette's payroll CPM network should look like the diagram below. If your diagram is not exactly the same as this check that it is **logically** the same.

6.2 Drawing Brigette's activity network as a CPM network

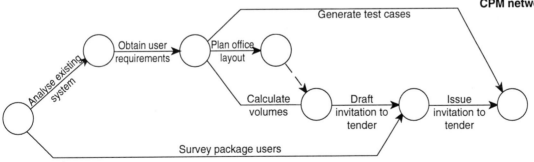

A solution is given in Figure 6.13. If your solution is not exactly the same as this do not worry. Just check that it is **logically** the same and that it follows the CPM conventions of layout and node numbering etc.

6.3 Drawing a CPM network

Free float and interfering float for each of the activities are shown in Table B.7 below. Note that activity A has no free float since any delay in its completion will delay the start of activity C. Activity C, however, has a 2-week free float so

6.4 Calculating activity floats

long as activity A keeps to time. Float must be regularly monitored as a project progresses since a delay in any activity beyond its free float allowance will eat into the float of subsequent activities.

Table B.7 *Activity floats*

Activity	Total float	Free float	Interfering float
A	2	0	2
B	3	0	3
C	2	2	0
D	3	3	0
E	3	3	0
F	0	0	0
G	0	0	0
H	2	2	0

6.5 Shortening a project duration

Shortening activity F to 8 weeks will bring the project completion date forward to week 11 – i.e. it will save 2 weeks on the duration of the project. However, there are now two critical paths, 1–5–6 and 1–2–4–6, so that reducing the duration of activity F any further will not shorten the project duration any further. If we wish to complete the project earlier than week 11 we must save time on path 1–5–6 and path 1–2–4–6.

6.6 Drawing a precedence network (Figure B.6)

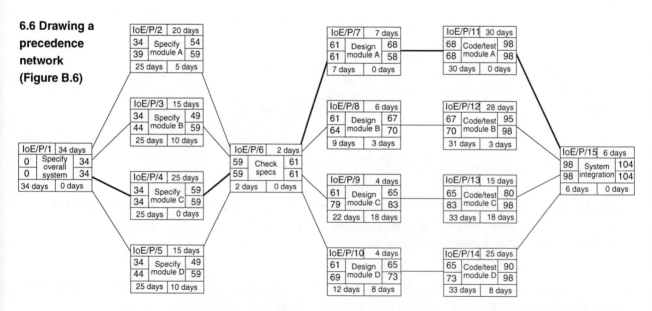

Figure B.6 *Amanda's precedence network.*

Chapter 7

Among the factors that she might consider are the following.

Application factors

- Will the package need to interface with other (existing) systems?
- Are there likely to be large differences between alternative packages?

Staff factors

- Do the staff at the college have experience in evaluating or procuring packages of this type?
- Do the Brightmouth College have experience of using similar packages?

Project methods

- Can we use standard methods for this project?
- Does the college have established procedures for this type of project?

Hardware factors

- Will the project involve the purchase of new hardware?
- Will we be able to test candidate packages on the same hardware configuration as we will be operating?

Changeover factors

- Can we run a pilot system before complete changeover?
- Will the master files be convertible from the existing system?

Supplier factors

- Have we experience of purchasing software/hardware from the likely suppliers?
- How well established are the suppliers we are considering?

Environment factors

- Are there any plans for reorganization within the college that could affect the system?
- Are there likely to be any changes in government legislation that could affect the project?

7.2 Amanda's risk reductions strategies

The following are illustrative of the actions that Amanda might consider.

- **Changes to requirements specification during coding.** This risk could be reduced by ensuring the original specification agreed at a senior level and adopting a high change threshold.
- **Specification takes longer than expected.** Review time estimates or break the activity down into smaller components and estimate each of them. Draw up contingency plans for shortening critical activities later in the project.
- **Staff sickness affecting critical activities.** Check availability of suitable agency analysts and programmers.
- **Staff sickness affecting non-critical activities.** Draw up rota of stand-by staff who may be recruited from other projects.
- **Module coding takes longer than expected.** Scrutinize estimating procedures and compare estimates with similar past projects.
- **Module testing demonstrates errors or deficiencies in design.** Use more stringent methods to validate design – formal methods or structured walkthroughs may be appropriate.

7.3 Calculating expected activity durations (Table B.8)

Table B.8 *Calculating expected activity durations*

	Activity durations (weeks)			
Activity	*Optimistic (a)*	*Most likely (m)*	*Pessimistic (b)*	*Expected (t_e)*
A	5	6	8	6·17
B	3	4	5	4·00
C	2	3	3	2·83
D	3·5	4	5	4·08
E	1	3	4	2·83
F	8	10	15	10·50
G	2	3	4	3·00
H	2	2	2·5	2·08

7.4 The forward pass to calculate expected completion date

The expected duration and the expected dates for the other project events are shown in Figure 7.2. An expected duration of 13·5 weeks means that we expect the project to be completed half way through week 14, although since this is only an expected value it could finish earlier or later.

7.5 Calculating standard deviations

The correct values are shown in Figure 7.3. Brief calculations for events 4 and 6 are given here.

Event 4:   Path A + C has a standard deviation of $\sqrt{(0·50^2 + 0·17^2)} = 0·53$

Path B + D has a standard deviation of $\sqrt{(0·33^2 + 0·25^2)} = 0·41$

Node 4 therefore has a standard deviation of 0·53.

Event 6:   Path 4 + H has a standard deviation of $\sqrt{(0·53^2 + 0·08^2)} = 0·54$

Path 5 + G has a standard deviation of $\sqrt{(1\cdot17^2+0\cdot33^2)} = 1\cdot22$
Node 6 therefore has a standard deviation of 1·22.

The z value for event 5 is $\dfrac{10-10\cdot5}{1\cdot17} = -0\cdot43$, for event 6 it is $\dfrac{15-13\cdot5}{1\cdot22} = 1\cdot23$
7.6 Calculating z values

Event 4: The z value is 1·89 which equates to a probability of approximately 3%. There is therefore only a 3% chance that we will not achieve this event by the target date of the end of week 10.
7.7 Obtaining probabilities

Event 5: The z value is $-0\cdot43$ which equates to a probability of approximately 67%. There is therefore a 68% chance that we will not achieve this event by the target date of the end of week 10.

To calculate the probability of completing the project by week 14 we need to calculate a new z value for event 6 using a target date of 14. This new z value is

$$z = \frac{15-14}{1\cdot22} = 0\cdot82$$

This equates to a probability of approximately 20%. This is the probability of not meeting the target date. The probability of meeting the target date is therefore 80% (100% − 20%).

Chapter 8

Smoothing analyst/designer demand for stage 4 is reasonably easy. The design of module D could be scheduled after the design of module C. Stage 2 is more problematic as scheduling the specification of module D to start after the completion of B would delay the project. Amanda might consider doing this if whoever is specifying module A could also be allocated to module D for the last six days – although she may well decide that drafting an extra person in to a specification activity is unsatisfactory.
8.1 Smoothing resource demand

If the activities are scheduled at the earliest dates then the plan still calls for four analyst/designers as shown in Figure B.7.
8.2 Drawing a revised resource histogram

    By delaying the start of some activities, however, Amanda is able to ensure that using three analyst/designers are sufficient except for a single day. This is shown in Figure B.8.

    Note that if the specification of module C were to be delayed for a further day, the project could be completed with only three analyst/designers although its completion day would, of course, be delayed.

When activities are
scheduled at their earliest
start dates the shaded
area of each bar
represents the activity's
total float.

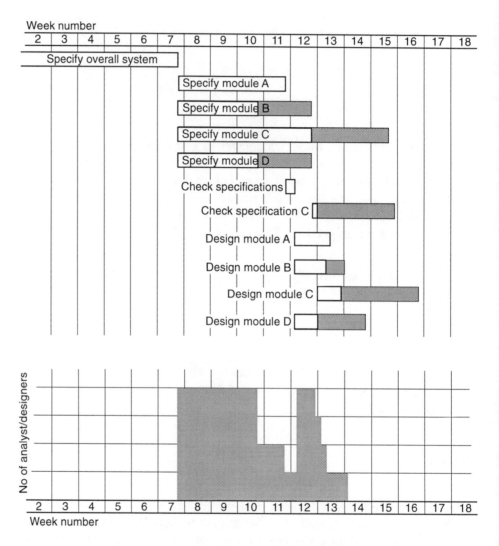

Figure B.7 *Amanda's revised bar chart and resource histogram.*

**8.3 Identifying critical
activities**

The critical path is now as shown in Figure B.9. Note the lag of 15 days against
activity IoE/P/4 ensuring that its start is delayed until an analyst/designer is
expected to be available.

However, the availability of an analyst/designer for IoE/P/4 is dependent upon
IoE/P/3 or IoE/P/5 being completed on time – these two activities are therefore
also now critical in the sense that a delay in both of them would delay IoE/P/4
which is on the normal critical path. These two activities, although not on the
critical path, are, in that sense, critical.

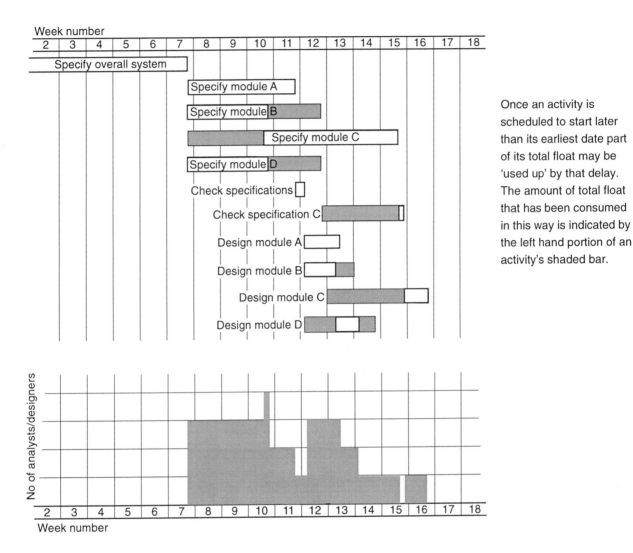

Once an activity is scheduled to start later than its earliest date part of its total float may be 'used up' by that delay. The amount of total float that has been consumed in this way is indicated by the left hand portion of an activity's shaded bar.

Figure B.8 *The effect of delaying some activity starts.*

Belinda must specify module B as she will then be available in time to start the specification of module C. This leaves Daisy for the specification and design of module A. Belinda cannot do the design of module B as she will still be working on the module C specification when this needs to be done (6 days between days 56 and 66). This will have to be left to Tom as he should be free on day 60.

Can you think of any other way in which she might have allocated the three team members to these activities?

8.4 Assigning staff to activities

8.5 Calculating project costs

The easiest way to calculate the total cost is to set up a table similar to Table B.9.

Table B.9 *Calculating the cost of Amanda's project*

Analyst	Daily cost (£)	Days Required	Cost (£)
Amanda	300	110*	33,000
Belinda	250	50	12,500
Tom	175	25	4,375
Daisy	225	27	6,075
Gavin	150	30	4,500
Purdy	150	28	4,200
Justin	150	15	2,250
Spencer	150	25	3,750
Daily oncost	200	100	20,000
Total			90,650

* Note that Amanda's time includes an additional 10 days for preproject planning and post project review.

Calculating the distribution of costs over the life of the project is best done as a per week or per month figure rather than as daily costs. The expenditure per week for Amanda's project is shown as a chart in Figure 8.9.

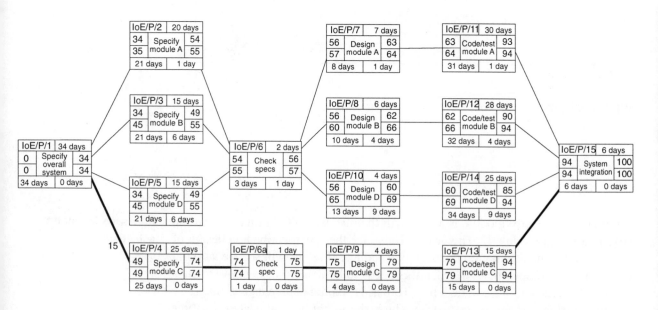

Figure B.9 *The critical activities after delaying the start of module C.*

Chapter 9

There are many reasons why the proportion of lines coded is not a good indicator of completeness. In particular, you should have considered the following:

- the estimated total number of lines of code may be inaccurate
- the lines of code so far written may have be easier, or harder, to write than those to follow
- a program is not generally considered complete until it has been tested – when 100% of its lines of code have been written a program will still be incomplete until tested.

With more knowledge of what has been done and what is left to complete it may be possible to make a reasonable estimate of completeness. The programmer may be able to make such an estimate.

At the end of week 8 the scheduled completion dates for drafting and issuing the tender need to be revised – note both need to be changed since they are both on the critical path (Figure B.10).

Subsequently, Brigette only needs to show the completion of each of these two remaining activities on the timeline chart – the project being completed by the Thursday of week 11 (Figure B.11).

Among the items most likely to be affected by the change are test data, expected results and the user handbooks.

Stages 1 to 6 will be basically the same except that an estimate on the effect of the project's timescale may need to be included in steps 3 and 4. Step 7 may not be required as system acceptance may not have taken place yet and acceptance testing of the changes will be included in that.

The release of software in step 8 will not be needed if the system is not yet operational, although master copies of products will need to be updated.

There may be several different system designs which meet the users' requirements and one may be selected which is more elaborate and involves more processing.

Essential housekeeping and security driven requirements may become apparent – e.g. additional validation of the input to ensure that the database remains consistent.

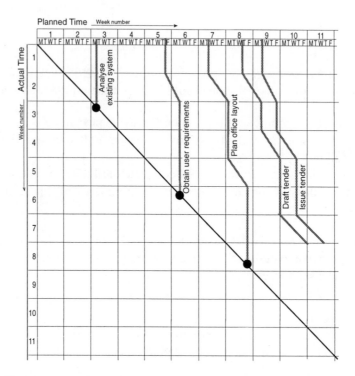

Figure B.10 *The revised timeline chart.*

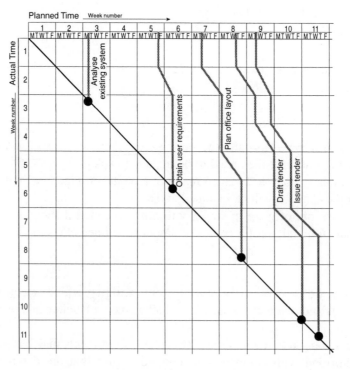

Figure B.11 *The completed timeline chart.*

Chapter 10

An analyst/programmer is expected to be able to carry out both analysis and programming tasks. It is likely, however, that the kinds of analysis tasks undertaken will be restricted. They may, for example, do the analysis work for enhancements to existing systems but not of completely new applications. Making this broad assumption, a list of tasks and responsibilities might be as follows.

- Carry out detailed investigations of new requirements for existing computer applications.
- Analyse the results of investigations and review the solutions to problems experienced, including the estimation of relevant costs.
- Prepare systems specifications in accordance with organizational standards.
- Conduct appropriate systems testing.
- Prepare functional module specifications.
- Produce and modify module structure diagrams.
- Code and amend software modules.
- Carry out appropriate unit testing.
- Produce and amend user documentation.
- Liaise with users, carrying out appropriate training in the use of computer applications where required.

A problem here is that the programmers who make most use of reused components will, as a consequence, be producing less code themselves. You also want to encourage programmers to produce software components that other people can use: this may help the productivity of the organization but not that of the current project that they are working on!

You need to have a method, like function point analysis, which measures the functions and features actually delivered to the user. You also need to have some way of measuring the code used in the application which has been taken from elsewhere. Percentage targets of the amount of reused code to new code could be set and staff rewarded if the targets are met. As an alternative, the savings made by reuse could be measured and a profit-sharing scheme could be operated.

Programmers could be encouraged to produce and publish reusable components by a system of royalties for each time a software component is reused.

This exercise was designed to be thought-provoking. Some thoughts that have come out of discussion on this topic are given below.

- To some extent material wants and, therefore, the motivation to obtain more money to satisfy these wants can be generated through the marketing and

advertising of new types of goods and services – but how likely is this to be at the very top?
- Large salaries are associated with status, esteem and success. It could be that these are the real reward.
- Historically, wealth has been associated with power, e.g. the ownership of land.

The essential point is that for many people money is not just a means of satisfying material wants.

10.4 High and low motivational incidents

This will obviously depend on individual experiences.

10.5 Social loafing

Among other ideas, the effects of social loafing can be reduced by:

- making the work of each performer individually identifiable
- involving and interesting group members in the outcome of group efforts
- rewarding individuals for their contributions to the group effort (rather like sports teams who pick out a 'clubman of the year').

10.6 Effect of IT on the Delphi technique

Developments in IT which assist cooperative working, especially the advent of electronic mail and groupware such as Lotus Notes, may be able to cut quite considerably the communication delays involved in the Delphi technique.

10.7 Classification of types of power

More than one type of power may be involved in each case.

(a) Some **expert** power is involved here, but for those who are subject to the audit, the main type of power is **connection** power as the auditor will produce a report that will go to higher management. External auditors may have **coercive** power.
(b) Here, power will mainly be **expert**- and **information**-based, but as the consultant will report to higher management **connection** power also exists.
(c) This sounds pretty **coercive.**
(d) Brigette may have some **connection** power. The technical expertise that is involved in her job may mean she has some **expert** power. She has little or no **coercive** power as she is not the manger of the staff involved. She might be able to exert some **reward** power on the basis of an informal 'I'll do you a favour if you'll do me a favour' arrangement!
(e) Amanda is unlikely to have direct **coercive** powers although she may be able to institute disciplinary procedures. Through the system of annual reviews common to many organizations she may have some **reward** power. **Connection** power, through her access to higher management is also present.

Her access to users may mean she has **information** power. If she brings specific expertise to the project (e.g. analysis skills) she may have some **expert** power. By acting as a role model that other project team members may want to emulate she may even be displaying **referent** power!

(a) The clerk will know much more than anyone else about the practical details of the work. Heavy **task-oriented** supervision would therefore not be appropriate. As the clerk is working in a new environment and forging new relationships, a considerable amount of people-oriented supervision/support may be needed initially.

(b) Both task-oriented and people-oriented management would be needed with the trainee.

(c) The experienced maintenance programmer has probably had considerable autonomy in the past. The extensions to the systems may have a considerable, detailed, impact on their work. A very carefully judged increase in task-oriented management will be required for a short time.

10.8 Appropriate management styles

Chapter 11

(a) Carry out an investigation to find out what the users' requirements really are. This may uncover that there are different sets of requirements for different groups of users.

(b) Organize the requirements into groups relating to individual qualities and attributes. These might be, for example, functionality (the range of features that the package has), price, usability, capacity, efficiency, flexibility, reliability and serviceability.

(c) Some of these requirements will be of an absolute nature. For example the package will have to hold records for up to a certain maximum number of employees. If it cannot, it will have to be immediately eliminated from further consideration.

(d) In other cases the requirement is relative. Some of the relative requirements may be more important than others. A low price may be desirable but a more expensive package cannot be ruled out straightaway. This can be reflected by giving each of the requirements a score out of 10 for importance.

(e) A range of possible candidate packages needs to be identified. If there are lots of possibilities, an initial screening, e.g. by price, may be applied to reduce the contenders to a manageable shortlist.

(f) Practical ways of measuring the desired qualities in the packages have to be devised. In some cases, for example with price and capacity, sales literature or a technical specification can be consulted. In other cases, efficiency for instance, practical trials could be conducted, while in yet other cases a survey of existing users may be able to provide the information required.

11.1 Selection of payroll package for college

(g) It is likely that some packages are going to be deficient in some ways, but that this will be compensated by other qualities. A simple way of combining the findings on different qualities is to give a mark out of 10 for the relative presence/absence of the quality. Each of these scores can be multiplied by the score out of 10 for the importance of the quality (see (d)) and the results of all these multiplications can be summed to give an overall score for the package.

11.2 Relationships between the different quality factors

- **Indifferent** – usability and reusability would seem to have little bearing on each other in spite of the similarity in their names. (Although it is usually possible to identify at least a tenuous complementary or conflicting relationship between two quality factors if you try hard enough).
- **Complementary** – a program that demonstrated flexibility might also be expected to have a high degree of maintainability.
- **Conflicting** – a program may be highly efficient because it exploits the architecture of a particular type of hardware to the full, and so not be easy to transfer to another hardware configuration.

11.3 The same software quality criteria often appear for more than one software quality factor. What is the significance of this?

The presence of the same software quality criterion for more than one software quality factor would indicate that the software quality factors are complementary.

11.4 Possible quality specifications for a word processing package

There are many that could be defined and just two examples are given below. One point that may emerge is that the package may be best broken down into a number of different function areas, each of which may be evaluated separately, such as document preparation, presentation, mail merging and so on. For example:

- **quality** – ease of learning
- **definition** – the time taken, by a novice, to learn how to operate the package to produce a standard document
- **scale** – hours
- **test** – interview novices to ascertain their previous experience of word processing. Supply them with a machine, the software, a training manual and a standard document to set up. Time how long it takes them to learn how to set the document up.
- **worst** – 4 hours
- **planned** – 2 hours
- **best** – 1 hour
- **now** – 4 hours

or

- **quality** – ease of use
- **definition** – the time taken for an experienced user to produce a standard document
- **scale** – minutes
- **test** – time user who has experience of package to produce the standard document
- **worst** – 45 minutes
- **planned** – 40 minutes
- **best** – 35 minutes.

This topic of evaluation is an extensive one and the pointers above leave all sort of unanswered questions in the air. Readers who wish to explore this area should read one of the more specialist books on the topic.

11.5 Availability and mean time between failures

Each day the system should be available from 18.00 – 8.00 hours, i.e. 10 hours.
Over four weeks that should be $10 \times 5 \times 4$ hours = 200 hours.
It was unavailable for one day, i.e. 10 hours.
It was unavailable until 10.00 on two other days, i.e. 4 hours.
The hours available were therefore $200 - 10 - 4 = 186$ hours.

Availability would therefore be $186/200 \times 100 = 93\%$

Assuming that three failures are counted, **mean time between failures** would be $186/3 = 62$ hours.

11.6 Entry requirements for an activity different from the exit requirements for another activity that immediately precedes it

It may be possible for one activity to start before the immediately preceding activity has been completely finished. In this case the entry requirement for the following activity has been satisfied, even though the exit requirement of the preceding activity has not.

11.7 Entry and exit requirements

- **Entry requirements** – a program design must have been produced that has been reviewed and that any rework required by the review must have been carried out and has been inspected by the chair of the review group.
- **Exit requirements** – a program must have been produced that has been compiled and is free of compilation errors; the code must have been reviewed and any rework required by the review must have been carried out and has been inspected by the chair of the review group.

It may be noted that the review group may use checklists for each type of product reviewed and these could be regarded as further entry/exit requirements.

11.8 Application of BS EN ISO 9001 standards to the software environment

- **Control of equipment** – in the software environment, this would include the software tools involved. Of particular concern, for example, would be the compilers used. These would need to be known to work correctly and also to work in the same way as compilers of the same language in other machine environments in order to assist portability.
- **Testing status** – there would be concern that software components which are being updated are not released to users before adequate testing has taken place. These issues are addressed by change control and configuration management procedures.
- **Distribution** – some concerns here would be to do with the security of physical copying and distribution of magnetic media. Configuration management would also be important to ensure that the version of the software that is being shipped has all the correct components.

11.9 Bearing in mind the criticisms of BS EN ISO 9001 that have been mentioned, what precautionary steps could a project manager take when some work where the quality is important is contracted out?

The project manager could check who actually carried out the certification. They could also discover the scope of the BS EN ISO 9001 certification that was awarded. For example, it could be that certification only applied to the processes that created certain products and not others.

Perhaps the most important point is that the project manager will need to be reassured that the **specification** to which the contractors will be working is an adequate reflection of the requirements of the client organization.

11.11 What are the important differences between a quality circle and a review group?

The quality circle would be looking at the process in general while the review group would look at a particular instance of a product. The use of review groups alone could be inefficient because they could be removing the same type of defect again and again rather than addressing, as the quality circle does, the task of stopping the defects at their source.

Index